DATE DUE

MODERNISM AND POPULAR MUSIC

Traditionally, ideas about twentieth-century modernism – whether focused on literature, music, or the visual arts – have made a distinction between "high" art and the "popular" arts of best-selling fiction, jazz and other forms of popular music, and commercial art of one form or another. In *Modernism and Popular Music*, Ronald Schleifer instead shows how the music of George and Ira Gershwin, Cole Porter, Thomas "Fats" Waller, and Billie Holiday can be considered as artistic expressions equal to those of the traditional high modernist art practices in music and literature. Combining detailed attention to the language and aesthetics of popular music with an examination of its early twentieth-century performance and dissemination through the new technologies of the radio and phonograph, Schleifer explores the "popularity" of popular music in order to reconsider received and seemingly self-evident truths about the differences between high art and popular art and, indeed, about twentieth-century modernism altogether.

RONALD SCHLEIFER is George Lynn Cross Research Professor of English and Adjunct Professor in Medicine at the University of Oklahoma. Among his other books, he has written *Modernism and Time: The Logic of Abundance in Literature, Science, and Culture 1880–1930*, also published by Cambridge University Press.

MODERNISM AND POPULAR MUSIC

RONALD SCHLEIFER

CAMBRIDGE
UNIVERSITY PRESS

CAMBRIDGE UNIVERSITY PRESS
Cambridge, New York, Melbourne, Madrid, Cape Town,
Singapore, São Paulo, Delhi, Tokyo, Mexico City

Cambridge University Press
The Edinburgh Building, Cambridge CB2 8RU, UK

Published in the United States of America by Cambridge University Press, New York

www.cambridge.org
Information on this title: www.cambridge.org/9781107005051

First published 2011

Printed in the United Kingdom at the University Press, Cambridge

A catalogue record for this publication is available from the British Library

Library of Congress Cataloguing in Publication data
Schleifer, Ronald.
Modernism and popular music / Ronald Schleifer.
p. cm.
Includes bibliographical references and index.
ISBN 978-1-107-00505-1 (hardback)
1. Modernism (Music) 2. Popular music – United States – History and criticism. 3. Jazz – History and criticism. 4. Gershwin, George, 1898–1937 – Criticism and interpretation. 5. Holiday, Billie, 1915–1959 – Criticism and interpretation. 6. Porter, Cole, 1891–1964 – Criticism and interpretation. 7. Waller, Fats, 1904–1943 – Criticism and interpretation. I. Title.
ML3477.S35 2011
781.6409′041 – dc22 2011008369

ISBN 978-1-107-00505-1 Hardback

for my twin brother, Robert Schleifer,
with whom I have shared music all of my life;
and to the memory of our father, Cy Schleifer,
who brought music into our lives

Contents

Figures

Preface

Modernism and Popular Music is a study that aims at enlarging our sense of cultural modernism by including within a working definition of modernism popular art forms – particularly, popular music – along with the usual high art practices in music and literature with which we are all familiar. To this end, I have tried to widen our sense of twentieth-century modernism by discussing it in the context of the relationship between Enlightenment modernity and the experience of the early twentieth century. This relationship is particularly clear in the study of music, because much of what we assume is "natural" about music really emerged in the early modern period of the seventeenth and eighteenth centuries. At that time, as I mention in the Introduction, methods of musical notation, musical instruments as we know them today, the very idea of a musical key, standardizations of "tempered" musical tuning, the creation of the modern shape of leisure in which listening to music can be understood as a focused leisure activity *separate* from other activities, and even the conception of a composer all emerged. Music is also an art form, as I argue throughout this book, that more forcefully than the other arts emphasizes the *materiality* of the production and consumption of art. Such an emphasis on materiality, I contend, is also a particular feature of the modernist arts in the new twentieth century, where all kinds of "defamiliarization" – in painting, prose, atonal music, poetry – became an important aspect of the arts. (Such defamiliarization was also a feature of post-Newtonian science of the early twentieth century as well.) Finally, the existence of performance as the primary modality of popular music underscores the performativity of modernist art forms – and, indeed, of the "modernist" intellectual disciplines such as literary criticism, psychoanalysis, semiotics, ordinary-language philosophy – more generally.

The very existence of popular music in performance is a function, in part, of remarkable technical innovations in the recording and dissemination of popular music in the early twentieth century: its commodification in the forms of sheet music, records, microphones, and even that strange commodification of public broadcast. (It strangely exists as a commodity without a tangible price tag.) These innovations related to popular music take their place among the vast number of technical innovations of the second Industrial Revolution of the turn of the twentieth century that affected and transformed virtually all aspects of human life, its forms of knowledge, its quotidian experience, its formal and informal social relations. In other words, the study of the "best" popular music of the early twentieth century allows us to see more clearly than we otherwise might particular defining features of twentieth-century modernism: the historicity of its received ideas about the world; the strategies of defamiliarization – in this musical study, I call this "rhythmic decomposition" – that the powerfully changing world of finance capitalism and widespread availability of commodities gave rise to; the disturbances occasioned by the democratization of social organization, including the emergence of a new social class of lower-middle-class information workers (engaged in the institutions of finance capital) possessing an individualist ideology that made certain kinds of material self-fulfillments personally and popularly imperative; and the need, in any comprehension of these phenomena, to pursue a "performative" as well as a causal understanding.

In pursuit of this goal of articulating a more comprehensive understanding of twentieth-century modernism – including, as I note in Chapter 4, its "structure of feeling" – I present in the Introduction to this book an aesthetics of popular music. In this discussion, I address Theodor Adorno's explicit dismissal of popular music as "trash" both by articulating what is valuable in popular music (at its "best") and by specifying elements that might condition the realization of those values. In this discussion, I follow Adorno's own analysis of the strategies and assumptions that govern and realize a modernist aesthetics for high art, and particularly for art music. In his work, Adorno describes three criteria for an aesthetics appropriate for modernist art in the twentieth century. Specifically, he notices the powerful strategies of modernist art to achieve a dialectical "wholeness" by means of decomposition – as noted above, in the context of popular music I describe this as "rhythmic decomposition" – and the particularly modernist art form of "montage." In the Introduction, I pursue these categories in order to describe the power and importance of "modernist" popular music – what I mean by describing the music I study as the "best" instances of popular music – and in the chapters of Part II focused on Gershwin, Porter, Waller, and Holiday I demonstrate the ways that, in close readings of their music and lyrics, these criteria can help us situate these musicians as "modernist" artists.

I also argue that at the heart of the difference between the art music Adorno valorizes and popular music, which he denigrates, is the category of pleasure. More specifically I argue, following Colin Campbell, that the provocations of "desire" and "pleasure" as well as articulations of "suffering" and "truth" – which Adorno claims are ends of art – are legitimate goals of art, and the aim and achievement of the best popular music. In this discussion, I take the opportunity of quoting Adorno's powerful observation in *Aesthetic Theory* that "the need to lend a voice to suffering is a condition of all truth."[1] Needless to say, I do not want to suggest that tragic suffering cannot help us define important art forms and, indeed, important ways of understanding personal and social life. Nevertheless, pleasure also has an important place in understanding art and life; Campbell is clear on this, especially in discussing Wordsworth and Romanticism more generally. In *Modernism and Popular Music* I describe the pleasure of popular music in relation to the emotions it arouses (again, at its "best") that celebrate and to some extent redeem, in the words of Robert Witkin, "life that is mutilated and suppressed by *modernity*."[2] Of course, such pleasure also inhabits much of "high" modernism, and I also note, in passing but repeatedly, that pleasure was the particular end of many high modernist artists: Joyce most of all, but also William Carlos Williams, Aaron Copland, Virginia Woolf, Wallace Stevens, and many others. In fact, the description of the pleasures Joyce affords is the work of the Conclusion to *Modernism and Popular Music* which returns to "high" modernism, but in fact the pleasures of modernist art – both popular and unpopular – are a constant in my argument.

The inclusion of pleasure within the aesthetics of popular music, I believe, also helps describe how popular music opened up a social space to find community and home in the modern world for many people who simply did not have access to either leisure or the arts before the abundances of the second Industrial Revolution. In fact, I cite Witkin's particularly strong discussion of Adorno's relation to popular culture that explicitly describes how popular music creates such a space of celebration for people who have been traditionally excluded from the space of public life. I think particularly of Jews, like the Gershwin brothers, homosexuals, like Cole Porter, Africans and African-Americans, like Thomas Waller and Billie Holiday, and women, again like Billie Holiday – all of whom were able to achieve quotidian emotional and intellectual pleasures in the popular arts that came, in the modernist era, to surround us all. That is, the new wealth of the new twentieth century afforded many hitherto disenfranchised groups and individuals the possibilities of leisure, self-realization, and, indeed, individual and social pleasure, and it is important to examine – as part of modernism – the highest achievements of this new freedom.

Closely related to this concern, I have developed this definition of aesthetics both in hopes it would answer another important question, of the way that modernism in general and popular music particularly challenges the received "universal" ideas of Enlightenment modernity – ideas that seem "natural" and self-evidently true – and to demonstrate the ways that popular music reasserts universals in a different way. I do this, as I mentioned, by emphasizing the pleasures art affords, which means emphasizing – in a gesture that comports well with the progressive democratization of social formations in the early twentieth century – the audiences of the arts as well as their composers. In part, this shift in focus follows from Campbell's argument that social (and by implication aesthetic) formations beginning in Enlightenment modernity need to be understood in relation to a "consumptionist" as well as a "productionist" ethos. Campbell is particularly good and useful in relation to the examination of the similarities and differences between Enlightenment modernity and twentieth-century modernism, and throughout Part I of the book I work to make their relationship clear and pertinent to our understanding of the early twentieth century. One place I pursue this relationship is in noting that Sigmund Freud, with his focus on the "satisfaction" of needs, participates in the "productionalist" ethos of modernity while Jacques Lacan, with his focus on the "pursuit" of desire, participates in the "consumerist" ethos of modernism. This abstract contrast is readily apparent, as I argue, in the music of Cole Porter. In this, as in much else concerning modernism, the value of using popular music to comprehend experience, understanding, and social formations in the early twentieth century, is clear.

My focus on consumerism, as I argue, reinforces a *performative* conception of pleasure that informs the aesthetics of popular music I present. Such a sense of performativity, focusing on the audience for music as well as the author of music, is, I suggest in the book's conclusion but also implicitly throughout the book, an important element of modernism, high and "low," altogether. The phenomenon of performativity is ubiquitously examined in *Modernism and Popular Music*. It is a significant aspect of my attempt to include more fully within a working concept of modernism some popular art forms along with the usual high art practices in music and literature with which we are all familiar. To this end, I discuss speech-act theory in the Introduction to emphasize the performative nature of pleasure, particularly in relation to the aesthetics of popular culture. In other chapters I also make clear the essentially performative elements in the writing of music by the Gershwins and Porter by emphasizing the ways their writings pursue pleasure, improvisation, and playfulness in a manner similar to the self-evident performativity in the actual musical performances of Waller and Holiday. (In the Conclusion I note that in 1929 Eugene Jolas emphasized in a similar way the performative aspects of Joyce's writings.) The focus on the concept of performativity also sharpens, I hope, the book's large contention that the "performative" human sciences – such as psychoanalysis, sociology, literary criticism, ordinary-language philosophy – are themselves productions of modernism.

An important concept, closely related to the performative aesthetics I develop, is the concept of "semantic formalism." This concept grows out of an observation that Igor Stravinsky made about Beethoven, that his music creates a "language structure" that reflects or organizes the phenomenal world.[3] Daniel Albright has observed that Stravinsky is accomplishing "the deep equivalence of the natural and the artificial,"[4] and such modeling of the natural, I also argue (following Mary Poovey and my own argument in *Intangible Materialism*), is a distinguishing feature of modernism. Moreover, Albright's mention of the "natural" also ties the idea of semantic formalism more closely to the distinction between the (more or less) pure formalism of Enlightenment modernity and what I am calling the semantic formalism of twentieth-century modernism. As with the definition of the aesthetics of popular music, this elaboration of semantic formalism governs local as well as global arguments in *Modernism and Popular Music*. Both locally and globally, it is particularly useful in relation to a ubiquitous criticism of popular music, that it depends inordinately on clichés in words and music. In Chapter 3 on the Gershwins, but also throughout *Modernism and Popular Music*, I describe in some detail how authors *inform* cliché with meaning by making clear that cliché is a formal device – like the received forms of popular music – that can be "semanticized."

Here, then, are the aims of this book: to locate popular music within a working comprehension of twentieth-century modernism, and in so doing to demonstrate the ways that the study of popular music makes clearer what an operational definition of "modernism" might look like. Such an operational definition would include a historical understanding of changes in experience, knowledge, and social relations in the early twentieth century; a sense of the materiality of these changes, including strategies of "defamiliarization" in order to discern them; the continuities and discontinuities between Enlightenment modernity and twentieth-century modernism; the place of pleasure and consumerism in the new world of modernism; the "essential" operation of performance – even the *accidents* of performance – within any working definition of modernism; and a sense of modernism's freedoms as well as its oppressions.

But along with all this, popular music is, in the word of Simon Frith, simply *fun*, pleasures bound into the rhythms of everyday life. This book, as I mention in the Acknowledgments, has been a particular pleasure for me. Here, in concluding this Preface, I would like to describe one moment in *Modernism and Popular Music* when I am having fun with scholarship. One such gesture appears, virtually silently, in Chapter 4 on Porter when I conjure up the Heideggerian battleship of ponderous philosophical pronouncement to talk about Porter's nicely crafted music under the category of "thing." I do this, in part, to underscore implicitly the opposition between seriousness-truth and playfulness-pleasure that governs my own and others' discussions of popular music (both pro and con). But in its very cumbersomeness, I hope, my calling up of Heidegger's hieratic seriousness in the context of Porter's musical fun implicitly valorizes pleasure in the face of ponderous truth. (Such valorization, I believe, is the work of the popular signifyin' that Waller performs for us.) The pursuit of "ponderous truth" is found in Adorno as well as Heidegger, and found more particularly in German Idealism, which writers about popular music repeatedly revert to in their understanding of the opposition between "serious" music and "popular" music. While there might not be much playfulness about Lacan, whom I hear in Porter in Chapter 4, surely there is a twinkle in Bakhtin's eyes, who rings through the Gershwins' music and lyrics in Chapter 3, and no doubt there is great pleasure, and the pleasures of virtuosity, in the African American signifyin' which I listen for in Waller and in the virtuosities of the stride piano in Chapter 5. Finally, with Billie Holiday, in Chapter 6, I celebrate the pleasures of bringing things together, including what seemed to be missing or lost, recoveries that all have the feel to them of new beginnings, of Pound's "making it new." Wallace Stevens articulates such "modernist" beginnings, I note in Chapter 4, as "this beginning, not resuming, this / Booming and booming of the new-come bee." It is my great hope, then, that *Modernism and Popular Music* will afford its readers (and its listeners!) a sense of recovering what we already knew, the community and space of shared music, art as the enactment of celebration, and the importance and pleasure of the music that most people in America born before the 1960s grew up with and have lived with all their lives.

Acknowledgments

Working on this book has been one of the pleasures of my professional life. In 1995 my friend Russell Reising called and asked if I would like to join him in going to the conference for the International Association for the Study of Popular Music that was meeting that year in Kanazawa, Japan. Like myself, Russ is an English professor (in American Studies), though unlike me he has wide knowledge of rock 'n' roll of the 1950s and 1960s. I was excited to travel to Japan with Russ – who studied Asian languages in college – and was delighted to put together a talk about Cole Porter, whose music I've loved from early on when I was a saxophone player with my brother Robert in a small combo dance band which played all the old standards. I also played Porter, Gershwin, and Waller to my two infant sons, Cyrus and Benjamin, on the piano, and with my wife Nancy and our lifelong friends David and Stephanie Gross and Roy and Carolyn Male, who would sing these tunes wonderfully. It is these kinds of experiences – which I like to imagine most all of us have participated in – that create the power of popular music. Unlike other eras, where people also came together to sing – Colin Campbell, in *The Romantic Ethic and the Spirit of Modern Consumerism*, lists "singing" among the "basic list of 'pleasures'" that "human beings in all cultures seem to agree on" – we are able to add to our parlor music, because of "modernist" technological innovations, experiences of heard and remembered *performances* in recordings and covers of all the songs we sing. But as in all times, we shared our music in performance ourselves.

After Russ called, I couldn't wait to organize a paper around "Do do that voodoo that you do so well!" Two years later Russ called again, and we took Cyrus and Benjamin, and James Reising – along with our friend Robert Markley and his son, Stephen – to Sydney. There I presented a paper on the Gershwins' music and lyrics. Two years later Russ and I were in Turku, Finland, where I talked about Waller. Two years after that it was Montreal, where I discussed Billie Holiday. The next conference was in Rome, where I discussed the concept of musical modernism altogether. Finally, we were scheduled to go together to Liverpool in 2009, after late drafts of this book were finished, where I had planned to talk about the relationship between classical modernity and popular music. Unfortunately, the death of my father, Cy Schleifer, at the age of 94 prevented my attending the Liverpool IASPM meeting.

These IASPM meetings, as all know who attend them, are remarkable for their intellectual excitement, warm friendliness, and diversity. In *Putting Popular Music in Its Place* Charles Hamm discusses the important impact these meetings have had, a "turning point," he says, in musicology: "both [the journal] *Popular Music* and IASPM moved quickly and decisively towards the privileging of theoretical, critical, and ideological discourse." As someone who works in literary and cultural modernism, literary theory, and cultural studies, I found myself wonderfully welcomed in this interdisciplinary organization. I found early on that the kinds of interests in language and poetry I brought to these meetings were useful to many, and the combination of historiography and musical analysis I encountered has been an important influence in my studies of literary and cultural modernism, especially *Modernism and Time: The Logic of Abundance in Literature, Science, and Culture 1880–1930* and my more recent work focusing on materialism and economics at the turn of the twentieth century. The many friends and colleagues I met at IASPM include Hasse Huss, Walter Everett (whom I met earlier, again introduced by Russ, at the Beatles 2000 conference in Jyväskylä, Finland), Sheila Whiteley, Catherine Rudent, Derek Scott, Toru Mitsui, Jacqueline Warwick, Stephen Valdez, Steven Baur, Jim LeBlanc, and Matthew Bannister, among many others. As well as from these encounters, this book has greatly benefited from the three anonymous readers who my long-time (and remarkably patient) editor at Cambridge, Ray Ryan, brought to my work. The readers corrected, focused, and clarified my argument to such an extent that on one or two occasions I have paraphrased their comments to sharpen my argument. Several other people also were instrumentally helpful in responding to parts of the manscript: I want to thank Robert Schleifer, Cristina Reyes, Derek Scott, Anne Jacobs, Walter Everett, and Russell Reising for helpful suggestions.

A shorter version of Chapter 4 of this volume appeared as "'What Is This Thing Called Love?': Cole Porter and the Rhythms of Desire," in *Criticism*, 41 (1999), 7–23. Some pages from Chapter 1 appeared in a longer article, "The Beatles, Postmodernism, and Ill-Tempered Musical Form: Cleaning My Gun; or, The Use of Accidentals in *Revolver*," in *'Every Sound There Is': The Beatles' Revolver and The Transformation of Rock & Roll*, edited by

Russell Reising (Hants, GB: Ashgate Publishers, 2002), pp. 222–33. I thank the editors and publishers of these essays for permission to include revised versions in the present volume. As well as at the IASPM meetings, I also had the pleasure of invitations of long-time friends, Professor Karen Klein, Professor Nancy West, and Dr. Sul Lee, Dean of the University Libraries here at Oklahoma, to discuss popular music of the 1930s at Brandeis University, the University of Missouri, and the Bizzell Library Society of the University of Oklahoma. In addition, I presented "Fats Waller and the Music of Modernism," a more literary version of Chapter 5 than was the presentation in Turku or the chapter here, at the 2004 Twentieth-Century Literature Conference in Louisville, Kentucky. Conversations with people at these sites nicely complemented discussions with musicologists and ethnomusicologists at IASPM and helped shape *Modernism and Popular Music*. The shared music with another long-time friend and weekly chess partner, David Levy, informs my work in subtle ways. And as always my wife, Nancy Mergler, has supported me in this work in small and large ways.

In addition, the following lyrics and poems are included here with the kind permission of their owners:

BUT NOT FOR ME (from "Girl Crazy") Music and Lyrics by GEORGE GERSHWIN and IRA GERSHWIN © 1930 (Renewed) WB MUSIC CORP. All Rights Reserved. Used by Permission of ALFRED MUSIC PUBLISHING CO., INC.

"Variations on a Theme by William Carlos Williams" from COLLECTED POEMS OF KENNETH KOCH by Kenneth Koch, copyright © 2005 BY The Kenneth Koch Literary Estate. Used by permission of Alfred A. Knopf, a division of Random House, Inc.

"The Red Wheelbarrow" and **"This is Just to Say"** By William Carlos Williams, from THE COLLECTED POEMS: VOLUME I, 1909–1939, COPYRIGHT © 1938 BY New Directions Publishing Corp. Reprinted by permission of New Directions Publish Corp.

I am dedicating this book to my twin brother, Robert Schleifer, with whom I have shared music from the very beginning, and to the memory of our father, Cy Schleifer, who many times when we were boys met us on Bleecker Street after our music lessons and took us to the Italian fish market for clams and good cheer before driving us home. He gave us music and much more.

Introduction: popular music and the experience of modernism

This is a book about the "cultural modernism" of the early twentieth century. Part I examines the place of popular music within conceptions of modernism, and Part II examines what I call "the rhythms and semiotics of language and sound" in the music of the Gershwin brothers, Cole Porter, Thomas "Fats" Waller, and Billie Holiday, with occasional references to modernist writers William Butler Yeats, T. S. Eliot, Ralph Ellison, William Carlos Williams, Virginia Woolf, and others. The emphasis of *Modernism and Popular Music* is primarily linguistic or textual in that I am pursuing an account of how a "revolution in words," as I note in the Conclusion, transformed or marked the ways in which sensibility, mind, belief, perspective, society, economics, and human experience more generally came to be understood in the early twentieth century. I argue, however, that this revolution, which is usually associated with poets, writers, artists, linguists, and philosophers – as well as twentieth-century composers of "art" music – is just as evident, if not more so, in the work of the great songwriters and jazz performers who came to prominence in the United States between the two World Wars. These artists did not merely reveal the basic contents of this shift in how the world was (or could be) comprehended or "felt." Rather, in their role as "alchemists of the vernacular," as Alfred Appel has described them,[1] they opened up a powerful social space through which fundamental problems of equality, difference, desire, reason, authority, self, and language were not merely expressed, but questioned and negotiated. And they did this, above all, by foregrounding the dynamics of performance and gesture in the experience of human being.

Modernism and Popular Music is a "literary" study insofar as it takes the lyrics and verbal performances of the musicians seriously, but it doesn't focus on literature in any conventional way. Rather, it focuses on non-verbal performances and verbal performances that aspire to the condition of music. In so doing, it offers two global arguments. One is that popular arts can and should be included in any working concept of twentieth-century cultural modernism. A second global argument is its contention that the ways that musical lyrics/poetry emphasize the material aspect of language can and should help us understand the other verbal arts of poetry and fiction. Both of these arguments assume that focusing on the best music/lyric composition and performance in the 1930s can teach us to hear poetic language of the early twentieth century in new and better ways, and that the "musical modernism" of popular music makes this clear. In one explicit example, I mention that Walter Benn Michael's contention about the material "reality" of William Carlos Williams's language – an argument that can be found in much criticism of modernist poetry – is almost immediate and self-evident when we listen to Cole Porter. Thus, while the book doesn't focus on literature in that it doesn't offer the standard kinds of analyses of particular poetic texts – though it does do so for Gershwin and Porter and for Waller's and Holiday's performative texts – it does emphasize the power of language, including the "language structure" of music, and particularly the power of modernist language in the early twentieth century.

MODERNITY AND MODERNISM

"Modernism" is a term that is still a site for contest, yet most people who examine it agree that it witnesses a remarkable moment in our history that marks the particular cultural crisis of the early twentieth century. That crisis was the need felt by many working in the arts and sciences to rethink and redefine received conceptions about human life, social value, and scientific knowledge. In *Modernism and Popular Music* I turn to the popular music of the 1930s to examine what seems to me to be participating in the same or a similar phenomenal crisis: the felt need to rethink and redefine received conceptions of aesthetic modernism in the particularly American context of the rapid urbanization of the United States. This urbanization was based upon huge influxes of people from eastern and southern Europe and from the American south into American cities (and especially New York City); the great American economic boom that followed World War I; and the remarkable technical innovations that produced a host of new consumer goods (including the innovation of installment buying that put many of these products in the hands of large numbers of people and helped create the boom). To this end the book begins by comparing the phenomenon of what I am calling "Enlightenment modernity" in the "early modern" period of the seventeenth and eighteenth century to the "cultural modernism" of the twentieth century. These two signal moments in our cultural history share many qualities – individualism, secularism, trust in reason or instrumentalism – even while they differ in many respects, most notably, as I argue here, in the power of consumerism in the later period. (Such consumerism, I also suggest, conditions the validation of performance along with production.) In this discussion I am, I know, generalizing across a host of local questions about the particular terms and issues I examine – particularly notable in remarkably different national and political contexts – but it is my hope that such generalizations give rise to a finer sense of the experience and values of early-twentieth-century Europe and, especially, the United States.

In any case, *Modernism and Popular Music* begins with this comparison at least in part because so many of our self-evident received ideas emerged in the time of seventeenth- and eighteenth-century "modernity," that particular time of transition from the medieval world to the "modern" world. Especially notable in the context of this study is the fact that our received ideas of music, at least in Europe and America, really begin in the seventeenth and eighteenth centuries when methods of musical notation, the inventions of musical instruments as we know them today, the very idea of a musical key, standardizations of "tempered" musical tuning, the creation of the modern shape of leisure in which listening to music came to be understood as a focused leisure activity,[2] and even the conception of a composer – the "author" in Michel Foucault's famous essay "What Is an Author?" – all emerged.[3] What also emerged then and culminated in nineteenth-century thinking about music and nineteenth-century performances of *concert* music – Charles Hamm describes this historical period as "Concert Life (from *c.* 1740 to World War I)"[4] – is the clear distinction between art music and popular music. This distinction is probably most clear in Theodor Adorno's contention that the popular music of the 1920s and 1930s – he, like most people in the 1930s, called all the popular music of that time "jazz"[5] – was simple "bad music" and "artistic trash."[6]

These two aspects of Enlightenment modernity – namely, the origin of aesthetic expression in the individual "genius" of a particular author and the organizing structure of experience based upon the putative "clear and distinct" differentiation between spheres of understanding – came into question at the turn of the twentieth century. They did so for a host of overdetermined reasons. Thus, mathematical physics, that great invention of Descartes and Newton based upon both clear and distinct ideas (embodied in mathematical notations) and the abstractions of interchangeable parts, had exhausted itself with success. (In the same way late in the nineteenth century chronological linguistics, based as it was upon a distinct sense that the *origin* of phenomena – such as their earliest, simplest manifestations or simply their "authors" – was the adequate explanation of them, had exhausted itself through success.) In addition, the powerful idea of individualism, manifest most of all in the industrial entrepreneurs of the first Industrial Revolution and the soul-searching of Protestant Christianity, was overwhelmed by the manifest *social* nature of wealth, value, and power. Thus, Marx and Engels ask in *The Communist Manifesto*, "What productive forces slumbered in the lap of social labor?"[7] Moreover, the idea of individualism was overwhelmed as well by the sheer abundance of consumer goods, burgeoning knowledge, and possibilities of experience in the new twentieth century.[8] And finally the arts themselves – and, for my purposes, the art and order of music – came face to face with the tumult of urban life, abundant consumerism, and all kinds of new ways of knowing. This resulted in the particular commercialization of popular music in Tin Pan Alley in New York, with its combination of Jewish American and African American musics, that Part I also examines.

As well as the two explicit global arguments I have mentioned – the importance of understanding the popular arts as part of twentieth-century modernism, and the ways that musical modernism can help us read modern poetry – *Modernism and Popular Music* also presents an implicit argument about twentieth-century cultural modernism in its focus on the popular music of America in the early twentieth century. One significant difference between the first Industrial Revolution of the eighteenth- and nineteenth-century development of capitalism centered in Britain and the second Industrial Revolution of the late nineteenth and early twentieth century was the fact that the vast majority of the technological innovations of the second Industrial Revolution, unlike the first, were made and developed *outside* of Britain. Kenneth Hudson suggests that cultural modernism was especially notable in America; in a parallel fashion I note in Chapter 1 that the United States was the first "modernist" nation instituted on principles of Enlightenment modernity. "The history of industry and commerce," Hudson argues,

> becomes increasingly complicated after c.1870 as licensing agreements, cartels, international groups, import controls, and government direction and intervention have increasingly to be taken into account. All combine to produce a situation which makes the world of Watt, Brunel and their contemporaries seem very small and simple . . . If one is concerned with the history of iron-making between c.1700 and c.1850, all the essential developments can be documented by studying British sites. If, however, the field is cornflakes, tractors or telephones then the

early shrines are to be found in North America. The same is true regarding most electrical appliances, safety razors, escalators, passenger lifts, linotype and monotype printing, roll-film cameras, aeroplanes, cinemas, petroleum extraction and refining, incandescent lamps, typewriters and refrigerators.[9]

And the same is also true regarding the popular arts of music, cinema, and radio.

That is, what is often described as the commodification of aesthetic experience – and what I suggest in Chapter 2 could also be described more widely as the commodification of desire and pleasure – might fruitfully be understood as the transformation of Enlightenment notions of "autonomous" aesthetic experience into the complicated phenomenon of "popular" aesthetics. Such a transformation realized itself most fully in the strange combination of the laissez-faire ideological individualism of American culture and the powerful social-collaborative production of wealth and value in the United States. The popular aesthetics I describe later in this chapter is complicated precisely because it is an interested rather than a disinterested aesthetics insofar as it traffics, explicitly, in pleasure. That is, popular music calls into question the austere aesthetics of Kantian disinterested judgment in a manner similar to the ways that, in Europe, Heisenberg, Einstein, and even the mathematical infinities Russell describes called into question the Kantian "pure" reason of late-eighteenth-century philosophy. In any case, implicit in my argument is the possibility that a rethinking of modernist aesthetic judgment necessitates focus on American "popular" experience.

THE MUSICIANS

Part II of *Modernism and Popular Music* focuses closely on four American musicians, the Gershwin brothers, Cole Porter, Thomas "Fats" Waller, and Billie Holiday. To call the Gershwin brothers "a musician" underlines the problematics of individualism, just as focusing on Holiday's performances of what seems to be other people's compositions also does. In both cases what is in question – as in the less obvious cases of Porter's attempt to tap *common* sources of what seems to be individual feelings and Waller's play with what seems to be other people's language – is the very origin of feeling and expression. In the Gershwins, I examine the art of quotation as I similarly examine another kind of quotation in Waller's participation in the African American tradition of "signifyin'." And both my examination of sources and resources of desire in Porter, based upon Jacques Lacan's interrogation of desire in language, and the more or less technical focus on the "semantic formalism" manifest in the language and rhythms of Holiday's singing underline the problematics of clear and orderly distinctions between nature and culture, biological need and interpersonal demand, the clarity of facts and the overdeterminations of language. Such orderly distinctions, as Bruno Latour has argued, created the basis for the edifice of Enlightenment modernity and its ongoing tradition through the first half of the twentieth century.[10] All of the examinations of popular music in Part II – quotation in the Gershwins, signifyin' in Waller, and the use of Lacan's modernist revision of the relationship between psychoanalysis and linguistics to examine the power of desire in Porter – are examples of the emphasis I give to language and textuality in *Modernism and Popular Music*.

This is perhaps most explicit in the concept of "semantic formalism," which is explicitly examined in Chapter 6 in relation to Holiday, but which really runs throughout my discussions of the place of popular music and performance in any working understanding of modernism. If the clear and distinct ideas of Enlightenment modernity are essentially formal – and for that reason, seemingly timeless and universal[11] – then one feature of twentieth-century modernism is a new type of comprehension that discovers or realizes particular, timely meanings as, in fact, constitutive of those forms. Mary Poovey describes this in the context of her cultural history of "facts," noting that in the late nineteenth century a "fact" became, across many different fields of understanding, not simply an instance of a pre-existing form, but a "model" in which form and particular instance were simultaneously "enacted" or "realized," as it were.[12] In discussing the musical achievement of Beethoven, Igor Stravinsky makes a similar point in his description of the possibilities of "a reflective system between the language structure of the music and the structure of the phenomenal world," which Daniel Albright describes as realizing "the deep equivalence of the natural and the artificial."[13] In this, Stravinsky is suggesting that the logic of music's language – or really Beethoven's particular musical language – creates the meaning-experience it seems to represent. Thus, the procedure of semantic formalism, *realizing* as it does the equivalence of the natural and the artificial, is powerfully performative insofar as it is an enactment as well as a representation. Later in this chapter I offer a formal description of the aesthetics of popular music in terms of the relationships among formal features in its modernist aesthetic. But it is important to remember that those relationships, above all, are *performed*.

The performative nature of popular music – the ways that it is more explicitly performative in its experience and in the ways that it is studied – is a basic assumption of *Modernism and Popular Music*. That is, throughout this book I particularly focus on performance in terms of the pleasure it creates, its improvisatory "form," the very thematics of performance in its finest achievements. The performative nature of popular music is closely tied to quotation – not only in Gershwin and Waller, but even in the Lacanian sense of the "quotation" of meaning, value, and even desire in our psychological lives – and performances of quotation bring together what seem to be somehow antithetical: semantics (content) and formality (structures). (This is particularly notable in the quotations of cliché.) That is, quotation is both formal and meaningful, a speech act that says something and does something, as Jonathan Culler demonstrates in his fine discussion of use and mention.[14] ("Mention" is the philosophical description of quotation.) The very concept of desire in Lacan and in Porter's musical performances hovers between the standardization of need and the semantics of demand in Lacan's topology of need/desire/demand. And Waller's signifyin', in a different register from the Gershwins' quotation, is both a formal repetition and a semantics.

Formalism of one sort or another, as I have mentioned, is necessarily clear and distinct: it offers the possibility of mathematical physics – and the hope of mathematical biology and mathematical sociology or economics – as well as the elaborations of harmony and development that are the result of the formal organization of sound in notation and strict composition, both of which are crowning achievements of Enlightenment modernity. Semantics, on the other hand – like its closely related science, phenomenology, that emerged in the late nineteenth century – replaces clarity and precise distinction with different kinds of overdeterminations. Twentieth-century "facts," in Poovey's history, are overdetermined in this way, and the linguist and semiotician A. J. Greimas makes such overdetermination clear when he argues that the "edifice" of language "appears like a construction without plan or clear aim" in which, for instance, "syntactic 'functions' transform grammatical cases by making them play roles for which they are not appropriate; entire propositions are reduced and described as if they behaved like simple adverbs."[15] Greimas summarizes this situation by asserting that "discourse, conceived as a hierarchy of units of communication fitting into one another, contains in itself the negation of that hierarchy by the fact that the units of communication with different dimensions can be at the same time recognized as equivalent" (82).[16]

That there might be a semantic formalism – or what Elmar Holenstein has called "phenomenological structuralism"[17] – seems, in the context of Enlightenment modernity (with its seemingly absolute distinction between nature and culture), a contradiction in terms. Yet the high modernist music of Arnold Schoenberg is just such a contradiction, a kind of phenomenological structuralism. And in humbler ways, the transformation of the clichés of the music and words of Tin Pan Alley into the felt meanings of the Gershwins, Porter, Waller, and Holiday also combine the repetitions of form and unique events of meaning in their enacted, performed achievements of semantic formalism. When I turn to what makes particular music "good" in my discussion of popular aesthetics near the end of this Introduction – as I claim that the performances of the popular musicians I treat here are particularly good – I will return to this sense of art forms conditioning and enacting the very meaning of experience.

Latour's global argument in *We Have Never Been Modern* is precisely that such an "absolute" contradiction between formal repetition and unique events – between, that is, the universal laws of nature and the inalienable rights of subjects – was the source of the power of Enlightenment modernity in science and politics precisely because the "moderns" asserted the absolute difference between nature and culture, the global and the local, yet at the same time *acted* as if there were no contradiction at all and thereby *enacted* modernity.[18] Latour argues that Enlightenment modernity governed itself by consistently acknowledging the anxiety of confusing these oppositions, even while it "performed," more or less unconsciously, their confusion. Similarly, Andreas Huyssen identifies as a defining feature of the high modernism of the early twentieth century the "conscious strategy of exclusion, an anxiety of contamination by its other: [namely,] an increasingly consuming and engulfing mass culture."[19] Thus, he describes modernist artists as particularly outraged by popular culture even while, as many recent scholars have noted, the high modernist arts freely appropriated the semantics of popular culture.[20] Popular music also enacts this contradiction inhabiting high modernism in its combinations of sound and sense, of music and the personality of its performers, of personal meanings and impersonal forces, and, of course, its appropriation and transformation of the banalities of Tin Pan Alley. Perhaps a better way of describing this is to note that the popular arts of the new twentieth century at their best, in large part because of the emancipation concomitant with its intense consumer culture, challenged the received universals of Enlightenment modernity, even while they reasserted different *kinds* of universals – of quotidian celebration, of communal solidarity, of achieved personal agency of those deprived of it – in the enactments of performance.

Most notably, popular music does so by shifting attention from the composer to the audience: it is precisely this that scandalizes Adorno in his high modernist disdainful observation that popular music and "jazz" cater "to the socially determined predisposition of the listener."[21] Thus Richard Middleton argues that

> Adorno assumes without question the superiority of certain kinds of listening, notably what he calls 'structural' or 'integrative' listening. Just as he privileges a particular mode of production (focused on the bourgeois composer), a particular kind of musical form (integrative, self-generating), and particular parameters of musical language (those foregrounded by notation), so he privileges the concomitant mode of listening . . . For Adorno, 'after Beethoven' any type of listening other than contemplative cognitive effort is necessarily regressive. Other listening modes – for instance, those where music is associated with activities of various kinds, the sounds perhaps impinging on muscles, skin, nerves as much as conscious thought processes – have a long and continuous history, however; and, still, as anthropologists have shown, a living ethnography.[22]

David Brackett, in his important study of popular music, more generally emphasizes the audience rather than the composer by citing Roland Barthes's contention that "a text's unity lies not in its origin but its destination,"[23] but he does not add what Barthes goes on to say in this essay, "The Death of the Author," that "this destination cannot any longer be personal: the reader is without history, biography or psychology" (148).[24] Such an impersonal audience, I think, is one way to distinguish achieved from banal popular music. The banality of the worst popular music resides, at least in part, in the fact that it never semanticizes its clichés, but leaves them empty ciphers that are charged, so to speak, to trigger automatic yet seemingly "personal" responses. The best popular music calls for responses that are not automatically personal, but that allow one to recover the social – and often utopian – meaning in seeming cipher-clichés. It is precisely this process, I argue later, that allows the recovery of celebration and community in achieved art. In any case, Barthes's *impersonal* sense of audience – like Middleton's *social* sense – is another way that the chapters of Part II are tied together. Chapters 3 and 4 focus on the impersonality of composition by focusing on just the kind of cliché and received ideas that Adorno hated: after all, he lauds Schoenberg as "a radical composer inspired by a drive for expression."[25] These chapters focus on the ways that the Gershwins' collaborations complicate the personal expressiveness of their music/lyrics and the ways that Porter's syncopations articulate patterns of desire which seem beyond personal "demand." And chapters 5 and 6 focus on the impersonality of performance. They focus on Waller's riffing on other people's music and lyrics and the ways that Holiday complicates the relationships between words and music.

Moreover, the chapters of Part II also complicate the clear and distinct differentiation between text and performance. That is, popular music necessarily shifts the locus of significance from score or text to performance. It is no accident, as I argue in Chapter 2, that the people who talked about the music of the 1920s and 1930s – all kinds of people from Irving Berlin to Theodor Adorno – used the term "jazz" to refer both to the self-consciously improvisational music that grew out of the African American community and the Tin Pan Alley "standards" of Berlin, Kern, Gershwin, Rogers, Porter, Arlen, Youmans, and others that grew out of the received practices of popular musical forms at the turn of the century. It is no accident because popular music was (and is) performance oriented: as both Middleton and Brackett argue, popular songs "circulated primarily as recordings" rather than scores[26] and call for different kinds of analysis and understanding from music circulated by means of authored scores.[27] Hamm also notes that popular music necessarily calls for an analysis of the arts which is "based upon economic and social relationships" that call for analytic periodization that does not present a progressivist understanding culminating in the "Concert Life" of art music as the apotheosis of Enlightenment conceptions.[28] All of these scholars are suggesting that the clear and distinct difference between popularly circulating demotic music and the "museum art" of concert music is, in fact, a function of the assumptions and strategies of listening brought to them and not an *absolute* distinction.

THE STRUCTURE OF THE ARGUMENT

In these ways, then, parts I and II of *Modernism and Popular Music* offer both counterpoint and harmony. Moreover, if music, as Middleton argues, impinges on "muscles, skin, nerves as much as conscious thought processes" and can be associated with "living ethnography,"[29] then the particular ethnographic senses of music presented in Part II harmonize with the general sense of cultural modernism examined in Part I. In Part II I examine four "musicians" in relation to sociality, subjectivity, semiotics, and aesthetics reconceived in relation to the conditions of the early twentieth century. In these analyses I am suggesting that the enormous transformations in the lived life of the early twentieth century that can be grasped under the category of cultural modernism, most markedly in the United States, created senses of a *new sociality*, a *new subjectivity*, a *new semiotics* – literally "new," since semiotic science, in Charles Sanders Peirce and Ferdinand Saussure, is part and parcel of cultural modernism altogether – and a *new aesthetics*, which I am calling "anagogic" insofar as it instances a more general sense of a transformation in experience altogether.

In these categories I am guided by J. Hillis Miller's examination of the "grounds" of literary study. Miller notes that literary criticism has developed four "basic" or "grounding" assumptions about how to interpret literary texts that present themselves as *needing* interpretation because such works present to readers texts which seem "irreducibly strange, inexplicable, perhaps even mad."[30] In short, Miller says, literary criticism developed in relation to works that present themselves as "anomalies of literature" that must be "made lawful" so that "the unaccountable [is made] accountable" (21). High modernist art forms, in particular, emphasize such "anomalies" in their self-conscious pursuit of the "new." In any case, Miller is writing at a particular moment in our intellectual history, a moment of "poststructuralism," and he offers a structuralist and poststructuralist response to "the terror and dread readers may experience" (20) when they confront such texts. In his argument "current criticism tends to propose one or another" of three grounds for normalizing such texts:

> the more or less hidden *social* or *ideological* pressures which impose themselves on literature and reveal themselves in oddnesses; *individual psychology*, the more or less hidden psychic pressures which impose themselves on a work of literature and make it odd, unaccountable; *language*, the more or less hidden rhetorical pressures, or pressures from some torsion within language itself as such, which impose themselves on the writer and make it impossible for his work to maintain itself as an absolutely lucid and reasonable account. (21; italics added)

To these three categories – organized, as they are, with a sense of creating a rational structure of accounting – he adds "a fourth possibility . . . [which is] exceedingly difficult to name in so many words." This possibility, he says, "for the disturber of narrative sanity and coherence, a disruptive energy neither society nor individual psychology nor language itself, is properly religious, metaphysical, or ontological, though hardly in a traditional or conventional way" (21).[31]

It is hardly conventional because it doesn't explain or "account for" the unaccountable the way that, say, the social meaning of ideological hegemony or the psychological meaning of the unconscious might make itself visible in the encountered disturbance. Miller's first three "grounds" make the unaccountable *accountable* precisely by making it reasonable, in the same way that Newtonian physics makes what William Blake took to be the miracle of the sunrise reasonable or the way that Adorno argues, in Theodore Gracyk's summary of his essentially high modernist position, that music – and art more generally – creates "the 'illusion' of its coherence and meaning" even while it fails. The example given by Adorno that Gracyk cites – important to my discussion of well-tempered music in Part I – is the fact that "the homophonic tradition that arose with the adoption of diatonic scales and equal temperament guaranteed conflict because 'harmony is never fully attainable . . . given the strict criteria of what harmony is supposed to be.'"[32] In this example the "hidden" dialectical (and ideological) truth Adorno describes *makes sense* of the failure of harmony, it makes that failure *reasonable*. Miller's fourth possibility doesn't make sense but reveals, in a poststructuralist gesture, senselessness altogether. The fourth possibility simply *names* the "disturbance" itself, "an ontology without ontology," as Miller says, the very "possibility" of meaninglessness itself: "something encountered in our relations to other people, especially relations involving love, betrayal, and that ultimate betrayal by the other of our love for him or her, the death of the other" (21).

Besides the fact that Miller's discursive description sounds like most of the themes of what in Chapter 2 I call the "second wave" of Tin Pan Alley that included the musicians I study here – themes in which the expressive content of popular music narrowed almost exclusively to personal emotion[33] – his "fourth possibility" subsumes all the rest insofar as it names the "ground" of encountered meaninglessness. He argues that each of these four "grounds" offers explanations or accountings of all the others, so that, for example, "social explanations see human psychology, language, and religion as epiphenomena of underlying and determining social forces" (22; Miller describes each of these grounds in similar terms). But his fourth ground does so in a different manner by revealing the possibility that all experience can be both "new" and strange; and it does so by functioning as an *anagogic* mode of accounting that demands that all phenomena be grasped in a new way.[34]

Miller is describing the ways that sensible accountings are "disturbed," as he says, by terrifying senselessness, but I want to argue that sensible accountings might also be upset by the complacent senselessness that is often found in cliché and received ideas. Even in the face of such clichés, as in the face of terrifying anomalies, such a new way of apprehension – that "makes it new!" in the slogan that captures the energy of both Enlightenment modernity and twentieth-century modernism – is possible. And such apprehension, I argue, is the work of the best popular music of the 1930s. In the chapters of Part II, I take each of Miller's grounds as the focus of discussion: the Gershwins' interaction with the *social* world of New York, Porter's enactments of the *psychological* rhythms of desire, Waller's *linguistic* engagements with music and with his world in African American signifyin'. But the final chapter, focused on the great performances of Billie Holiday, describes her ability to bend language to musical sound and make those sounds create an anagogic sense that we inhabit a *world* of music where nothing is not musical (just as Dante used the term "anagogic" to describe the fact that we inhabit a world of faith where there is nothing that does not exist in relation to faithfulness).

It is in this same way, I contend, that the new twentieth century – and I suspect the new eighteenth century as well – presented to its inhabitants and listeners the repeated experience of "modernity." Jean-François Lyotard has argued that "modernity, in whatever age it appears, cannot appear without the shattering of belief and without discovery of the 'lack of reality' of reality, together with the invention of other realities."[35] Despite Lyotard's apocalyptic sense – it is surely T. S. Eliot's as well, and Stephen Dedalus's, if not Joyce's, and Huyssen's sense of high modernism altogether – there are other ways of inventing "other realities" without shattering belief. One is the way in which the best popular music of the early twentieth century did it – as did other "high modernists," Joyce, Ellison, and Flannery O'Connor – by *realizing* cliché so that shared commonplaces can come to seem to be real in a new way and powerfully affective. Holiday turned the commonplaces of most of whatever she sang – more often than not written "by often less-than-first-rate lyricists," as Gunther Schuller notes[36] – into powerful music in this way, and the other musicians studied here found in commonplace ideas about sociality, feeling, and verbal intercourse similar kinds of musical modernism.

This, then, is my argument: that the finest music of the 1930s can find its place within a working sense of modernism and, indeed, can inflect and help shape that sense. The reinvention of love in the Gershwins, the modernist lyric poems of Porter, the punctuation of language in Waller, the semantic formalism of Holiday all exhibit this sense. Throughout these chapters I note available recordings of the music I discuss – I only wish I could have included the music with the book, texts and performances together. It is my hope that readers might share the music with me, as friends have always shared popular music, listening together, singing together, making origin and destination wonderfully the same. This is how we hear, play, and sing the music of our time.

THE AESTHETICS OF POPULAR MUSIC

Finally, to conclude this Introduction I explore the aesthetics of popular music – the elements of which, I hope, emerge throughout the following pages – and particularly the grounds for choosing the musicians I study in *Modernism and Popular Music* besides the categories that Miller articulates. As I have already suggested and will continue to argue in the section concluding this chapter and in the chapters that follow, the essence of popular music is performative: its ability, at its best, to impinge, as Middleton has argued, "on muscles, skin, nerves as much as conscious thought processes."[37] Such performativity, I have also suggested, is part of – perhaps at the base of – Adorno's objection to popular music, what he called "jazz." Before I turn to Adorno's aesthetics in order to describe an aesthetics of popular music (that, among other things, valorizes my choice of musicians in this book), let me say a few words about what I mean by the performative nature of popular music, and especially the particular nature of the *pleasures* of popular music. (Art for Adorno, it seems to me, yields truth rather than pleasure.)

In his study of the origins of consumer desire in Enlightenment modernity, Colin Campbell distinguishes (as I do in Chapter 4) between need and desire. He describes this opposition in terms of the contrast "between need and want [that] can be related to the difference between activities which aim to relieve discomfort and those which yield pleasure."[38] (Comfort, he argues throughout his book, is the goal of utilitarianism while pleasure is the goal of Romanticism [see particularly 193 and Chapter 9, "The Romantic Ethic"].) In his argument, Campbell calls the opposition of need to want "the difference in meaning between the concepts of need and satisfaction on the one hand, and those of desire and pleasure on the other. The former relate to state of being and its disturbance, followed by action to restore the original equilibrium . . . The paradigm for this model is . . . hunger. By contrast, pleasure is not a state of being so much as a quality of experience . . . The paradigm for this model is . . . sexual activity" (60).[39] The former describes Freud's definition of "pleasure" as the restoration of equilibrium (see, for instance, *Beyond the Pleasure Principle*), while the latter describes the working of desire as defined by Jacques Lacan and enacted in the music and lyrics of Cole Porter (see Chapter 4). Lacan is particularly useful in describing cultural modernism in relation to desire precisely because he emphasizes the performativity of pleasure. In his focus on need, Freud seems closer to the formal universals of Enlightenment modernity.

Pleasure, Campbell argues, organizes itself in a very different way from objects of need. "Objects," he writes,

possess utility or the capacity to provide satisfaction. It is, in this sense, an intrinsic attribute of real things: food can relieve hunger, clothes provide warmth, houses shelter, people affection. Pleasure, on the other hand, is not an intrinsic property of any object but is a type of reaction which humans commonly have when encountering certain stimuli. Pleasure is not even a property of stimuli, but refers to the capacity to react to stimuli in a certain fashion. To search for satisfaction is thus to engage with real objects in order to discover the degree and kind of their utility, whilst to search for pleasure is to expose oneself to certain stimuli in the hope that they will trigger a desired response within oneself. Hence, whilst one typically needs to make use of objects in order to discover their potential for satisfaction, it is only necessary to employ one's senses in order to experience pleasure, and, what is more, whereas an object's utility is dependent upon what it is, an object's pleasurable significance is a function of what it can be taken to be. (61)

In this sense, then, pleasure is necessarily *performed*: it is an event rather than an object (or a "thing," to repeat Porter's – and Lacan's – term I examine in Chapter 4), and as an event it necessarily encompasses production and consumption, performer and audience. For this reason many of the defining elements of "classical" or "art" music, as opposed to "popular" music – elements of notation, key, author, and so forth I mentioned earlier and explore in greater detail in Chapter 1 – are less important in studying popular music and its pleasures than its elements of enactment, performance, and what Simon Frith calls "*fun*": "the ideal of cultural experience," he writes, "is *fun*; pop provides routinized pleasures, more intense than the everyday but bound into its rhythms, and legitimized emotional gratification, a play of desire and discipline."[40] The defining aesthetic elements of popular music that "perform" pleasure include a dialectical sense of *wholeness*, *rhythmic decomposition*, and *montage*: the event of (musical) pleasure is a rhythmic "meaningful whole" that unfolds itself in juxtaposition and "breaks."[41]

I am adapting these terms from Adorno, who uses them to describe the art that is possible for modernism. I follow Adorno here because, despite his disparagement of popular music, he offers a remarkably powerful account of aesthetics in the culture of modernism. As Robert Witkin has noted,

Adorno has done more than any modern thinker to place the arts, both 'serious' and 'popular' at the very centre of a theory of modernity . . . In the process of developing his critical theory, Adorno provided a way of thinking about the homologous relationship between art and social life that will continue to influence the sociology of the arts long after the specific generalizations he made in relation to the popular music of the mid-twentieth century have been superseded.[42]

In studying modernist aesthetics, Adorno posits the touchstones for aesthetic value that I have mentioned. First of all, he emphasizes the *wholeness* of art even in the context of the dialectic of parts and whole that governs his working sense of the power of art and its reflective structuring of experience. Thus, in one critique of popular music, he sums up the difference between popular and "good serious music" thus:

> in Beethoven and in good serious music in general – we are not concerned here with bad serious music which may be as rigid and mechanical as popular music – the detail virtually contains the whole and leads to the exposition of the whole, while, at the same time, it is produced out of the conception of the whole. In popular music the relationship is fortuitous . . . [so that] the whole is never altered by the individual event and therefore remains, as it were, aloof, imperturbable and unnoticed throughout the piece.[43]

Such non-fortuitous "wholeness," as I am arguing, in which "the detail virtually contains the whole and leads to the exposition of the whole," defines the anagogic as I describe it throughout *Modernism and Popular Music*, but particularly in the final chapter focused on Billie Holiday. Such wholeness is enacted: it describes the performative "event" of pleasure.[44]

In addition, Adorno also emphasizes the "crisis" of such wholeness that is not an accidental occurrence that happens to a work of art, but part of its very nature – or at least part of its very nature within the culture of modernism. "It is the very moment of formal completion," he writes,

> at the greatest distance from the formlessness of nature, that the natural moment, that of the not yet formed and of the unarticulated, returns in strength. On the closest inspection of a work of art its most objectivized forms and images are transformed into a swarm of elements, texts dissolving into sheer words. When you think you have the basic details of a work of art firmly in your hands, they suddenly melt away into the indeterminate and the undifferentiated.[45]

This description comes close to asserting "the deep equivalence of the natural and the artificial" that Albright discerns in Stravinsky's articulation of what I am calling semantic formalism.[46] The melting into the indeterminate and undifferentiated that Adorno describes is also enacted – which is to say it is *performed* – in the Gershwins' uses of cliché described in Chapter 3. Cliché, as I note, is at the heart of popular music – just as its "standardizations," as I note in Chapter 1, are at the heart of Adorno's critique of popular music as well – but the utopian hopes of community and "pity," as I describe it later, can be discovered within the clichés of everyday life as a kind of redemptive gesture. The very dialogics of the Gershwins' words and music that I describe in Chapter 3 creates both the "swarm of elements" Adorno describes and a demotic American community for the new century.

More radically, the melting into the indeterminate is powerfully enacted in the sensuousness of music more generally that can be discovered in both the lyrics and the music of Cole Porter, his transformation of words into sound – "Do do that voodoo that you do so well!" – that returns to us to the "swarm of elements" Adorno is describing. "What is called reification," Adorno writes, "gropes, where it is radicalized, towards the language of things."[47] The great power of the modern lyric, Adorno writes elsewhere, enacts "the virtual elimination of mere content, [so that] the subject sounds through language in such a way that language itself becomes audible."[48] In Porter, sensuous music sound rings through words so that the subject – and particularly, as I argue following Lacan, the impersonal subject of desire – reveals itself in art. Moreover, in both Porter and Gershwin – and in music, popular or not, more generally – such a realization of the sensuous *quality* of sound is accomplished through rhythm and beat, the "breaks" I mention in a moment and the "beat" of music I describe in the concluding section of this chapter. Claude Lévi-Strauss describes this rhythm more generally in a discussion of the "musical emotion" that I cite at length in Chapter 4. In his analysis, he particularly discusses the manner in which music brings together or juxtaposes the physiological or "natural" rhythms of our bodies and the semiotic or "cultural" rhythms of our understanding.[49]

Such rhythmic juxtapositions create a montage effect; they enact montage in their very rhythmic gestures of syncopation and counterpoint. It is striking that Adorno valorizes the particularly modernist aesthetic form of the montage: "all modern art," he writes, "may well be montage."[50] Such montage, as Fredric Jameson argues, "is the moment of triumph of the constructional principle itself," and he goes on to quote from Adorno's *Aesthetic Theory*: "the aesthetic constructional principle, the peremptory primacy of the planned whole over detail as such . . . now stands as the correlative [to the seeming surface disorder]."[51] The signifyin' I trace in Waller and, to a lesser degree, in Armstrong's scat singing, creates this kind of montage in a triumph of the constructional principle in the face of racism. Such triumph is the achievement of popular music at its best, in which the particularities of performance – the "swarm of things" – seem to overwhelm "wholeness." In the case of the popular music of the 1930s, this "wholeness" is simply the "wholes" of received ideas and received musical forms, and the achievement of the "constructional principle" is to then construct (or "realize") a new sense of wholeness in a montage which, in popular music, encompasses audience as well as performer.

These elements of wholeness, rhythmic decomposition, and montage that I am borrowing from Adorno describe at least some of what is basic to a modernist aesthetic, and they are found in – indeed, they are *performed* by – the popular musicians studied in this book. As Adorno states in *Aesthetic Theory* to Jameson's delight – Jameson adds the italics to the following citation – "art remains alive only through its essentially social powers of resisting society; *unless it submits to reification, it becomes a mere commodity*."[52] But it is possible, I believe, that the commodification of art that so troubles Adorno can be redeemed. It is my contention that it is redeemed – at least at moments – in Gershwin, Porter, Waller, and Holiday, and, indeed, in other performances of the "best" popular music. These musicians, I am arguing, achieve some of the "best" popular music of the 1930s precisely because they participate in – they enact and perform – a modernist aesthetics that, as Stravinsky said, creates "a reflective system between the language structure of the music and the structure of the phenomenal world."[53]

Let me make this clear. Part of the reason that Adorno thinks a popular enactment is impossible, I believe, is because he always assumes, as I note in Chapter 1, that art is always tied to terror of suffering rather than to the pity that suffering and its artistic representation arouse – or, for that matter (as in all the musicians here), to the *pleasure* that the fellow feeling of both pity and art give rise to. Thus, in *Negative Dialectics* he asserts that "the need to lend a voice to suffering is a condition of all truth."[54] As an exile from Hitler's Germany, a Jew, a survivor in the face of horrendous devastation, Adorno, I suspect, was not able to recover the celebration and community that art creates – its pleasures – as well as its lonely truth.[55] In his sympathetic examination of Adorno's relation to popular music, Witkin sums this up in ways that may justify my use of Adorno's aesthetics in describing what I am calling the best popular music of the 1930s. "The emotions that surface in the blues and in jazz," Witkin writes,

> celebrate a life that is suppressed and mutilated by modernity, and jazz has as much claim to being considered a medium of resistance as does the art of the high priests of modernism. The principal difference is that this suppressed life, the life of the body rather than the life of the mind, has a space in which it can be lived, namely the space of the interpersonal, the domestic and the leisured world. Its dynamic is not that of a negative dialectics aimed at the totalitarian collective, but of a sensuous and charged affectivity, lived and celebrated on the margins of

rational-technical modernity, configured in relation to it and always rubbing up against its grain.[56]

Witkin sums up the aesthetics of wholeness, rhythmic decomposition, and montage I have been tracing in Adorno in his powerful juxtaposition of Adorno and Winthrop Sargeant. Adorno cites Sargeant enthusiastically, Witkin notes (110), yet he misses the sense of celebration and achievement that Sargeant finds in popular music. America's "most characteristic arts," Sargeant wrote,

> – the comic strip, the skyscraper, journalism, jazz, the tap dance, the 'happy ending' movie – all lack the element of 'form' that is so essential to tragedy, to the symphony, to the novel, to the opera, to monumental architecture and even to some of the less pretentious arts of other nations . . . The European 'composition' is a complex structure of organized sound, fixed more or less immutably as to form. It perpetuates the message of a creative mind through generations, even centuries . . . The form in which the message is cast is subject to a process of intellectual development. Its composers themselves are highly trained professionals, the greatest of them capable of extraordinary feats of technique which average people marvel at but can scarcely hope to duplicate. (cited in Witkin 112)

Both Sargeant and Witkin are celebrating comic rather than tragic art that gives itself over to its audiences and their communal laughter and pleasure.

That is, Sargeant is praising non-monumental art, "a music," Witkin notes, "that he identifies with performance and not with composition" (113). "When players, dancers and audience alike are hanging desperately on to their sense of rhythmic orientation on the one hand," Sargeant notes, "and are violently disturbing it (or listening to it being violently disturbed) on the other, the result is jazz in its purest form" (cited in Witkin 114). Such human comedy can be discerned in Joyce and Williams, but not so clearly in the monumental art of Eliot and Schoenberg. And it achieves its effects in bringing together senses of wholeness and rhythmic decomposition in the seemingly "accidental" form of montage. In popular music, such montage realizes itself in what Sargeant calls the jazz "break," the musician improvising against the strict – Adorno calls it the "standardized" – beat of the received music. Waller performs such breaks verbally, playing, as we shall see, words against music; Holiday performs them harmonically and rhythmically, playing beat against beat. But even Gershwin and Porter "improvise" against standard forms in their written music: the Gershwin brothers play with musical and verbal quotation to create a montagelike music; and Porter plays words into sound – into swarming things – to realize what Lacan describes as restless desire (rather than Freud's more traditional satisfaction of a need). It is this *power* of popular modernist music that Sargeant comprehends more fully than Adorno (who grasps, I believe, the power of modernist art forms more generally). Thus Sargeant notes that "the phenomenon of simultaneous rhythms, playing against each other, is, of course, not limited to the break . . . The break merely represents the principle of syncopation operating on somewhat larger spans of musical structure . . . Indeed certain types of hot jazz may be said to consist of an indefinite series of breaks" (cited in Witkin 113).

The space in which art "can be lived" that Witkin describes (179) is ordinary and popular, but it is also, as I suggest in what follows, a particularly urban space, particularly the New York of the Gershwins with which I begin, that is inhabited also by Waller and Holiday and is the space that the Protestant Porter felt both drawn to and not quite part of. This is why, at least in part, I have not included the blues that Witkin mentions as part of my examination of the modernism of popular music. Certainly the music of Robert Johnson, Bessie Smith, and others could be configured within the discussions that follow. But the twentieth-century cultural modernism I discuss was a particularly metropolitan phenomenon – Raymond Williams, among others, makes this argument[57] – and the blues essentially was a rural and, more strikingly, a railroad traveling music, focused most of all on the freedoms of movement.[58] Commercial popular music, as I note in Chapter 2, was quintessentially urban, as was its lower-middle-class audience and the ideology of that class (urban but not quite bourgeois). In short, the "space" in which the popular music of twentieth-century modernism was lived – "the space of the interpersonal, the domestic and the leisured world" Witkin describes – was the urban space of Gershwin, Porter, Waller, Holiday, Tin Pan Alley, and radio broadcasts from New York and other urban centers.

A NOTE ON INTERDISCIPLINARITY

The chapters of Part II focus on the music and musicality of the Gershwins, Porter, Waller, and Holiday, yet the organization of these chapters and their focuses, based as it is on Miller's sense of the "grounds" of *literary study*, emphasizes that the interdisciplinarity of their analyses are inflected by and towards the interpretive work of literary studies. Still, I hope that the work of *Modernism and Popular Music* will appeal to students of cultural history, popular music studies, sociology, semiotics, and musicology. The last of these disciplines is both important and, in relation to this book, a case study for interdisciplinarity. Richard Middleton, among many others, has focused on the encounter of musicology with popular music studies. Popular music studies, he notes, are powerfully interdisciplinary. In *Studying Popular Music* he devotes an important chapter on what he calls "the musicological problem," focusing on the ways that the terminology, methodology, and ideology of musicology developed in relation to the "classical" tradition of music that "centred on the work of the Austro-German 'great masters' from Bach and Handel to Mahler, Richard Strauss and Schoenberg [– a tradition which formed] the core of the emerging bourgeois concert repertory. It found its philosophical grounding," Middleton concludes, "in the aesthetic and historical theories of German idealism."[59]

It is a "problem," Middleton argues, because in relation to this historical tradition musicology developed a particular vocabulary for studying music that was based upon music that depended, primarily, on the "notational centricity" (104) of written notation for its composition. The basis of written notation, he argues, "encouraged reification . . . [so that] the score comes to be seen as 'the music'" (105), and both performance is downgraded and the author is emphasized above the audience in the analysis of music.[60] "Western musical analysis," he argues (following the argument of Charles Keil), "by virtue of its dependence on notation," focuses on syntax and the syntactic: "it centres . . . on the hierarchic organization of quasi-linguistic elements and their putting together (com-position) in line with systems of norms, expectations, surprises, tensions and resolutions" (115).[61] In contrast to this, Keil argues, "non-notated musics – and *performances* of written music to some extent – foreground *process*. They are much more concerned with gesture, physical feel, the immediate moment, improvisation" (Middleton's paraphrase, 115). In a later study, Middleton notes that "mainstream methods" of musicology have had "a tendency to formalism,"[62] and he suggests that "a theory of gesture" – understood "as possessing affective and cognitive as well as kinetic aspects" (105) – is necessary. Such a theory, moreover, would necessarily be interdisciplinary, looking "outside musicology, to anthropology and cultural theory – for example, to Lévi-Strauss's theory of 'correspondences' between musical and somatic structures,"[63] among others. (In Chapter 4, I examine Lévi-Strauss's theory in relation to desire in Porter.) Although Middleton doesn't mention it, Keil argues that the "basic unit" of the classical tradition in Western music is the "'sound term' (phrase)" while the "basic unit" of popular music (his chief example is jazz) is "gesture (phrasing)."[64] This opposition instantiates the more general opposition between the "embodied meaning" of the classical tradition with the "engendered feeling" of musical traditions "outside the West [that] are almost exclusively performance traditions"

(338). Such engendered feeling, of course, is the pleasure I discussed earlier. In Chapter 6, I analyze the ways that Billie Holiday "'gestures' with her voice."

A theory of gesture is necessarily "interpretive" in the same way that semiotic science, as Greimas describes it, focusing as it does on overdetermined definitions and borders, calls for interpretation that does not come after and "interpret" some pre-existing fact, but creates, in its act (or "gesture") of interpretation – in its *semantic formalism* that equates the natural and the artificial – the possibility of grasping a phenomenon as a "fact" in the first place.[65] Thus, Keil suggests in one example that "gesture" is not a label for a pre-existing action, but the very act of grasping an action *as* a gesture: "when a jazz saxophonist comes up with a triple forte screech, is he having reed trouble or is it the climax of his solo? Only the gesture's place in the overall process can determine the answer" (345). If it were the "accidental" screech of reed trouble, it is not a gesture at all, but a simple accident. A gesture, one might say, is a complex accident, purposeful and aleatory at the same time (insofar as a screech might be unintentional and yet still purposeful), and essentially *subject* to interpretation.

J. L. Austin describes how an act might be purposeful and unintentional at the same time,[66] and, in fact, Austin's speech-act philosophy stands behind this discussion and the sense of the performativity of popular music I am following throughout this book. In his work, Austin distinguishes between "constative" meaning, that asserts propositions about the world that can be judged true or false, and "performative" meaning, that by means of a particular act (or even a "gesture") of language performs an act that cannot be judged true or false but rather successful or unsuccessful. (He describes such success as "felicitous"[67] and with that description we can assimilate the opposition of constative and performative to the opposition of truth and pleasure I have been pursuing in aesthetics.) His examples of performative language include the "I do" of a marriage ceremony or "I bet you five dollars it will rain tomorrow." The act of saying these things *enacts* what is said.[68] As I argue more fully in a moment, a working sense of the performative aspect of language is crucial to literary studies insofar as any performance *calls for* interpretation, just as Keil calls for interpretation when he wonders whether the "gesture" of a triple forte screech is reed trouble or the climax of a jazz solo. He concludes that "only the gesture's place in the overall process can determine the answer" (345). The gesture's place in a process is precisely the interpretation of performance.

Such performativity situates the "jazz" of popular music – its wholeness, decomposition, and montage – within modernism. Here is the argument.

The very "revolution of the word" that Colin MacCabe finds in Joyce's modernism is the fact that in "the *classic realist text*," he argues, everything inside quotation marks was subject to interpretation since it is *performed* by characters in the classic novel, while the narrator's language – like the transcendental nature of Enlightenment "truth" I examine in Chapter 1 – "transcended" local manifestations of "quoted" language: "the text outside the area of inverted commas claims to be the product of no articulation, it claims to be unwritten,"[69] which is to say *unperformed*. To conceive of all of a literary text – including its seeming transcendental and authoritative narrator, who simply tells the "true" story – as a performance of language subject to interpretation was indeed a "revolution of the word": "in place of a discourse," MacCabe argues, "which attempts to place and situate everything, we have discourses which are determined in their situation by the reader" (28). In this way, language becomes "gestural" in the same way that the *place* of the jazz saxophonist's triple forte screech can only be determined by the listening audience encountering the performance. Similar "revolutions of the word" were Bakhtin's and Freud/Lacan's equally "modernist" insights (governing my discussions of the music of Gershwin and Porter) that words in their performances might convey more than a speaking subject consciously intends, revealing social forces, drives, and linguistic structures beyond the speaker's conscious understanding. (MacCabe's argument depends on Freud and Lacan.) For this reason the philosophy of language (as in Austin's ordinary-language philosophy), psychology, sociology, dialogics, like literary studies, are all *interpretive* sciences engaging performance.[70] So is the study of popular music (as opposed to musicology). All of these are also, I am suggesting, sciences of and within cultural modernism.

The more or less formal "syntactic" analysis of traditional musicology is not interpretive in the way that these "modernist" sciences are. Middleton emphasizes this when he focuses on the terminology of musicology: the vocabulary "mainstream" musicology developed, he notes, focuses on certain elements of phonic organization "in musicology's typical corpus, and [is] an impoverished vocabulary for others."[71] Such terminology emphasizes certain "facts" about music and obscures others, and it does so by creating, as we have seen, a "hierarchic organization of quasi-linguistic elements and their putting together (com-position) in line with systems of norms, expectations, surprises, tensions and resolutions" (115).[72] For Middleton, the terminology of traditional musicology obscures the kinetic functioning of music – "listening modes . . . where music is associated with activities of various kinds" rather than cognitive processes (58) – while remaining remarkably powerful in its examination of the *formal* aspects of musical composition. Such formalism, at least apparently, relies less on "interpretation" than on analysis of the cognitive import of music and pre-existing ("transcendental") forms by which the cognitive import is understood. Gesture, as Steven Mithen has argued, lies at the core of music and, he speculates, as the evolutionary basis of language that might be described as "proto-cognitive" rather than cognition itself. He even describes the emphasis on prosody at the expense of semantics in infant-directed speech and suggests that such speech answers "the emotional and linguistic needs" of infants even without clear (and formally discernable) cognitive meanings.[73] Gesture, then, emphasizes the performed rhythms of music: Keil's essay almost exclusively uses bass and drum in his examples of "tension" and "vital drive" so that, as he notes (in a description that encompasses Billie Holiday's singing), "in music concerned with process, constant repetition, the use of clichés, and exceedingly small tonal repertoires can sometimes be employed to create great tension and vital drive."[74] Middleton's sense of such performed rhythms means "that how we feel and how we understand musical sounds are organized through processual shapes which seem to be analogous to physical gestures," a theory of "musical gestures – deep structures or principles which give unity to a music culture – [that] are underlaid with still deeper generating 'gestures': kinetic patterns, cognitive maps, affective movements. But these," he continues, "are probably specific to a culture too: people seem to learn to emote, to order experience, even to move their bodies, through locally acquired conventions."[75] In such musical gestures in the popular music of the 1930s, I am arguing, we might also discern or "interpret" other cultural values: the particular sociality, subjectivity, linguistic play, and the very shape of experience of cultural modernism.

The theory of gesture that Middleton advocates should not, and does not in his argument, replace traditional musicology. "The rehabilitation of a more kinetically oriented mode of analysis does not mean," he argues,

> . . . that other modes are always irrelevant. To return to the opening of Beethoven's fifth symphony for a moment: as well as functioning gesturally, the passage obviously carries a range of connotations (fate, heroism, and all that); and at the same time stands at the beginning of a large-scale musical argument [that traditional musicology analyzes], which will not be completed until the very end of the final movement, and which for its full assimilation certainly does demand the techniques of structural listening. What I would suggest is that these three areas – gesture, connotation, argument – operate in different repertories in diverse ratios and interrelationships; and analysis needs to reflect that.[76]

Moreover, these three areas are emphasized in different disciplines: formally analyzing argument is the work of traditional musicology, discerning the function of connotation is the work of semiotics, and teasing out the relationships among gestures and meanings and affects – gestures and their contexts, as Keil says – is the work of highly interpretive disciplines. Specifically, the work of literary studies – or cultural studies inflected by literary studies – teases out relationships between performance and text, performance and context: between performative and constative utterances in the vocabulary of speech-act theory or among understanding, history, and experience in the vocabulary of cultural studies more generally. John Casti describes these *kinds* of disciplines in relation to the *predictable* certainties of physics, the *explanations* of the "semi-physics" of biological sciences, and what he calls the *metaphysics* of the "postulation," "assumption," and "presupposition" – terms which sometimes represent "out-of-the-blue assumption[s]" – of the "social and behavioral arenas" of what I am calling literary and cultural studies.[77]

Another way to say this is to note that the four "grounds" of literary studies that Miller describes and by which I organize the modernist "ethnography" in Part II of this book shift and slide as primary and secondary modes of understanding, base and superstructure, as each is postulated, assumed, and presupposed. Such presuppositions are *gestures* of interpretation. Middleton bases his argument for a theory of gesture on the work of János Maróthy, who "defines rhythm as 'a repetition of any element, whereby heterogeneity can be made coherent'; its periodicities 'reveal the identity hidden in difference.'"[78] Such a sense of rhythm is radically interpretive insofar as the "identity" of any particular repeated element is defined in the process of recognizing – which is to say *grounding* – a seemingly repeated identity in fields of difference. One can "ground" culture – cultural modernism as I describe it in *Modernism and Popular Music* – in terms of sociality, subjectivity, semiotics, or aesthetics (taken large, anagogically, as "experience" itself). But such grounding is necessarily gestural insofar as it is "proto-cognitive," embodying and leading to meaning at the same time, in a single "gesture" of presupposition, assumption, and postulation, a gesture of semantic formalism.

Interdisciplinarity is gestural in a similar fashion. It brings disciplines together in counterpoint and harmony, yet it always contains a "gesture" of grounding, of finding the inflection of a particular discipline that shapes and focuses its questions and answers. The literary "grounds" I pursue in *Modernism and Popular Music* create this kind of inflection for my study of cultural modernism in terms of the experiential aesthetics of the popular music and language of the new century. In *Modernism and Time*, which focused on the sciences and literature of the new twentieth century, I inflected my study of cultural modernism in a similar fashion. But in both the sciences and the popular arts of the new century I am trying to describe the transformations in understanding, experience, and history that were conditioned by the repertoires of cultural phenomena I examine that seemed to burst forth, new and strange, but also as a kind of outlandish repetition, a century ago. The "high" modernism of Schoenberg and Picasso, Stravinsky and Stein, is new and strange; but there is also a "popular" modernism, in Gershwin and Williams, Waller and Joyce, Holiday and Woolf, playing across the experience of the new with outlandish repetitions of the ordinary and quotidian: "routinized pleasures," as Frith says – city walks, a refrigerator note, the syncopation of a standard chord progression – "more intense than the everyday but bound into its rhythms."[79] It is instances of these last "modernist" texts – organized around ordinary pleasures – that can be found in the American popular music of the 1930s and that help us understand cultural modernism more generally.

PART I

Musical modernism: popular music in the time of jazz

CHAPTER I

Classical modernity and popular music

MODERNISM'S OTHER CONSTITUENCY

In his remarkable book *Rites of Spring: The Great War and the Birth of the Modern Age*, Modris Eksteins argues that the inaugural performance of Igor Stravinsky's *Rite of Spring* in 1913 in Paris stands as a "landmark of modernism, . . . one of the supreme symbols of our centrifugal and paradoxical century, when in striving for freedom we have acquired the power of ultimate destruction."[1] That historical performance remains a "supreme" symbol of *unpopular* music: the ballet that enacted the clashing and blending of an ancient pagan Russian myth and the rhythms of sounds of modern Paris – "its crash, clash, cling, clang, bing, bang bing" as one reviewer described it (cited in *Rites of Spring* 9) – with its cars and horns and massive dissonance, at the eve of World War I to an audience that was shocked and dismayed. At that performance in May 1913 in what Eksteins describes as "the newly constructed, ultramodern Théâtre des Champs-Élysées" (16) men in tuxedos and women in evening dresses rioted, ripping chairs out of the concert hall and breaking windows and electric chandeliers while hearing (but barely hearing, since there was so much tumult) Stravinsky's strange rhythms and chords and watching the dancers' curious stiff movements and gestures. Carl Van Vechten describes the furor this way:

> Cat-calls and hisses succeeded the playing of the first few bars, and then ensued a battery of screams, countered by a foil of applause . . . Some forty of the protestants were forced out of the theater but that did not quell the disturbance. The lights in the auditorium were fully turned on but the noise continued and I remember Mlle. Piltz [dancing the part of the chosen maiden] executing her strange dance of religious hysteria on a stage dimmed by the blazing light in the auditorium, seemingly to the accompaniment of the disjointed ravings of a mob of angry men and women.[2]

Such a scene is the very enactment of unpopular music where "the Comtesse de Pourtalès . . . as Cocteau tells it [got] up, coronet askew, waving her fan, and exclaim[ed]: 'I am sixty years old and this is the first time anyone has dared to make fun of me'";[3] it enacts, as much high modernism does (or did), a sense of art as scandal, as aiming, as George Steiner has noted, at "difficulty."[4]

Carol Oja offers a spirited comparison between *Le Sacre du printemps* and George Gershwin's *Rhapsody in Blue*. Stravinsky's work premiered in the United States in Philadelphia in 1922, and had its first New York performance in January 1924, "just two weeks before the debut of *Rhapsody in Blue*."[5] Oja describes the ways that Stravinsky and Gershwin were compared: Paul Whiteman, who commissioned Gershwin's *Rhapsody*, called the event "An Experiment in Modern Music" (652), while others in "the budding modernist scene in America" emphasized the opposition between high and low art (655), and depicted Aaron Copland, for instance, "as elevating jazz into art, while Gershwin kept it at the base level of popular entertainment" (656). Oja argues that "ardent highbrows . . . saw Gershwin as a threat to the basic value system on which they had been weaned: that of European high art" (661–62).[6] Such a divide between "high" art and popular art distinguished, in the judgment of many of Gershwin's "serious" contemporaries (as in Andreas Huyssen's argument), "high modernism" from the popular arts. Theodor Adorno, as I suggested in the Introduction, is an extreme spokesperson for the "unpopularity" of high modernism. In *The Philosophy of Modern Music*, he argues that "because the monopolistic means of distributing music stood almost entirely at the disposal of artistic trash and compromised cultural values, and catered to the socially determined predisposition of the listener, radical music [i.e., high modernist music] was forced into complete isolation during the final stages of industrialism."[7]

Popular music is different from such unpopular modernism: it aims at simplicity rather than difficulty, even when it is complex, as it often is in George Gershwin and Cole Porter; it aims at reassurance, rather than scandal, even when it is disturbing, as it often is in Fats Waller and Billie Holiday; it aims, most of all, to express ordinary and everyday moments, rather than extraordinary moments of epiphany and revelation – the beginning of time in Stravinsky, the end of time in Olivier Messiaen – even as it reminds us, at its best, that the ordinary is worthy of powerful attention. At its worst – or, perhaps, in its own ordinariness – the popular presents the simplicities and reassurances of cliché. And much of the Tin Pan Alley music – which Gershwin and Porter wrote within and against and which Waller and Holiday struggled with in their performances – embodied, in its banal sentiments and forced rhymes, such cliché. But if "high modernism," as Eksteins and many others have noted, articulated a kind of "destructiveness" – a horror, as Yeats noted, of the "filthy modern tide" (Adorno also bemoans the "filthy tide" of popular culture)[8] – then the "everyday modernism" of the best popular music after World War I aimed at recovering certain kinds of human truths, about love, sorrow, ordinary unhappiness, that seem sometimes less apparent in the noisiness of high modernist theatrics. That is, the shock and dislocations of cultural modernism and high modernist art, as Cornel West has suggested,[9] shocked most of all those whose position in society was established and threatened: people like Matthew Arnold, frightened at the "anarchic" power of the working classes in late Victorian England; or Yeats and T. S. Eliot, with their pretensions to aristocratic culture; or Adorno, with his disdain for the popular arts; or even, in a different register, the Comtesse de Pourtalès, whose outrage Eksteins's narration of the response to *Rite of Spring* describes. For others – Eastern European Jewish immigrants in America, who had been literally dislocated and marginalized in Europe for generations; or homosexual "inverts" or "perverts" as they were described in the last decades of the nineteenth century,[10] who also had been socially ostracized in the communities they lived in; or black men and women, whose families had been literally transported to American plantations and later dislocated from the rural south to northern urban centers such as St. Louis, Chicago, and Harlem; or women in general, who suffered generations of oppression and circumscribed opportunity – for such people the possibilities of personal and social fulfillment offered by the remarkable wealth of modernity's second Industrial Revolution were not shocking but promised the potential transformation of everyday life.[11] That is, the seeming debased standardizations of all sorts of commodities in the second Industrial Revolution that took place in the generation around the turn of the new twentieth century was, for many – indeed, for the vast majority of people in Western Europe and America – enrichment and empowerment.

The advent of "popular" music in the new twentieth century makes the contradiction inherent in the commodification and popular dissemination of art particularly clear. This can be seen in the historical and ideological analysis of the definition of popular music that Richard Middleton has set forth. Following Frans Birrer, Middleton neatly describes four "standard" criteria for defining popular music: that it is "inferior"; that it is "not something else (usually 'folk' or 'art' music)"; that it is associated with a particular social group; that it "is disseminated by mass media and/or in a new mass market." He demonstrates that "none of these categories are satisfactory."[12] Instead, he describes the *process* of popular music as "an active tendency" "within the context of the *whole musical field*" (7), a tendency, conditioned by social struggle (including the social struggle that West suggests is part and parcel of high modernism), to create a sense that "the pattern of elements that it organizes comes to seem 'natural'; [and] in this form it usually spreads widely through society" (9). Most important in this analysis, Middleton describes the "commodification" of music: "By the 1890s," he writes, a "moment of 'mass culture'" can be seen to occur,

> characterized by the development of monopoly-capitalist structures. National lineages remain important, but as one pole of a tension counterbalanced by a growing internationalization of culture, associated particularly with an emerging American hegemony. This shows itself both in musical content – the impact of ragtime, jazz, Tin Pan Alley songs, new dance forms, and so on – and new methods of mass production, publicity, and distribution: in short, a drive towards 'one-way communication' in homogeneous markets . . . By the First World War, musical production and dissemination are coming to be concentrated in a new alliance consisting of a centralized publishing system (in New York's Tin Pan Alley and London's Denmark Street), the quickly developing gramophone companies (by 1910 dominated, world-wide, by Victor of the USA, and the Gramophone Co. of Britain) and, a little later, the new medium of radio. (13–14)

Middleton goes on to say, that "as for the avant-garde, we can see the development of modernism as precisely an outraged and deliberately esoteric response to the new drive towards total commodification" (14).

Such commodification, I am suggesting, has a positive as well as a negative side: even Marx acknowledges this when, in *The Communist Manifesto*, he describes the enormous positive forces unleashed by capitalism.[13] And that positive side, articulated in simplicity, reassurance, and expressions of the ordinary, made available to many people and classes of people who had not participated in or benefited from the "Age of Europe" art forms that they could take to heart. In other words, in *Modernism and Popular Music* I am pursuing a definition of *popular* music that assumes that its very "popularity" is a function of the fact that it takes up aspects of our lives that everyone shares, what Stephen Dedalus describes in *A Portrait of the Artist as a Young Man* – he is defining the terror and pity of tragedy – as "constants" in human affairs:

> Pity is the feeling which arrests the mind in the presence of whatsoever is grave and constant in human sufferings and unites it with the human sufferer. Terror is the feeling which arrests the mind in the presence of whatsoever is grave and constant in human sufferings and unites it with the secret cause.[14]

It might well be that high modernism, in its iconoclastic pursuit of the "new," takes up the *terror* of whatsoever is grave and constant in human affairs – not just in "suffering," but in personal and social human life in general – while the popular arts at their best take up the *pity* of whatsoever is grave and constant in human affairs. The term "pity" is particularly interesting in this regard. It was a powerfully positive term in English and other European languages until the advent of cultural modernism in the early twentieth century, when it subsequently became a term of condescension and dismissiveness. It is found in Chekhov and Tolstoy, in Stowe, and most powerfully in Wilfred Owen's World War I poetry, which aims to articulate, as he says, "the truth untold, / the pity of war, The pity war distilled." Owen's is a "popular" art: it is not as difficult or arcane or, most of all, as ironic as that other high modernist World War I poem, *The Waste Land*.[15] Rather, it seeks in received poetic forms to describe the common experience of suffering.[16]

At the base of this study is my intuition that popular music is a special case of the popular arts precisely because it is a *performance* art as well as a *commercial* art while other popular "arts" – illustration, formulaic genre fiction, mass-produced architecture, cinema, even the skyscrapers Winthrop Sargeant mentions[17] – although capable of achieving notable insights and communion in and with their audiences, are not performative in the same way. Throughout *Modernism and Popular Music* I repeatedly return to and emphasize the ways that popular music and its pleasures are performative, especially in the ways that, as I mention in the Introduction, literary studies teaches us to attend to the performative impulse in language and action. Here, though, I want to mention Aaron Copland's insights about "musical imagination" in the United States and in the Americas. In his 1952 Norton Lectures entitled *Music and Imagination*, Copland argues that the distinguishing feature of American music – both in composition and in performance – is its rhythms. To analyze this, he examines a pre-Enlightenment musical form, the Elizabethan madrigal, emphasizing, as he does, the madrigals' creation at the very beginning of standardized notation for music. This Enlightenment standardization occasioned "notational speculation" that allowed their composers "a new toy by means of which they were enabled to experiment with all manner of unprecedented rhythmic combinations."[18] "The rhythmic complexities of the Elizabethan madrigalists," he argues, " . . . were firmly grounded in English speech rhythms. By retaining these independently in each vocal part a delightful freedom of cross-rhythmic irregularities resulted. And since English is a strongly accented language – with qualitative rather than quantitative values – a rich and supple variety of rhythm was obtained" (92–93). Copland goes on to argue that

> the polyrhythmic structures of Elizabethan composers are different in kind from those that typify American music. They were concerned with the creation of a supple and fluid pulse in which no single strong beat dominated the overall rhythmic flow. Our polyrhythms are more characteristically the deliberate setting, one against the other, of a steady pulse with a free pulse. Its most familiar manifestation is in the small jazz band combination, where the so-called rhythm section provides the ground metrics around which the melody instruments can freely invent rhythms of their own. (93)

Copland concludes his discussion of the "rhythm-inspired music" of America (95) by examining *improvisation*, the very essence of music as performance rather than text. He notes that baroque music often included the improvisation of individual keyboard performers, but "the idea of *group* improvisation was reserved for the jazz age" (96). Now, the very idea of *group* improvisation is communal and "popular," entailing those active "listening modes" that Middleton describes "where music is associated with activities of various kinds, the sounds perhaps impinging on muscles, skin, nerves as much as conscious thought processes."[19] Rather than an individual author, popular music entails different kinds of *enacted* collaborations – musicians and producers, musicians and media, musicians and (often dancing) audiences[20] – all of which create the fellow feeling of communal "pity," articulated, as I mentioned, in simplicity, reassurance, and expressions of the ordinary that are *popularly* made available to many hitherto disenfranchised people and classes of people, art forms, as I said, that they could take to heart.

It is to examine this other constituency of modernism – the constituency of common, ordinary, and, often, hitherto disenfranchised people – and its *other* response to the powerful cultural changes of the new twentieth century that I discuss in *Modernism and Popular Music* the work of the most popular and most enduring composers of the 1930s in relation to cultural modernism – to its social world, its sense of subjectivity, its language, its experience of music. I'm thinking of the composers and performers I've already mentioned: the Gershwin brothers, who introduced the musicality of indigenous African American music of the southland to popular commercial music in New York in the 1920s; Cole Porter, who incorporated jazz rhythms within his ballads and lyrics; Fats Waller, like the Gershwins a native New Yorker, who refined the particular northern and urban music of the stride piano that grew out of the cultural situation of Harlem; and

Billie Holiday, of Philadelphia and New York, who sang the songs of all the rest with haunting virtuosity. I have chosen these musicians in part because they embody in their popular art the sociality, the subjectivity, the language, and the overarching "experience" that came to be felt and lived within the cultural modernism of the new twentieth century. In part I have chosen them because they exemplify, individually and together, the dialectic of performance and text that, as I argue, defines the historical phenomenon of popular music. (Middleton also makes this dialectic central to his discussions of popular music.) And I have chosen them, as I suggested in the Introduction, for the sheer pleasure they provoke and participate in.

In other words, I have chosen the Gershwins, Porter, Waller, and Holiday for the remarkable quality and the thoroughgoing popularity of their work. In Chapter 3 I take the opportunity of citing Aaron Copland's striking description of the fine jazz improvisation of Lenny Tristano that avoids what Copland describes as two "pitfalls" that prevent the "freedom" of performative improvisation, "the conventionality of jazz harmonic formulas, and . . . over-used melodic formulas."[21] As I suggest in the follow chapters, the Gershwins and Porter avoid conventionality of harmony and melody even while they work, seemingly, within their confines, and they do so, I argue, by *enacting* modalities of performance in their music. And Waller and Holiday in their realized performances transform those conventions into the achieved freedom of popular music, which, I am suggesting, is best understood in relation to popular performances. Thus, finally, I have chosen them for their abiding popularity, their ubiquity in the experience of most people living in America in the middle twentieth century. To some extent, Part I's title, "Musical modernism" – and the musical modernism I focus on throughout this book – is about everyday modernism rather than the "high modernism" of unpopular culture. To this end, I examine music most everybody born before the 1960s knows: George and Ira Gershwin's "I Got Rhythm," Cole Porter's "Night and Day," Fats Waller's "Ain't Misbehavin'," Billie Holiday singing both her blues "Fine and Mellow" with Lester Young and singing the Gershwins' "They Can't Take That Away from Me."

ENLIGHTENMENT MODERNITY AND TWENTIETH-CENTURY MODERNISM

Before I focus on this music in Chapter 2, though, I want to describe more fully the concept of modernism and, at the end of the chapter, to examine more fully the structure I follow in this book which I outlined in the Introduction, presenting one way of grasping or configuring twentieth-century modernism. "Modernism" is a particularly overdetermined term. It refers to the advent of Enlightenment modernity in Europe in the sixteenth and seventeenth centuries – especially the seventeenth century with its Thirty Years War, almost coincident with the life of René Descartes, that saw the beginnings of the modern nation state and secular science in the context of its great religious strife. And it also refers to twentieth-century modernism, what I am calling cultural modernism or twentieth-century modernism, the remarkable transformation of the arts, politics, and everyday life in Europe and North America in the years between 1875 and 1945. Cultural modernism is marked by remarkable transformations in social relations, scientific understanding, technological development, and the very experience of life itself that manifested itself – among other ways – in the great scandals in the arts such as the riot at Stravinsky's *Rite of Spring* I mentioned in the beginning of this chapter.[22] Such a transformation of experience was occasioned by the momentous technological innovations of this period – which included, among other important "inventions," the bicycle, advertising agencies, telephones, airplanes, mass market journalism (and the first compulsory education laws in England), automobiles, postgraduate education in the United States, finance capital and the limited corporation in Great Britain (which really became law a little earlier, in 1855), the radio, and a host of other things.[23] In one telling example – though the mass marketing of sheet music by Tin Pan Alley in New York is certainly another telling example I will return to – the invention of the incandescent light bulb in 1879 literally transformed the relationship between night and day. Stravinsky's stage and concert hall in Paris were illuminated by light bulbs. The light bulb created the possibility of "night life" – in Harlem, St. Louis, New Orleans, and even in Peru, Indiana, where Cole Porter grew up. Relatively suddenly, the diurnal rhythms of life were transformed into something else, what Susan Buck-Morss, speaking of Walter Benjamin, that great spokesperson of cultural modernism, describes as a "second nature," which, as she says, distinguished itself from the "first epoch" that "evolved slowly over millions of years." It is, she says, a "second" epoch, "our own, [that] began with the industrial revolution, and changes its face daily."[24] David Landes, in his global history of wealth *The Wealth and Poverty of Nations*, describes the kinds of technological transformations of the turn of the twentieth century, for which I am using the light bulb as a defining example, as comparable to the "Neolithic revolution" from 8000 to 3000 BCE, the "shift away from hunting and gathering

[that] made possible towns and cities, with all that they yielded in cultural and technical exchange and enrichment." The Neolithic revolution, like that of a "second nature" which Benjamin suggests, had at its "core," Landes says, "an enhancement of the supply of energy, because this feeds and changes all aspects of human activity."[25] Such energy, as Stravinsky and Eliot both knew, is at the heart of modernist music and art. Such energy, in a humbler example, powered the microphone that made the intimacies of Billie Holiday's performances possible and the record player that had allowed her to imagine herself a singer in the first place; it also powered the steamers that allowed Porter to travel the world and the radio that allowed Waller to be heard throughout the United States.

Still, the music of George and Ira Gershwin is perhaps the best example of the enormous social upheavals and transformations that accompanied – that, in fact, *was* – modernism. Moreover, in the Gershwins – and especially in the introduction of the "blue note" to popular music that George developed in the early part of the century and in George's more general knowledge and admiration of African American music – the very affinity between the transformative power of Enlightenment modernity of the seventeenth century and that of the cultural modernism of the twentieth can be seen. Writing about Bob Dylan, Wilfrid Mellers notes that

> the 'alienation' of the blues – the basic conflict between black and white sources – is epitomised in the phenomenon of 'blue' notes: for repeatedly the 'natural' flat thirds and sevenths of pentatonic and modal melodies collide with the sharpened sevenths and *leading* notes demanded by Western dominant–tonic harmony, the more so because the natural thirds and sevenths can never do more than approximate to the harmonically tempered intervals.
>
> Significantly, the phenomenon of blue notes repeats a process that had happened, in a wider and more complex context, in European history when the mystically orientated theocracy of the Middle Ages was being engulfed by the Renaissance and by the humanistically and scientifically centred modern world. The new post-Renaissance harmony called for sharpened sevenths and thirds to define cadence and mark temporal progression; while music-makers trained on folk monody and on liturgical polyphony intuitively favoured the natural, flatter intervals. Simultaneous or near-simultaneous clashes of minor and major thirds, known as false relations, occurred. Blue notes are an exactly comparable technique, likewise springing from a clash between two views of the world. They are indeed *false* relations which, in the context of history, may prove to be symptomatic of a change no less crucial than that between the Middle Ages and the modern world. Moreover, it might be valid to suggest that the evolution of temperament, and especially equal temperament, in European music was a fall from Eden, from grace to disgrace: without which, of course, the splendours and miseries of modern 'Faustian' man would have been musically inconceivable.[26]

In a moment I discuss musical temperament more fully (and especially Bach's well-tempered clavier), but now I want to emphasize, the way Mellers does, that modernism – both seventeenth-century Enlightenment modernity and twentieth-century cultural modernism – marks eras of powerful transformation. A most striking, if negative, similarity can be seen in the parallel between the thirty years' religious wars, 1618–1648, and our own thirty years' ideological wars, 1914–1945.

The America of Gershwin and his younger contemporaries – America in the new twentieth century – underlines the affinities between Enlightenment and cultural modernism. This is so because the United States in many ways was the first nation instituted upon the principles of Enlightenment modernity, the first "modernist" nation, and – as Carol Oja notes – because even though European "cultural" modernists in the early twentieth century "shared the common passion . . . to 'make it new!' as the poet Ezra Pound put it," they had stronger ties to the past than the Americans, who "perceived themselves as possessing a greater opportunity than their European contemporaries for genuine innovation, uninhibited by historical accretions."[27] That is, America in the new twentieth century seems to have been participating in both Enlightenment and cultural modernism simultaneously.

In the Enlightenment, what was transformed was indeed the worldview, and especially the place of "man" as Mellers says – the gender is important – within the world. The gender is important because one of the tenets of the new worldview of the Enlightenment was that the general or universal case, in politics and everyday experience as well as in science, governed each and every specific instance. This is most clear, I think, in the criteria for determining scientific and other kinds of truth in the work of Descartes and others. Superseding "tradition" and "common sense," these new criteria were *generalization*, *accuracy*, and *simplicity*. Still, as many have argued,[28] some time around the turn of the twentieth century a new mode of comprehension arose supplementing received Enlightenment ideas concerning the nature of understanding and explanation. Those received ideas revolved around Descartes's conception of "clear and distinct ideas" and the larger assumption, central to Enlightenment science from Newton to Einstein, that the criteria for scientific explanation entailed three global concerns: generalizability, accuracy, and simplicity. These received ideas were and are closely tied to the politics of the Enlightenment, which entailed a curious combination of liberation, based upon remarkable notions – above all *secular* notions – of individualism and equality; and domination, based, at best, upon an unreflective sense of the self-evidence of Enlightenment truth and of the "naturalness" of male European experience and, at worst, upon ruthless power disguised as disinterested reason. Bruno Latour, in his powerful analysis of Enlightenment modernity – and modernism in general – describes this as the great achievement of Enlightenment modernity, the "double task of domination and emancipation."[29]

I mention generalization first here because the sharpened sevenths and thirds of Enlightenment music most fully realized themselves in the tempered tuning that Johann Sebastian Bach – that towering Enlightenment figure – advocated in the early eighteenth century in the *Well-Tempered Clavier*, a temperament which standardized "pure" tones across different keys. It is the *purity* of its perceptions of the world – the constant guard against contamination, mixture, miscegenation – that, in the argument of Latour, most characterizes Enlightenment modernity, even if, as Latour argues, early modern scientists, politicians, and philosophers were happy to participate in such contaminations even when they decried them. Latour's intricate and, to my mind, mostly persuasive argument details how the absolute opposition and its violation between Nature (whose objects are self-evident and always themselves, always "pure") and Culture (which was the realm of hybridization, translation, and negotiation) allowed for the remarkable social and intellectual success of the Enlightenment modernity of Western Europe. Thus, he describes the ways that the ideology of modernization kept "the two constitutional guarantees of the moderns – the universal laws of things, and the inalienable rights of subjects"[30] absolutely separate even while in practice they supported, reinforced, and infiltrated one another. In *Pandora's Hope* Latour criticizes the "general" or "universal" category of modernism in a historical example – the work of Louis Pasteur near the beginning of twentieth-century modernism – that demonstrates this "modernist" procedure of asserting and abandoning the "subject-object" dichotomy.

> We want to have a substance *in addition* to attributes . . . [But] the relation of substance to attributes does not have the genealogy that the subject–object dichotomy forced us to imagine: first a substance out there, outside history, and then phenomena observed by a mind. What Pasteur made clear for us . . . is that we slowly moved from a series of attributes to a substance. The [yeast] ferment began as attributes and *ended up being a substance*, a thing with clear limits, with a name, with obduracy, which was more than the sum of its parts. The word 'substance' does not designate what 'remains beneath,' impervious to history, but what gathers

together a multiplicity of agents into a stable and coherent whole. A substance is more like the thread that holds the pearls on a necklace together than the rock bed that remains the same no matter what is built on it.[31]

Bach is a notable musical example of the simultaneous sense of the absolute hierarchical separation of the universal from the particular and, as Latour contends, their mutual support. Although Bach was, as I argue in a moment, remarkable for his commitment to the "purity" of his compositions (as exampled in the *Well-Tempered Clavier*), he was also a master improviser in whom "the extempore organ tradition reached its apogee."[32] In fact, Andy Hamilton points out that "many of Bach's compositions can be seen as 'worked-up' versions of an improvisation or series of improvisations" (327). Hamilton goes on to note that baroque improvisation in general distinguishes itself from the twentieth-century jazz improvisations of popular music in that it is a thematic rather than a harmonic variation technique. It is just such harmonic improvisation that allows Waller and Holiday – as well as Louis Armstrong and Miles Davis – to improvise on Gershwin and Porter; it also allows the group improvisation Copland noticed. Still, Bach's extempore music – like the jazz and popular music I study here – remained "popular" in the ways I will argue later in this chapter that "classical" music in the nineteenth and twentieth centuries did not. It remained popular, that is, insofar as his extempore music responded to the moment rather than the universal or "general" idea; insofar as in its repetitions and variations – its art of "quotation" – it was not necessarily precise or "accurate"; and insofar as in its imitations it lacked the self-contained "simplicity" of Enlightenment knowledge and science. In short, the "popularity" of popular music betrays the tenets of general, accurate, and simple truths. Both Pasteur's science (participating in twentieth-century modernism) and Bach's music (participating in Enlightenment modernity) instantiate Latour's contention that modernist ideological assumptions both assert and undermine absolute distinctions between Nature and Culture, text and performance.

Still, Bach's most self-conscious aim was to purify music, to make each scale ring clear on that early modern technological innovation, the new, undefined musical machine of the Enlightenment, the clavier. In fact, one feature that might well distinguish Enlightenment and twentieth-century modernisms is the self-conscious embracing of mixtures and "impurities" in the early twentieth century.[33] This is certainly true of George Gershwin, who in 1929 described his aim of capturing in his music the "clashing and blending" of the "rhythms of these interfusing peoples" he found in New

York after World War I. Thus he announced that his goal was to "write an opera of the melting pot, of New York City itself, which is the symbolic and the actual blend of the native and immigrant strains. This would allow for many kinds of music, black and white, Eastern and Western, and would call for a style that should achieve, out of this diversity, an artistic and an aesthetic unity."[34] But it is also clear in the *performances* of popular music more generally: in the syncopations of Porter, the signifyin' of Waller, and the ensemble performances of Holiday. More generally, the phenomena of contamination, mixture, impurity, as Latour argues, is precisely what we can see as the very motor of Enlightenment modernity from the vantage of the twentieth century even as the earlier Enlightenment ideology strove to discover pure, transcendental essences amid the welter of worldly appearances. Thus Enlightenment science sought, as Elizabeth Ermarth has argued, "to chart both the differences and similarities in nature which give rise to those generalizations in science and art that we call laws. In formulating such laws no attempt is made to save the appearances. In fact, we might say that in reducing the welter of particulars to some abstract regularity, scientific and realistic generalizations represent an attempt to save the essences."[35]

ENLIGHTENMENT MODERNITY, TEMPERED MUSICAL FORM, AND POPULAR MUSIC

The phenomenon of "impurity" Latour describes might well help us to delineate features of Enlightenment modernity and twentieth-century modernism in relation to popular music. As Mellers noted, pre-modern "music-makers trained on folk monody and on liturgical polyphony"[36] followed their ears rather than written music, as do many performers of popular music to this day. This is not the case for musicological analyses, which depend on reading scores rather than listening to music (or depend on the interchangeability of reading and listening that I noted in Adorno's practice [Introduction, note 60]). In fact, David Brackett argues that "in musicological analysis" – a practice that traces its origins to the mid nineteenth century –

> the written document representing the piece of music, the "score," tends to function as the main source for analysis. However, the [popular] songs under consideration [in his book, *Interpreting Popular Music*] circulated primarily as recordings. Recordings tend to foreground the *temporality* of the musical text, as well as to emphasize one particular (and frequently, in some respects, simulated) performance rather than an idealized set of instructions for a performance. As a written

document, a score is a spatialized representation of a piece, which . . . lends itself to an analysis of structure. Modern popular music, which circulates primarily in recorded form, seems unsuited to analytical methods that stress spatial metaphors rather than temporal ones, and that favor visual methods as opposed to aural ones.[37]

As I noted in the Introduction, Middleton also describes the "notational centricity" of traditional musicology[38] and argues that, in its performative nature, one of the defining features of popular music is the absence of such "centricity."

A contributing element to such notational centricity is the tempering of the music scale, which I discuss in greater detail later in this chapter. Such tempering, as I have already suggested, is one, among many, of the great transformations that took place during the advent of Enlightenment modernity that have come down to us as a "natural" way of organizing experience, what Ermarth calls a generalizing and I would call a "transcendental" organization insofar as it transcends accidental differences of time and space. The notion of "transcendence" is also useful in understanding the opposition between "classical" and "popular" music I am examining here. Brackett summarizes Simon Frith's catalogue (one that is also encountered in Middleton and Birrer)[39] of "the critical discourse associated with the three main musical categories into which the musical field is conventionally partitioned – art music, folk music, popular music." These categories, Brackett argues,

all produce different conventions of aesthetic value. "Art" music revolves around providing a transcendent experience; however, only those with the right training can experience the real meaning of "great" music. "Folk" music revolves around providing an authentic experience of community. "Popular" music values are created by and organized around the music industry – musical value and monetary value are therefore equated, and the sales charts become the measure of "good" pop music.[40]

As I noted in the Introduction, in a later essay, Frith qualifies the category of popular music by describing the element of "fun" in pop which "provides routinized pleasures, more intense than the everyday but bound into its rhythms, and legitimized emotional gratification, a play of desire and discipline."[41] In fact, the very act of writing down the notation of music, as Charles Hamm argues, is part and parcel of the "modernist" distinction between "transcendent" art (or "classical") music and "ephemeral" popular music that especially works to guard against the "contamination" of the former. (Later I discuss the opposition between notation and performance in examining Paul Klee's remarkable assertion of the role of accidents in modernist art.)

A defining case of musical notation is that of the "accidentals" that occur in particular keys: the odd flatted third, E♭, of the blue note in the key of C; the B♭ of its seventh – "the 'natural' flat thirds and sevenths of pentatonic and modal melodies" that Mellers describes colliding "with the sharpened sevenths and *leading* notes demanded by Western dominant-tonic harmony."[42] The phenomenon of "accidentals" – indeed, its very name – reinforces the transcendental power of Enlightenment understanding by taking the general case as the essence of the particular case so that deviation from the general is simply seen as an "accidental" variation.[43] Such a conception of a transcendent general truth characterizes Enlightenment science, where Newton's almost mystical notion of force determines the action not simply of sublunary material, but of *anything* in the universe; it also characterizes Enlightenment politics, where woman is simply an "accidental" man and non-Europeans are "accidental" instances of an essential European humanity; and it also characterizes Enlightenment understanding of art where, as Kant has it, experience can become apprehended as "autonomous" and "disinterested." (In the study of music, Brackett notes that the focus on the "transcendental" score, resulting in or instantiating "the 'notational centricity' of Western musicology, has contributed to the neglect of much of the world's music outside of a narrow canon of work.")[44]

It is for this reason that Hamm notes that the "musical autonomy" of classical music made it "universal and eternal" as opposed to the ephemera of so-call popular music. "Early in the modern era," he writes,

> a distinction developed in the Western world between the music of the elite classes, comprising both classical ("high art") music and the less technically demanding genres of the bourgeois parlor, and that of the people, encompassing both folk and popular music (as these two terms came to be used in the twentieth century). Classical music, preserved in musical notation and performed by professionals for passive audiences, was understood to be universal and eternal, with a single repertory serving for the entire (Western) world. The music of the people, created and passed on chiefly in oral tradition, often in a participatory environment, was taken to be regional and ephemeral.[45]

Hamm goes on to argue that in its modernist conception

> music is autonomous; that is, its value resides in the musical composition itself and not in its reception and use. From this follows the notion that distinctions between "the best and highest" music and all lesser genres, as well as between "masterpieces" of the classical repertory and lesser pieces within this genre, are

> to be found in details of melody, harmony, form, rhythm, and instrumentation. As [Carl] Dahlhaus put it, the great works of classical music came to be seen as "ideal objects with an immutable and unshifting 'real' meaning," and the function of the scholar dealing with these objects "consists in the gradual unfolding of [this] meaning," a view grounded in nineteenth century German idealism and the concepts of genius and individual masterpieces.[46] (4)

This conception of music, Brackett argues, "emerged in the mid nineteenth century in Europe in tandem with a whole panoply of beliefs about what the musical experience should provide, about the relationship between performers, audiences, and composers. Audiences and scholars developed an aesthetic of distanced appreciation, and a belief in the autonomous art work and the primacy of 'absolute' music... These attitudes and beliefs were accompanied and accommodated by the context of the concert hall, a context which divorced the musical work from its previous social functions, and transformed musical performance into a sacred ritual."[47] Such a conception also elevates wordless music over lyrical music, even, paradoxically, in many analyses of opera. Hamm's focus on the very *notation* of "classical" music, the fact that its "autonomy" is captured in its written form, like Descartes's great invention of analytical geometry or Bach's preludes and fugues – or even the European colonization of the world – allows the "eternal" truths of Enlightenment knowledge, art, and politics to exist without regard to time and place.

This is clear in Bach. In a discussion of Bach's *Well-Tempered Clavier* examining precisely to what instrument "clavier" refers, Hermann Keller notes that while "there is music which can truly be brought to life only on the instrument for which the composer intended it" – he includes among his examples the fact that "many pieces of Karl Philipp Emanuel Bach only [sound good] on the clavichord" and "the piano sonatas of Beethoven only [sound good] on the pianoforte" – "the special charm of *The Well-Tempered Clavier* exists precisely in the fact that a mere keyboard instrument, whether it be now the clavichord, the harpsichord, or the pianoforte, must serve as the medium for a music whose content is to be sought beyond the sound."[48] This "transcendental" sense of music beyond its particular manifestation – a comprehension of "absolute music," which "means that it is the absolute, artistic *idea* expressed in the music that counts, not the technical way in which it is performed,"[49] very different from extempore performance – is a chief assumption of much of what we take to be the achievement of the Enlightenment and Enlightenment modernity.

In important ways, this can help us understand the often vague term "postmodern," which I have examined elsewhere.[50] If modernism attempted to create first of all the general laws of science that "transcend" and account for how the world works, but also to create the transcendental laws of "universal" ethics and "impersonal" aesthetics, then postmodernism attempts, among other things, to recover a sense of the power of local phenomena: how Beethoven's piano is necessary for his sonatas; how the particularities of gender or race or class need to be taken into account in relation to ethical questions; how the impersonal order of a beginning, middle, and end or of the seeming disappearance of the artist aren't the only ways to achieve aesthetic experiences. Such a sense of the power of local phenomena – as we shall see in the "popular" modernism of the Gershwins, Porter, Waller, and Holiday – manifests itself in particular performances and enactments of the social, psychological, linguistic, and anagogic aspects of music/lyrics and creates a distinct brand of cultural modernism in the 1930s. At its most outrageous, its critics think, postmodernism attempts to show that "transcendental" scientific laws can also be understood in relation to their own history and to the ethical and political ends they serve or have served in discovering seemingly disinterested truths about the world. (This is most clear, I think, in Enlightenment attempts to create "scientific" racism.) Certainly what is called postmodern often is a scandal to settled conceptions of art, the ethics of interpersonal relationships, and scientific "truth" itself.

The well-tempered scale is one instance of the homogeneous, transcendental regularity of Enlightenment modernity that emerges in the late seventeenth century precisely in order to *resist* the contaminations that can be seen in "postmodernism" and that, in fact, inhabited the "pre-modern" errors and superstitions of local "traditions" that Descartes's clear and distinct ideas were designed to combat. The well-tempered scale is opposed to a scale based upon the "just" intervals of notes of particular scales, which are governed by the cycle of fifths. As Ralph Kirkpatrick notes,

> systems of tuning more closely attached to the pure fifths and thirds of the natural overtone series either require more intervals than the twelve-note octave of the ordinary keyboard affords, unless given special subdivisions, or they favor only certain tonalities. This explains the infrequency in older music of tonalities involving more than three or four sharps and flats. So-called pure intonation based on the natural intervals is still instinctive to every good musician and is still commonly practiced by string players and singers. Thus, for example, in pure intonation, a rising G-sharp functioning as a leading tone would differ from a descending A-flat. The conventional keyboard, however, gives the same sound for both notes, creating a compromise to which the sensitive musical ear has only reluctantly become accustomed.[51]

The benefit from this "compromise," however, is not simply the wide range of possible keys and modulations created for keyboard instruments where they didn't exist before by means of the creation of an "essential" A♭ that may exist under two names (e.g., "A♭" and "G♯," in an example of Enlightenment nominalism that Adorno describes), but possesses a "transcendental" identity wherever it is sounded. Such a compromise has profound *political* consequences that helped to reconfigure what we still take to be "common sense."

The tempering of the scale was first described by Andreas Werckmeister, who published *Musical Temperament / or clear and correct mathematical instruction / how to tune a clavier, particularly organs, positives, regals, spinets, and the like in equal temperament* in 1691. Twenty years later, Mattherson wrote a book of exercises that allowed students to play all twenty-four keys (twelve tones, major and minor). And in 1722 Bach composed the twenty-four preludes and fugues of Book I of *The Well-Tempered Clavier*, in, as he says, "all tones and semitones, in major as well as minor, for the benefit and use of musical youth desirous of knowledge as well as those who are already advanced in this study."[52] (Bach composed Book II about twenty years later [dated 1744].) This tempering takes its place alongside Samuel Johnson's "tempering" of the English language with the publication of the *Dictionary* in 1754: henceforth, just as every A♭ will always "be" A♭, so the spelling of words in English will always be self-identical no matter what their pronunciation and, more importantly, no matter who their speaker is and where she comes from. Moreover, as Toby Miller notes in appropriating Bach's title for a study of the political economy of contemporary citizenship, "as a title and an intervention into musical technology, [*The Well-Tempered Clavier*] represents a move toward *politesse* and consistency over unruliness and difference, a move that was to typify the incorporation of music into popular education in the nineteenth century as part of a training in equable citizenship."[53]

Miller is examining the manner in which "the hold that popular music can have on a politics of identity" is "both different from and potentially unsettling for the project of government through culture exemplified by the pedagogic routine of *Das wohltemperierte Klavier*" (x–xi). In this he is arguing that particular instances of popular music "abjure," at least in moments, their "attention to an even-tempered structure and style in the service of 'the tissue of cultural values' [he is quoting Roland Barthes], preferring the directness . . . [of] a rawness . . . that transcends representational protocols, because it operates from a more elemental seduction and excess" (xi). That is, certain moments in popular music do not follow the "representational protocols" of equal tempering, and this omission has the effect or result of serving other purposes, other ends. Miller goes on to cite Jacques Derrida, who "reminds us," he says, that "moving out of tune is frequently rendered as a tonic delirium, 'a social disorder and a derangement, [Derrida notes,] an out-of-tune-ness of strings and voices in the head parasitising the voice of reason that speaks equally in each.'" Such out-of-tune-ness, Miller concludes, breaches "the unproblematic sweet reasonableness of *Das wohltemperierte Klavier* [which] is clearly akin to the ordered obedience of the desired subjects of civic culture" in the modern era (xi). In this way popular music participates in that modernist gesture – both in the seventeenth and the twentieth centuries – of "making it new."

The "modernist" order of reason Miller is describing on the level of politics and I have been describing on the level of aesthetics is thus neither universal nor transcendental, though one of its attributes is that it creates the impression that it is both. Moreover, what is striking for Samuel Johnson and Bach – as it is for Galileo with his telescope, and even for Descartes with his invention of mechanical compasses to perform mathematical operations – is that their "discoveries" of transcendental essences of spelling and sound are responses to historical and local technological innovations: widespread printing and keyboard music.[54] It might well be that the transformation, in Enlightenment modernity, of each royal subject into a citizen equal – as Thomas Jefferson says – to every other citizen is also a function of growing standardizations of communication and consumption. In any case, it is just such "standardization" that Adorno scorns in his discussions of popular music: "the fundamental characteristic of popular music," he writes, is "standardization."[55] In an analogous fashion, many of the innovations in the best popular music in the 1930s are responses to and the taking up of innovative means of creating, storing, and transmitting sound: the mass distribution of printed music from Tin Pan Alley in the early twentieth century, the advent of the gramophone record disk in 1910 that allowed inexpensive and widespread reproduction of music in the 1920s, the development of commercial radio at the same time, the intimacies of the microphone I have already mentioned. All these things helped *identify*, as popular music does, communication and consumption. The identification (or confusion) of communication and consumption is, in fact, parallel to the "postmodern" confusion of aesthetics, politics (ethics), and the more general epistemology (understanding) whose clear and distinct demarcation was the work of Immanuel Kant's great critiques and, in fact, the work and source of much of the great and good achievements of Enlightenment modernity. And insofar as twentieth-century cultural modernism participates in such identification or confusion, it offers what Lyotard describes as "states" or moments of postmodern, post-Enlightenment ethos (and understanding), power, and art.[56]

ACCIDENTS OF MODERNITY

It is my contention – one that I pursue in Chapter 2 – that one might discern a particular distinction between early modernity and twentieth-century modernism in the moment of popular music in the 1930s. This can be seen in differing modalities of this music, its existence as both performance and record (written as well as sound recordings, to which I revert in Part II). To examine these contrasting modalities I want to return to the seeming technological "conventionality" and the representational protocol of the *accidentals* of musical notation, which I have already touched upon. After all, the standardizing of tone and semitones – of every G♯ and A♭ – is precisely the work of modernist "tempering." In its general meaning, "accidents" are precisely the opposite to the essences of Enlightenment modernity: they are what the Enlightenment wants to forget, or at least to absorb within a system that accounts for them as essential to one extent or another. Musical accidentals can be seen, as Toby Miller notes, as a kind of "tonic delirium" and "derangement" as well as a "moment" in the achievement of the tempered order of reason. That is, accidentals – like the term "modernism" itself as I have described it, and, I am arguing, like the performative saxophone screech I mentioned in the Introduction – function as a counterpoint of different worldviews, particularly of literal and figural (or "performative") meanings. *Modernism* literally means "up to date," contemporary, and Ezra Pound's slogan for poetry and art in the early twentieth century, "Make it new!", clearly participates in this sense of the modern. But the term "modernism" also opposes itself to other senses in a performative gesture – it is opposed to the "pre-modern" sensibilities of medieval society I've already mentioned, for instance – where its meaning does not possess *positive* literalism, but is rather figurative and oppositional: in this sense *modernism* is, as Mellers says, a name for a particular worldview that defines itself in contrast with other worldviews. (In the same way, the "Age of Europe" Cornel West describes defines itself in contrast with its non-European "others.")

The accidentals of music – sharpened and flatted notes of song and chord outside the diatonic scale – explode (or at least threaten) the key signature of any particular piece they occur in and at the same time also articulate and present the material modality of the music, whether it be major or minor, Dorian or Lydian. Mode and key cross and interfere with one another; authentic or plagal modes underline the relationship (and counterpoint) between the simultaneous harmonies of key and the consecutive notes of musical scale. This is inscribed, as I have mentioned, in the very term "accidental," which is both a simple accident or arbitrary fluke of etymology, a material event to be disregarded in grasping the musical meaning of the term ("note or pitch outside the scale of the dominant key") and a meaning or sense contained within the term's use. The same contrapuntal combination of meaning and materiality can be seen, as the *Concise Oxford Dictionary of Music* notes, in the term "key" itself.

> Key. (1) As a principle in mus. comp., implies adherence, in any passage, to the note-material of one of the major or minor scales . . . – not necessarily a rigid adherence (since other notes may incidentally appear), but a general adherence, with a recognition of the tonic (or key-note) of the scale in question as a principal and governing factor in its effect. For instance we speak of a passage as being 'in the key of' C major, or F minor . . .
>
> The element of key crept into European mus. in the early 17th cent., as the **modes** gradually fell out of use: it remained of supreme importance to the end of the 19th cent. but in the 20th cent., many composers, led by **Schoenberg**, have abandoned tonality . . .
>
> (2) A lever on an instr. which is depressed by finger or foot to produce a note, e.g. on a [piano] by finger, on an [organ] by foot, on woodwind by finger (the levers covering the airholes).[57]

Unlike the "clavier," some instruments – the banjos and drums that play behind Louis Armstrong, for instance, but also the human voice itself, Billie Holiday singing – don't exactly have "levers," even if the frets on banjos might be called "modified key-levers" and might even be taken to be "accidental" keys, so to speak.

The more or less fortuitous example of the word *fret* is useful here. Thus, a word such as *fret* – like *accidental* or *modernism* for that matter – combines and contrasts two modes of meaning, one more or less literal (the definition of the word) and one more or less figurative.[58] The *Oxford English Dictionary* defines *accidental* as "present by chance; non-essential"; and it also defines it in music as a "sign of chromatic alteration." In this second definition, musical accidentals combine the "transcendental" meaning of music, its combinations and interrelations building up its non-local musical "sense," and the literal materialities in its soundings, the sound sensations in another way of understanding "sense,"[59] as in the accidental triple forte screech-sound of the saxophone that Keil mentions.[60] In the Enlightenment, musical mode became the "accident" of key: literally it was realized in the presence and absence of accidentals in a scale, and figuratively it was the "taming" (or "tempering") of sound to key, a way of reincorporating accidents into meaningful system.[61] If, as I have suggested, such "taming" of emotion and meaning by means of *standardizations* of sense is one of the great achievements of the culture of Enlightenment modernity, then the emphasis on *accident* signals a "new" kind of modernism, as does the popular music of the twentieth century more generally. The double meanings I have presented – of *fret*, of *accidental*, of *modernism* itself – underline the counterpoint of ("transcendental") meaning and ("local") materialism. Both Enlightenment modernity and twentieth-century modernism resolve this contradiction in relation to transcendental meaning, but in very different ways. If Enlightenment modernity seeks the elusive certainty that tormented Descartes by pursuing transcendental essences, then cultural modernism seeks what Paul Klee near the turn of the twentieth century defined as modern art, the quest to discover "the essential nature of the accidental."[62] Such "essential" apprehensions of the accidental, I argue, reside in performance rather than notation, and they allow Gershwin, Porter, Waller, and Holiday to take up and transform the ordinary, standardized music of Tin Pan Alley. In *Ulysses*, James Joyce has Stephen Dedalus describe the artist as a person for whom there are no accidents: "a man of genius," he says in the library chapter of *Ulysses*, "makes no mistakes. His errors are volitional and are the portals of discovery."[63] Such a sense of discovering simplicity, reassurance, and the ordinary – a sense that the ordinary is worthy of powerful attention in the seemingly meaningless "accidents" of the banal and of cliché – was the genius of American popular music in the 1930s. It is a way of making the ordinary "new." It is also the genius of American consumer culture, which makes non-essential *things* feel curiously essential to one's well-being. In Chapter 4, I examine the role of things in the creation of desire in Cole Porter's music as a kind of musical example, as I see it, that may help distinguish between Enlightenment modernity and the cultural modernism of the twentieth century. In this, I will argue that what characterizes twentieth-century cultural modernism – and distinguishes it despite its kinship with Enlightenment modernity – is a whole new kind of "accident," the accidents of abundance.

MODERNITY AND CONSUMPTION

The genius of American consumer culture, as I am describing it here, allows us more clearly to discern the place of popular music within twentieth-century cultural modernism. Colin Campbell traces the historical sources of consumerism in what he has called "the other Protestant ethic" of Enlightenment modernity. Describing this "other" tradition, he argues that

> there were two, and not one, powerful cultural traditions of thought and associated 'ethics' which developed out of English Puritanism in the eighteenth century. The first, which corresponds to that identified by Weber and is consequently commonly referred to as 'the Protestant ethic', stressed rationality, instrumentality, industry, and achievement, and is more suspicious of pleasure than of comfort; here the impact of Enlightenment scepticism produces an atheistic and empiricist outlook which finally develops into utilitarianism. The second, . . . incorporating an 'optimistic', 'emotionalist' version of the Calvinist doctrine of signs, develops first into the cults of benevolence and melancholy, and then into fully fledged Sentimentalism. For both, the culture-carriers are the middle classes, and each, in its own way, has a vital contribution to make to the accomplishment of the Industrial Revolution and the legitimation of an essentially 'bourgeois' way of life.[64]

For this reason, Campbell argues that "Romanticism itself played a critical role in facilitating the Industrial Revolution and therefore the character of the modern economy" (2) and that the "upheaval which went under the title of the Industrial Revolution had to be regarded as centring upon a revolution in consumption as well as production" (8). In his argument he is attempting to challenge the "productionist bias of both history and social science" (13) just as I am attempting to challenge the productionist bias of the literary and cultural history of twentieth-century modernism. Such a bias, as I suggested in the Introduction, is particularly notable in musicology which, with its notational centricity, has made the production of music its central focus at the cost of marginalizing its consumption, particularly in popular music. But such notational centricity, I have also noted, was also a central feature in the literary criticism of modernism a generation ago as exampled in Joseph Frank's influential contention of the centrality of "spatial form" in modernist literature (see note 37).

In his historical account, Campbell – following and supplementing Max Weber's argument in *The Protestant Ethic and the Spirit of Capitalism*[65] – argues that modern consumerism arose within Enlightenment modernity, and particularly in relation to the "Protestant ethic." "To stress the crucial part played by Puritanism in the evolution of modern hedonism may seem, at first sight," he writes,

> to be somewhat strange, yet as far as the emergence of sentimental hedonism is concerned, Protestant religion, and especially the harsh and rigorous form of it which is known as Puritanism, must be recognized as the primary source. This is precisely because as a movement it adopted a position of such outright hostility to the 'natural' expression of emotion, and consequently helped to bring about just that split between feeling and action which hedonism require. (74)

Such a split between feeling and action – like the split between the abstract commercial firm and its living owners effected, as Mary Poovey has argued, by the invention of double-entry bookkeeping in the early sixteenth century;[66] or the split between abstract tempering of the "clavier" and the particular scales tuned on violins, guitars, and voice – creates or participates in the conditions of Enlightenment modernity even as it also conditions hedonistic consumerism, which was fully realized in the second Industrial Revolution and twentieth-century cultural modernism. Here again – as in the wide-ranging demographics of modernism, in musical accidentals, and in the defining example of modernist popular music – is the dialectic of absolute distinction and local ("enacted") contamination by which Latour defines modernity. In a similar fashion, Romanticism, which is often taken as a dialectical response to the "abstraction and control" of the Enlightenment, as Jameson described it,[67] can also be understood, in Campbell's powerful argument, as the realization of its consumerist (as opposed to its productionist) manifestation.

I mention this because, as I contend in Chapter 2, popular music in the 1930s exhibited qualities of late Romanticism, which both literary high modernism and Adorno responded to in powerfully negative ways.[68] That is, its representations of achievable pleasure and happiness, its almost exclusive focus on romantic love,[69] its virtually exclusive focus on personal emotion to the exclusion of any social concerns – all these qualities of late Romanticism were not different from but part of aspects of Enlightenment modernity that were the stimuli and origin of much of twentieth-century cultural modernism. These were, indeed, decayed and debased aspects of what Witkin and Adorno call "bourgeois ideology."[70] But, Romanticism, as Campbell argues, can also possibly create "opportunities for the generation of idealism," including the very social idealism that Adorno articulates.[71] It is such "Romantic" and even "social" idealism, as I mentioned in the Introduction – the opening of powerful social space through which fundamental problems of equality, difference, desire, reason, authority, self, and language were not merely expressed, but questioned and negotiated – that can be heard and felt in the performative musics of the Gershwins, Porter, Waller, and Holiday as they are taken up and transformed into celebratory art, the pleasures of popular modernism.

CHAPTER 2

Twentieth-century modernism and "jazz" music

THE MODERNIST CULTURE OF DESIRE

Both Enlightenment and twentieth-century modernisms made things "new," but the intensity of newness, as both Stephen Dedalus and David Landes suggested, was particularly pronounced in the later era (or at least it seems that way to us, living in that later era). In fact, this intensity of feeling – of dislocation, of vague wonder, of free-floating anxiety, of inchoate need – seems to me to be a signal distinguishing feature between Enlightenment modernity and the cultural modernism of the early twentieth century. This feature has to do with the role of desire – again, dislocated, free-floating, vague, inchoate – within social, psychological, and linguistic cultural formations. In a review of Regenia Gagnier's study of aesthetics and economics in the late nineteenth century, John Coates notes that

> in the summer of 1930, as America spiraled into the Great Depression, R. C. Leffingwell, a partner at the Wall Street firm of J. P. Morgan, proposed what was to him an obvious solution to the crisis: People, he said, should "stop watching the ticker, listening to the radio, drinking bootleg gin, and dancing to jazz; forget the 'new economics' and prosperity founded upon spending and gambling, and return to the old economics based upon saving and working" . . . Leffingwell was wrong about what the economy needed. But he was right about one thing: in the decades leading up to the crash, two unlikely allies – art and economics – had united in a common front against the old order. Laissez-faire, balanced budgets, the puritan work ethic, sexual prudishness – one by one, these Victorian orthodoxies had been upended. What Leffingwell was hopelessly resisting was the seismic shift from a culture of production to a culture of consumption.[1]

A culture of consumption is a culture of desire, and the "seismic" difference between Enlightenment modernity and the cultural modernism of the early twentieth century can be seen in the role of desire within culture itself.[2]

This is most clear, I think, in that other seismic shift that Coates and Gagnier (whose book, *The Insatiability of Human Wants*, he is reviewing) both see, the shift from the *political economy* of the classical economics of Adam Smith, David Ricardo, and even Karl Marx to the scientific *economics* of the neoclassical economists of the late nineteenth century. As well as Coates and Gagnier, Lawrence Birken, in his book *Consuming Desire*, has argued powerfully that the great productivity of the second Industrial Revolution of the turn of the twentieth century created a world of abundant consumer goods that transformed the sense and experience of value altogether. In fact, the distinction between "use-value" and "exchange-value," so important to the classical economists, dissolves in the face of abundance. The significant feature of use-value is that it is, like Enlightenment values more generally, *universal*. The use of a pair of shoes *always* functions to protect the feet, everywhere and for everyone – in this it functions like the definitions in Johnson's dictionary and the precisions of musical tones for the "clavier" – and both Smith and Marx measure the value of this commodity by its *first* use, the pair of shoes without which one would walk barefoot.

The crucial nature of universal need in this argument is clear in Marx's analysis of political economy. At the heart of Marx's analysis of capital is the concept, borrowed from David Ricardo (but also implicit in Smith), of the labor theory of value. The labor theory posits that the value of a commodity can only be measured by the amount of human labor that is expended in creating that commodity; it focuses on its *production*. Marx argues that the creation of "surplus value" and the accumulation of capital are based on the discrepancy between the value of a day's labor as a commodity purchased from the worker at full value in terms of what it costs to produce that commodity – namely, the food, clothing, and shelter that allows the worker to live for a day – and the amount of value the laborer produces through his labor.[3] Thus, the subsistence of the laborer might require the value of six labor hours, all told, which the capitalist pays in full while he obtains the value of ten labor hours from the worker. The difference for Marx is "surplus value." At the heart of Marx's analysis, as it is at the heart of Smith's, is that workers have universal needs, "basic" needs: food, clothing, shelter. What makes these needs "basic" is precisely their simplicity and universality. Like the precisions of Enlightenment reason, they create the necessary and sufficient conditions for life and labor. Similarly, the concept of use-value in classical economics is directly related to this idea of basic need. As mentioned above, this conception assumes a theory of value that focuses on *production* rather than *consumption*: value is measured by the work of production, not the pleasures or fulfillments of consumption. For both Smith and Marx, the value of a pair of shoes is best measured in and by the first pair of shoes we acquire, the pair we need because it answers a basic necessity, not by shoes that give pleasures beyond necessity.

But what about a world in which we already have a dozen pairs of shoes, pumps, hiking boots, work shoes, sneakers? What about a world of abundance? How do we measure the value of a pair of Nikes compared to Reebok when, without them, we still wouldn't go barefoot? As Colin Campbell notes, in distinguishing between need and desire – pain and pleasure – "the choice between action directed toward maximizing satisfaction and that directed at maximizing pleasure is not likely to be especially apparent to people who rarely escape from the experience or threat of deprivation. This is because activity which relieves the discomfort of need also brings pleasure."[4] When we focus on the first pair of shoes, the *needful* pair, we are inhabiting the position of the individual in the Enlightenment world situated between the "accidental" material happenings in the world and an "essential" sense of the nature of things without regard to the seeming immaterial differences of ordinary occurrences. But when we focus on the value of the last pair of shoes we have acquired – what the neoclassical economics of the 1880s called (and still call) the "marginal" pair – the situation is significantly different. First of all, the last pair is neither necessary nor sufficient: the "last" pair can always become the "second-to-last" pair. In this situation Marx's crucial distinction between basic "use-value" and secondary "exchange-value" breaks down. Under these circumstances, the comprehension of economy – and of value – transforms its focus from the production of wealth to the consumption of wealth. As Birken has observed, "the marginalists started from the assumption that human beings were first of all consumers."[5]

Another way to say this is to note that with the transformation of a culture of production into a culture of consumption that Coates describes and Birken situates precisely at the time of the second Industrial Revolution around the turn of the twentieth century, *desire* replaced *need* as the site of value for large numbers of people, and the necessary and sufficient measures of Enlightenment reason are supplemented by other forms of reasoning. "In the classical conceptions of economics, then," Birken writes, "desire was subordinated to need, understood as a holistic value. Individual *taste* was not recognized, at the theoretical level at least. In striking contrast, neoclassical thought possesses no concept of need. Instead, it takes idiosyncratic desire as a given."[6] Under these conditions, the *generalization*, *accuracy*, and *simplicity* of Enlightenment truth are supplemented by other modes of understanding: *retrospective understanding* supplements generalization (see especially quantum physics, but also the African American signifyin' examined in Chapter 5), *alternating the levels of analysis* supplements accuracy (see especially cubism, but also the Bakhtinian dialogics examined in Chapter 3), and *overdetermination* supplements simplicity (see especially psychoanalysis, including Lacanian psychoanalysis examined in Chapter 4).[7] Such supplements are governed by desire rather than the strict "necessary and sufficient" truths of need; after all, desire by its nature (as I discuss it in relation to Cole Porter in Chapter 4) is never quite necessary and never quite sufficient. I say "supplements" because in an economy of desire, the discipline of need is not done away with but rather added to.

This transformation, as I have said, was conditioned by the material, social, and experiential abundances of the turn of the century, and, as Richard Middleton notes, it allowed for the mass marketing of a new kind of popular music that participated in the very cultural modernism manifest in the continuities and transformations of Enlightenment modernity in the early twentieth century. Tin Pan Alley governed the composition and publication of the vast majority of popular music in America from about 1900 until the advent of rock 'n' roll in the 1950s. Tin Pan Alley was a concentration of music publishers in New York; its name was coined by a lyricist for popular music, Monroe Rosenfeld, who sometimes also worked as a reporter, when the majority of music publishers moved from Union Square in Manhattan uptown to Twenty-eighth street in the early twentieth century to follow the theaters and live entertainment.[8] The name derives from the "pluggers" who performed the music for customers – early in his life George Gershwin had such a job – and Rosenfeld noted "that the sound of numerous upright pianos played simultaneously in a small space resembled the clashing of kitchenware."[9] The publishers of Tin Pan Alley "produced sheet music as systematically as factories poured out industrial goods"; retail sales "peaked in 1921 at $106.5 million ($47.8 million wholesale), a figure not exceeded for another twenty-six years."[10] In his history of popular music in America, Charles Hamm describes the concentration and standardization of music in this period. The music published by Tin Pan Alley, he writes, "is familiar even before one hears the song for the first time; the style is similar to that of thousands of other songs written before (and after) this particular song. The harmonies and the characteristic sound of the octave doubling in the right hand of the piano part had been heard in innumerable songs."[11] It is precisely this standardization of popular music that led Adorno to distinguish it absolutely from "modern" music.

In this study, I am focusing on what is called the second wave of Tin Pan Alley song, those songs written after 1921, the year that saw record sales exceeding one hundred million dollars, the first regular radio broadcasts from station KDKA in Pittsburgh, and the independent record company Gennett, the most significant of the "race" labels of the 1920s, win the legal right to produce phonograph disks without a license.[12] What is most striking about these second-wave songs was that the themes of the music changed. "As America moved into the 1920s and then the '30s," Hamm writes,

> the expressive range of popular song narrowed. Texts began dealing almost exclusively with personal emotions, almost never with events outside of the person. An increasingly large percentage of the most popular songs was concerned with one aspect or another of romantic love.
>
> One searches almost in vain for songs touching in any way on the great social and political issues of those years – the continuing desperate plight of the black American in white America; the struggle of working class citizens to combat by unionization and strikes their exploitation by management; the worsening situation of ethnic minorities in Central and Eastern Europe and the inexorable rise to power of totalitarian regimes in many of these countries.[13]

In part this narrowing was a function of the commercialism of popular music, which sought formulas that worked, including vague general emotional themes that anyone could identify with. In part, it was a function of the concentration of popular music in New York City, dominated almost exclusively by first- or second-generation Jewish immigrants, who strove to become part of America – the melting pot that Gershwin mentions – without emphasis on ethnicity and social strife. Thus Irving Berlin has been described as "the Norman Rockwell of melody,"[14] and more generally Jeffrey Melnick has argued that "Tin Pan Alley was organized by Jews in New York who figured out how to make the city the cultural heart of the nation, how to use the sounds of blackness as the basis of their own creations, and how to standardize all of this in an incredibly efficient popular culture enterprise."[15]

But most of all, I think, this narrowing was part of what Hamm calls the "urbanization of popular song." "The world that held Gershwin," Melnick has written, "and what we now call 'American popular song' or 'standards' or 'Tin Pan Alley,' was defined by its modern, urban, mixed-race character."[16] Such urbanization was part and parcel of the emergence of a new social class in the United States (and in Western Europe as well), the lower middle class of "white-collar" workers. In fact, one feature distinguishing between Enlightenment modernity and twentieth-century cultural modernism is that a central force in the cultural revolution of the Enlightenment – and particularly the Industrial Revolution beginning in the eighteenth century – was, as Colin Campbell describes it, "the middle or trading classes, together with artisans and sections of the yeomanry,"[17] while the central force in the cultural revolution of twentieth-century modernism – and particularly the second Industrial Revolution beginning in the late nineteenth century (and in post-Civil War America) – was the lower middle class of mostly information workers, who were significantly different from the petty bourgeoisie of traders, artisans, and independent yeomen. That difference was that this new class traded on skills rather than the "small" property of the petty bourgeois, and they didn't employ people for their own profit. In Britain, where labor was cheaper than in America, they did, however, employ house servants. In fact, as Eric Hobsbawm notes, this "class" distinguished itself from the working class in two ways: although its members were "often barely a financial hair's breadth above the better-paid skilled workers," they did not perform manual labor; and "they certainly belonged to what British social observers called the 'servant-keeping class.'"[18] Still, what is most striking about this class is that it was made up of people who were particularly urban, newly educated – many said, "partially educated" – city dwellers who had recently arrived from the country (Theodore Dreiser's Sister Carrie is a good example); and it was made up of people who lived by *performing* non-manual skills in teaching, advertising, typing, et cetera rather than *owning* property. They were neither managers nor workers and prided themselves on salaries rather than wages.

Much of English modernist literature focuses on this class; it is the social situation of Joyce's and Lawrence's protagonists, an advertising canvasser, a schoolteacher, and T. S. Eliot's clerk, the "young man carbuncular" in *The Waste Land*; and it is also the object of both satirical admiration in H. G. Wells's *Tono-Bungay* and disdain in the characters of Septimus in Virginia Woolf's *Mrs Dalloway* and Leonard Bast in E. M. Forster's *Howards End*.[19] One striking feature of this class is its ideology of individualism: cut off from traditional social networks – it is a class of newly educated (that is, newly literate) people streaming into cities at the time of the second Industrial Revolution – the class makes salvationist religion and the individualistic ideology of the "self-made man" its creeds. And it also makes material fulfillments of one sort or another – fulfillments of vague, inchoate, free-floating desire – its goal. In other words, the lower middle class emerges coincidentally with a consumerist society. As a class of workers primarily dealing with paper, documents, and semiotic systems of one sort or another, it is both the product and the motor of the transformation of industrial capital into finance capital. And, significantly, it is a class situated in a world where personal desire is both the result and the motor of the political economy. The second wave of Tin Pan Alley coincides with "the explosion of installment buying and living on credit of the 1920s" that Michael Tratner argues is part and parcel of an economy of desire.[20] Finally, I should reiterate that this class is the antithesis of the parallel class of the petty bourgeoisie – the class of entrepreneurial producers and savers – of Enlightenment modernity that Max Weber focuses upon in *The Protestant Ethic and the Spirit of Capitalism*.[21]

THE ESSENTIAL NATURE OF THE ACCIDENTAL

The early-twentieth-century economy of desire governs popular music more fully than it does classical music, and it does so in two important ways both related to Klee's insight about twentieth-century modernism, its focus on the "essential nature of the accidental." The first has to do with the immediacy of commercial popular music, the ways that, in the words of Timothy Scheurer, Tin Pan Alley pursued "the colloquial or vernacular style."[22] Thus Charles K. Harris, the first-wave Tin Pan Alley composer of "After the Ball" whom Hamm describes as epitomizing "better than any other songwriter the attitudes and methods of the first generation of Tin Pan Alley composers,"[23] wrote that songwriters should read newspaper headlines for trends and incidents for their music, even as the second generation made vague expressions of personal desire the trends and incidents of their music.[24] The second has to do also with the immediacy of popular music, not in terms of the ways that its lyrics often tie themselves to the "accidents" of particular incidents in the popular press and the musical romanticism of movies,[25] but in terms of the ways that popular music – and especially the "jazz" of the 1920s and 1930s (a term I more fully explain below) – emphasizes performance rather than composition: the "accidents" of improvisation.

These two kinds of "accidents" come together in the remarkable conjunction of African American popular "folk" music and Jewish American popular commercial music in Tin Pan Alley. "In 1929," Jeffrey Melnick writes, touching on four of the figures who loom large in the following chapters, George and Ira Gershwin, Louis Armstrong and Thomas "Fats" Waller,

> the great jazz trumpeter and vocalist Louis Armstrong established his stardom – after years of playing in bands from New Orleans to Chicago – with his appearance in the pit band for the African American musical revue *Hot Chocolates*. Armstrong's featured number was "Ain't Misbehavin'," a song cowritten by African American

songwriters Fats Waller and Andy Razaf, who had help arranging the number from another African American musician, Harry Brooks. According to Brooks, this song was a forthright attempt to copy the opening phrase and part of the bridge (the passage connecting verse and chorus) of "The Man I Love" (1924), written by George and Ira Gershwin.[26]

The "accidents" of immediate ordinary things – in Chapter 4, I describe the many "things" that appear in Cole Porter's music, "Just One of those Things," "You Do Something to Me," "What is This Thing Called Love?" – and the aleatory specifics of particular jazz performances both participate in the ordinary and specific occasions of desire. They also define the kind of *popular* modernism that manifests itself in the popular music of the Gershwins, Porter, Waller, and Holiday.

The accidents of the ordinary

The great modernist poet of the ordinary is William Carlos Williams. In his *Autobiography* he describes the relationship between his career as a physician and his career as a poet, and in so doing he offers a powerful reiteration of Klee's description of modernist art. "At times," he says, "we see through the welter of evasive or interested patter, when by chance we penetrate to some moving detail of a life . . . [T]he difficulty is to catch the evasive life of the thing, to phrase the words in such a way that stereotype will yield a moment of insight."[27] It is precisely such accidental chance moments that allow an ordinary accident to transform itself into poetry. Take, for example, his famous poem, "This is Just to Say":

This Is Just to Say

I have eaten
the plums
that were in
the icebox

and which
you were probably
saving
for breakfast

Forgive me
they were delicious
so sweet
and so cold[28]

Here's a poem that takes an ordinary occurrence, a note on a refrigerator door, and discovers in it the possibility that poetry can be found *anywhere*. Like his "Red Wheelbarrow," which asserts that "so much depends" on simply seeing what is already before us, "This is Just to Say" finds that bringing together the pleasure of fruit and the assumed goodwill of his companion can transform the stereotype of a "standardized" note into the insight that great goodwill can be found in ordinary relationships and ordinary things.

Such a procedure in its very nature lends itself to parody and systematic exploitation. It does so by opening itself up to bathos. Thus Kenneth Koch wrote a hilarious parody of Williams's poem, "Variations on a Theme by William Carlos Williams." In four stanzas he parodies the strengths and insights of Williams's small poem: the assumed goodwill of his companion, the excuse that offers no explanation, the sensuous pleasures of the fruit, and Williams's own double career as doctor and poet.

Variations on a Theme by William Carlos Williams

1

I chopped down the house that you had been saving to live in next summer.
I am sorry, but it was morning, and I had nothing to do
and its wooden beams were so inviting.

2

We laughed at the hollyhocks together and then I sprayed them with lye.
Forgive me. I simply do not know what I am doing.

3

I gave away the money that you had been saving to live on for the next
ten years.
The man who asked for it was shabby
and the firm March wind on the porch was so juicy and cold.

4

Last evening we went dancing and I broke your leg.
Forgive me. I was clumsy
and I wanted you here in the wards, where I am the doctor![29]

In Koch's poem, in contrast to Williams's "This is Just to Say," the title offers the "essence" of the poem. In Williams's poem, the title remains "accidental," part of the poem itself, but not quite its first line.

Like "This is Just to Say," Williams's "The Red Wheelbarrow" presents a single sentence that simply observes details in the environment and asserts value.

The Red Wheelbarrow

so much depends
upon

a red wheel
barrow

glazed with rain
water

beside the white
chickens.[30]

In this poem, the meaning of the poem's sentence – that much depends on the red wheelbarrow – is more than the addition of the particular meanings of the words of the sentence. Rather, it presents a meaningful whole and an overall effect. Williams breaks up words with his lines (wheel / barrow; rain / water) – he "decouples" words from their ordinary sense[31] – so that qualities of the adjectives stand out as the qualities of the objects, and not merely the addition of attributes. It is as if objects in his world – ordinary, more or less "accidental" objects – are apprehended whole and "glazed" with value, the essential nature of the accidental.

If this poem conveys a more or less vague sense of importance and significance, then we may ask, "What about the poem helps us to notice and attend to that importance?" My description of the way the poem decomposes nouns into adjective + noun (wheel + barrow; rain + water) may or may not present the "cause" of the "effect" of importance in the poem. But it calls attention to the poem's exploration of value in the world ("so much depends"). Even my metaphoric description of the poem – that objects in the world of this poem are "'glazed' with value" – offers an example of the descriptive power of metaphorical language and, at times, of cliché (discussed in Chapter 3). Such descriptive power asks us to notice explicitly the overall affectiveness of the poem – something that we might otherwise vaguely feel or dismiss. In this way, "The Red Wheelbarrow" *depends* on its listeners more fully than, say, *The Waste Land* – whose bardic voice overwhelms its listeners – or even more than Koch's poem, whose satire and humor still also depend on its audience.

In the fashion of Williams – and sometimes in the fashion of Koch – the best popular music of the 1930s transforms the stereotypes of Tin Pan

Alley songs into insight so that, as Alfred Appel, Jr. has argued, "to call Armstrong, Waller, et al., 'modernists' is to appreciate their procedures as alchemists of the vernacular who have 'jazzed' the ordinary and given it new life."[32] Sometimes, as in Waller, this transformation is accomplished by means of parody and satire – as when he begins the clichéd standard "Two Sleepy People" as "Two Sloppy People."[33] But often, even in Waller, these composers and performers achieve a transformation by discovering powerful – and often poetic – insight in the most ordinary of things. Thus, in "They Can't Take that Away from Me," a song that George and Ira Gershwin wrote in 1937 that I discuss in Chapter 3, the crucial moment is when the singer tells his beloved (Fred Astaire in the film *Shall We Dance*, singing to Ginger Rodgers), "The way you hold your knife, / The way we danced till three, / The way you changed my life."[34] In these lyrics, the rhyme of "knife" and "life" is quietly shocking.

Similarly, in Waller's music such ordinary and stereotyped things carry the weight of powerful feeling. I've already mentioned "Ain't Misbehavin'" and the way it connects Jewish American and African American music – and I return to this in a moment. But it also offers a striking double rhyme and the ubiquitous "radio":

> I don't stay out late,
> Don't care to go,
> I'm home about eight,
> Just me and my radio.

Equally ubiquitous here is what Jonathan Culler calls the vocative "O" of pure sounding, which I discuss in relation to the Gershwins in Chapter 3. In these lyrics, the "O" of "radio" is almost detached and made into pure singing sound. It is this quality – the *performance* – of returning sensible language to material sound that instantiates the "swarm of elements" Adorno describes, where texts dissolve not simply "into sheer words," as he says,[35] but into sheer *sound*. I discuss this at greater length in relation to Cole Porter and desire in Chapter 4.

More to the point, however, is Waller's most powerful and political song, "Black and Blue," examined more fully in Chapter 5. Near the beginning it offers the homely lines

> Even the mouse,
> ran from my house
> They laugh at you
> and scorn ya too
> What did I do (babe) –
> to be so black and blue?

These lines, in the singing of Louis Armstrong (in a 1929 recording with which Ralph Ellison begins his late modernist novel *Invisible Man*), transcend their bathos to achieve a sense of overwhelming sorrow. This is repeated in Armstrong's remarkable singing of the rhyme in the bridge,

> Ohh – I'm white, inside,
> that don't help my case,
> 'Cause I can't hide
> what is in my face –

where he cannot quite pronounce the word "face" and offers a moment of scat singing. The "Ohh" here and elsewhere, is also an example of scat.[36] Although I focus on Waller's modernist language in Chapter 5, here is a moment of powerful politics in his music. ("Black and Blue" is one of the few songs that Waller wrote but never recorded.)

A third example of the transformation of stereotype into insight can be seen in Cole Porter's "Night and Day" (1932). Porter makes most explicit the urban setting of his song, "In the roaring traffic's boom / In the silence of my lonely room"; he incorporates, as T. S. Eliot said Stravinsky did, "the scream of the motor-horn, the rattle of machinery, the grind of wheels, the beating of iron and steel, the roar of the underground railway, and the other barbaric noises of modern life'" into his music.[37] More to my point, however, is that Porter articulates *desire* in the very sounds of his rhymes. This is most clear in the song's bridge,

> Night and day,
> Under the hide of me
> There's an oh such a hungry yearning
> Burning inside of me,[38]

In the bridge not simply the feminine rhyme, "hide of me" / "inside of me," but the internal rhyme of "yearning" / "burning" seems to abandon its sense in the face of its sensuousness. It is this quality – the *performance* – of creating a *sensate* experience of yearning, of making it "sensible," that provokes the pleasure of his music. This is the "poetry" of emphasizing the qualities of experience in addition to attributes I mentioned in Chapter 1 (see note 31 to that chapter).

Here is a final example of the way ordinary things find their way into powerful music. Billie Holiday ends her 1939 blues "Fine and Mellow" with what is perhaps the homeliest of the everyday figures I am cataloguing:

> Love is just like the faucet
> It turns off and on
> Love is just like the faucet

It turns off and on
Sometimes when you think it's on baby
It has turned off and gone.[39]

The "faucet" here – like Gershwin's "knife," Waller's "mouse" and "face," Porter's city and his accidental musical rhymes – discovers music in the most ordinary of things. In the very rhymes of these songs, commonplace and homely as they are – Holiday's "on" / "gone"; Gershwin's "knife" / "life"; Porter's "yearning" / "burning"; Waller and Armstrong's not quite "case" / "face" – we can hear poetry in the most ordinary of things.

The discovery of music in ordinary life is a feature of popular music that is not usually apparent in high modernist music. Aaron Fox has analyzed such "songlike poesis"[40] in the everyday conversation of Texans – "the relationship between song and the 'ordinary' speech registers of everyday working-class life" (216) – and more specifically in "the submerged poetry" within the "accidental phrase[s]" of conversation (229). Such musical resonance, he argues, "involves a defamiliarizing movement away from 'ordinariness,' a movement in which poeticians have discovered the basis of verbal art's social power" (229). I would add that such defamiliarization also discovers verbal art's emotional, linguistic, and – as in Gershwin's rhyming of "knife" and of "life" – transformational power as well. And it does so, as defamiliarization always does, by *beginning* with the familiar and the ordinary.[41] Throughout his chapter "'Bring Me Up in a Beer Joint': The Poetics of Speech and Song," Fox offers detailed sophisticated analyses of both country music and country discourse, including "the poetic probing of conventional and hackneyed metaphors in song texts" (231) and the "semantic decoupling of words from their 'ordinary' sense" (233), even while he demonstrates the ways that "song and verbal art are sutured tightly together with everyday talk" (229). There is, then, in popular music – in the music of the thirties I am studying as well as the contemporary country music Fox examines – both the familiar and the unfamiliar, and that very combination, as in Joyce's, Williams's, and even Eliot's quotations of popular culture within their modernist language, marks powerful *modernist* moments in popular song.

Accidents of performance

What is striking about Fox's analysis of country music is the way that songlike poesis emerges from conversational speech that is both spontaneous and, once encountered, reflected upon. In a similar fashion,

Holiday's singing of the music of Gershwin, Porter and, less frequently, Waller, discussed in Chapter 6, emphasizes, within the *performance* of music, its power by combining songs we already know with singing that performs those songs in a particular way. This is true of jazz, and jazz improvisation, more generally. Adorno complained that "jazz" (meaning popular music) was a "static" repetition of the banal, "mechanical substitution by stereotyped patterns"[42] whose "standardization" reinforced a sense of "pseudo-individualism" that created the illusion serving the market that mass products could answer individual needs (458–59). "Good jazz," however, as Theodore Gracyk argues in response to Adorno, "requires both autonomy and cooperative production from its players, a combination that Adorno does not admit as possible within the culture industry."[43] It is just the possibility of "good jazz" – which is to say powerfully affective and intellectually startling popular music – that Holiday (as well as the other musicians I treat in *Modernism and Popular Music*) achieves by creating a *world* of music where there is nothing that is not musical, nothing that cannot bend sound to human feeling and meaning.

The issue of performance – which is to say, the issue of improvisation – returns to the discussion of the role of musical notation in the distinction between "classical" and popular music examined in the Introduction and Chapter 1. It also suggests a reason why, in the early twentieth century, the term "jazz" encompassed both what we now think of as *improvised* music and also the Tin Pan Alley music we now call "standards." Charles Hamm makes clear three different uses of the term "jazz" in the 1920s and 1930s.

1 Jazz (and blues) performed by black musicians for black audiences within the social context of black American culture. Phonograph discs of this music were marketed as "race records" by small independent record companies [such as Gennett which I mentioned earlier]. This music was rarely heard on commercial radio, and then only locally. Given the social structures of American life at this time, few whites (including Europeans) heard this music . . .
2 Jazz (and blues) performed by black musicians for white audiences within the social context of white American culture. By the late 1920s and through the 1930s, major record companies were distributing such music nationally, and some of it could be heard on network radio. Decisions of repertory and even musical style were usually made by white entrepreneurs and producers. [The music of "Fats" Waller and of Billie Holiday falls into this category.]
3 So-called jazz performed by white musicians for white audiences within the context of white American culture. This repertory made up the major share of all commercially recorded popular music in the 1920s, and was widely broadcast both locally and nationally.[44]

In a way the "so-called jazz" of Tin Pan Alley appropriated the term from African American culture.[45] This is clear in the way that Irving Berlin appropriated the term "ragtime" for his first big hit, "Alexander's Ragtime Band," which was hardly syncopated and not a rag. Yet it is also an appropriate term insofar as it was the basis of improvisation – both by "genuine" jazz performers (see the discussion of "I Got Rhythm" below) and by performers such as Waller, Holiday, and even Fred Astaire singing Tin Pan Alley standards. (Waller's improvisational singing – as opposed to his piano performances – was often primarily verbal; Holiday's was primarily musical, stylistic and rhythmic rather than harmonic.)

In his philosophical discussion of the aesthetics of improvisation, Andy Hamilton begins by describing Arnold Schoenberg's response to Ferruccio Busoni's 1910 *Sketch of a New Aesthetic of Music*. In that book, Busoni argues that "notation, the writing out of compositions, is primarily an ingenious expedient for catching an inspiration, with the purpose of exploiting it later. But notation is to improvisation as the portrait is to the living model."[46] In his response to this book Schoenberg, Hamilton notes, rejects this claim: "the portrait," he wrote in its margins, "has higher artistic life, while the model has only a lower life."[47] With this rejection, Schoenberg is validating the "transcendental" art of classical music over the ephemeral instances of popular music. That is, popular music is always performed: it is local, timely, and personal, and the radical immanence of performance sets it against ideals of "absolute" music.[48] Hamilton goes on to argue that

> the undervaluation of improvisation is one feature, and perhaps a contributory cause, of the 'museum art' ethos that dominates the world of Western art music, an ethos expressed by the very term 'classical music'. The saturation of the modern concert repertoire by masterworks of the eighteenth and nineteenth centuries is the semantically signaled end-product of post-Romantic historicism. The epithet 'classical' elsewhere refers to a period of particular excellence or influence; only in music is it ever simply equated with 'serious'.[49] (325)

The more or less improvised performances of popular music, and certainly the "jazz" of the 1920s and 1930s – untempered, rooted in a particular moment and, as we will see in Holiday, in a particular community, and much more idiosyncratic (if not "individualistic") than the strict readings of scores – offer, as I argue in what follows, another manifestation of twentieth-century modernism, the musical modernism of the succeeding chapters.

In those chapters I examine the music and lyrics of four musicians, but I also emphasize the musical performances of Waller and Holiday since they were performers in ways that the Gershwins and Porter were not. It is true that Gershwin was an accomplished pianist and Porter a serviceable one, but their music is distinguished by the performances of others. Still, there is a pronounced element of performativity in their work: the art of quotation I describe in Gershwin is a *performative* art, and the desire inhabiting Porter is governed by *enacted* restlessness. Still, it is no accident that Waller and Holiday were black, Gershwin and Porter white. I've already mentioned the fact that Gershwin introduced the "blue note" to commercial popular music, but the relation between black and white popular music in the 1920s and 30s is complicated. Jeffrey Melnick has written about the close and sometimes vexed interaction between Jewish American and African American music. He suggests that Berlin's first hit, "Alexander's Ragtime Band," could only fall into the category of so-called jazz, yet he argues that "Berlin inspired George Gershwin, Jerome Kern, Harold Arlen, and even the ultrasuave and Episcopalian Cole Porter (especially in 'Night and Day' with its insistent drum beats and mention of tom-toms) to experiment with the possibility of translating blackface into 'blackvoice.'"[50]

The creation of blackface characters by Jewish vaudeville in the new twentieth century is a particularly troubling fact in African American/ Jewish American relations, what Michael Alexander in *Jazz Age Jews* describes as Jewish participation "in an extremely problematic American tradition that no branch of scholarship can yet claim to fully comprehend."[51] Alexander discusses this phenomenon in relation to Al Jolson, who, he says, "was neither the first nor the last to perform in blackface, though he was the best." Jewish entertainers brought the "lowbrow" art of minstrelsy that ranked "somewhere between the freak show . . . and the raunchy burlesque circuit" to Broadway by infusing "blackface repertoire" with "the nostalgia for slavery and exile inherent in Jewish minstrelsy" (135). "By the 1910s and 1920s," Alexander argues,

> Al Jolson and other Eastern Jews in America had taken over the American project of depicting African-Americans, and had done so in their own unique way and for their own ends. Unlike the post-bellum minstrel tradition of hegemony and circumscription, Jewish minstrelsy in the 1910s and 1920s commonly represented "the scalawag servant with his surface dullness and hidden cleverness," as Gilbert Seldes noted in 1924. This more closely resembled the forms of minstrelsy of the antebellum period, which Eric Lott has understood as a means by which a white working class could have identified with enslaved African Americans. But Lott notes that whites could only identify with blacks in a period when there existed an institutional and hardfast division between black and white in the form of slavery. By Al Jolson's time, however, the racial barrier was growing ever more porous and

> to suppose that Jolson or his kind were trying to revive a barrier through blackface does not meet the basic facts of Jewish minstrelsy, including the liberatory themes of Jewish minstrel songs and performances. Rather, Jolson's acts were exercises in cultural fluidity and mutual longings for freedom.[52] (136–37)

Alexander goes on to say that "Eastern Jews in America maneuvered to see in African-American life their own story of exile and slavery" and that "Jewish depictions of blackness were explicitly and unambiguously understood by Jews as a form of identification"; "Jews believed they saw their own history reenacted before them in the form of African-American culture, and longed to participate in that culture" (137). Both Armstrong and Waller also participated in this tradition of minstrelsy, but, as Alfred Appel, Jr., points out, "Armstrong and Waller thrived in this environment ["of ethnic effrontery" directed at Italians and Jews as well as blacks] by turning the minstrel tradition upside down."[53]

Despite Alexander's argument, Jewish blackface entertainment was inherently and offensively racist, even while the appropriations of African American musical forms by Tin Pan Alley – the "blackvoice" Melnick mentions – though exploitative, rarely denigrated the music and its musicians. In some ways, that exploitation emphasized the American-ness of African American experience. Thus, Alexander argues in *Jazz Age Jews*, "when Jews helped jazz replace ragtime as the vogue music, the Jewish team of Rodgers and Hart expressed a similar belief that Americanization meant identification with imagined African-American culture" (164). The Jewish companies of Tin Pan Alley, Melnick argues, "with [their] reliance on 'black' sounds, . . . situated African American music at the heart of American popular song even though the rewards went almost completely to white composers."[54] The following chapters, in a way, reflect this situation: I emphasize the lyrics and music in Gershwin and Porter and the performance of music in Waller and Holiday. But I hope the chapters also reflect the ways that performance emphasizes both the *popularity* of the music I examine and positive links between African American and Jewish American music.

This is clear, I think, in the fact that, as I am arguing, in the 1920s and 1930s "jazz" was a term for popular music generally because the specific connotation of jazz as an improvised music also counts in the performances of popular music. "The properties of popular songs that made them vehicles for jazz," Peter Townsend writes, "have to do with the apparent contradictory values of simplicity and complexity. A song can be good material because it is simple enough to be improvised on fluently, or, on the other hand, because it is unusual or difficult enough to be interesting to improvise on."[55] Townsend goes on to say that some songs, because of their simplicity, "allow for a more expansive kind of improvisation," and he notes that "the master example of this kind is George Gershwin's 'I Got Rhythm', which has been improvised on in some form by every jazz musician who has played a note since the song was published in 1930" (10). In fact, David Yaffe offers a description of "I Got Rhythm" as an archetypal jazz form, which I should quote at length; in chapters 3 and 5 I examine its lyrics and music in relation to George and Ira Gershwin and its performance by Waller in an exemplary cutting contest. "To sever the ties between blacks and Jews," Yaffe argues,

> is to miss the collaboration that transformed George Gershwin's "I Got Rhythm" from a 1930 showcase for Ethel Merman to the "rhythm changes" used as a basis for Duke Ellington's "Cottontail," Charlie Christian's "Seven Come Eleven," Charlie Parker's "Salt Peanuts," Thelonious Monk's "Rhythm-a-Ning," and much more. Gershwin's 1–6–2–5 chord structure served as a guiding theme for the birth of bebop, and even if he was a Jew who was overt in his indebtedness to black music, the exchange worked both ways. Dizzy Gillespie's Minton's sessions would often start with playing the chords to "I Got Rhythm" – known as "Rhythm" changes – and survival on the bandstand depended on adapting those changes to the heat and structural innovations of the moment. To this day, calling for "Rhythm" changes is a universally understood directive on the bandstand; it is a common language of bop, and while Gershwin came up with his chord sequence borrowing from the swing and stride he heard from black musicians in Harlem, the beboppers returned the favor.[56]

Yaffe is describing the province of popular music, where music is both individual and communal, growing out of the moment it is performed, in my terms, in the time of jazz. That this music is modernist is also the burden of Yaffe's study, *Fascinating Rhythm: Reading Jazz in American Writing*, where he argues for the intimate relationship between literary modernism and popular music, "the affinities between the allusive, fragmented aesthetic of modernism and the often elliptical, associative logic of a jazz solo" (96).[57] In his juxtaposition of an "allusive, fragmented aesthetic" and an "elliptical, associative logic" he is describing features of modernist art close to those of wholeness, rhythmic decomposition, and montage I discuss in the Introduction.

What I am arguing is that the popular music between the wars, both white and black, itself is a manifestation of modernism, part of the historical moment I have been describing in this and the preceding chapters where economics, aesthetics, and the growing egalitarian culture of the lower middle class produced a particular kind of experience. The growing democracy of the new century – what Stephen Kern describes as "the progress of political democracy, the breakdown of aristocratic privilege, and the secularization of life"[58] – both nurtured this new class and its senses of real (and, as Adorno notes, sometimes pseudo) individualism and, in turn, was nurtured by this class, whose liberal and libertarian ideology comported so well with the individualism, self-expression, and spontaneity in what Hamilton calls "the aesthetics of imperfection" of jazz. "In other performing arts (drama, dance, perhaps poetry)," he writes, "improvisation is a very minor genre . . . But music does seem to be unique . . . The aspects of self-expression and spontaneity . . . come together in the fact that emotional expression in the finest improvised music is more *direct* than in its composed counterpart."[59] It is precisely the directness of popular music, I think, that allows us to discern the lineaments of twentieth-century modernism most closely.

THE STRUCTURE OF MODERNISM

In concluding this chapter, I want to sketch the organization of the following chapters of *Modernism and Popular Music* that I touched on in the Introduction, and in so doing offer the outlines of a "structure" of modernism altogether. If modernism – both Enlightenment and twentieth-century – finds itself imbricated in enormous transformations of social formations, subjectivity, languages (of music as well as discourse), and, in Mellers's global notion, worldviews, the music I examine here follows these categories in four notable exemplars of the popular American music of the thirties. In the Gershwins, as I mentioned early on in Chapter 1, the "clashing" of different cultures as they experienced it in the thriving metropolis of New York emphasizes the ways that *social life* was transformed in the early twentieth century. Such experience, as I note in Chapter 3, occasioned the reinvention of love. But equally important, the sense of quotations organizing their musical discourse presents an enacted performance of social life, the process of "an active tendency . . . within the *whole musical field*" that Middleton describes.[60]

I also mentioned early in Chapter 1 the intimacies of Billie Holiday's singing, which suggests a second global transformation in cultural modernism, the transformations of the nature of *personal experience* – and, indeed, emotional experience – that was concomitant with the transformations of social experience effected by the remarkable technological innovations of the period. As Virginia Woolf said, in a powerful description in

1924, "on or about December 1910 human character changed." And with this change, she writes,

> All human relations have shifted – those between masters and servants, husbands and wives, parents and children. And when human relations change there is at the same time a change in religion, conduct, politics, and literature. Let us agree to place one of these changes about the year 1910.[61]

Such changes affected our affectional lives: what passion, love, even despair might mean. And they may very well, as Colin Campbell almost suggests, transform the qualities of pleasure altogether. Another great *unpopular* modernist, Sigmund Freud, is the doctor and chronicler of these changes, which can be seen from a certain point of view as a sea-change in the very experience of subjectivity: thus W. H. Auden notes in his elegy for Freud that he created "a whole climate of opinion" under which "we conduct our differing lives."[62] What Freud describes in this "sea-change" is a performative conception of the subject – a psychological subject that emerges in relation to other subjects. Cole Porter captures this throughout his music in what I call in Chapter 4 the rhythms of desire in his work. There I focus on Jacques Lacan's "revision" of Freud that emphasizes the performativity of pleasure rather than the specific satisfaction of needs that I discussed in the Introduction.

A third aspect of modernism, closely related to the transformation of feeling that Woolf and Porter are both describing, is a kind of Copernican revolution that redirected the focus of understanding from the world to the forms of human experience; this is clear in the kinds of formalism that arose in the early twentieth century (epitomized in the Russian Formalism I have already mentioned), and especially what some philosophers have called the "linguistic turn" in philosophy. (In fact, the very "turn" to a focus on linguistic forms in philosophy itself can be seen as an instance of the "semantic formalism" I discussed in the Introduction.) This can be seen in Freud, who invented the "talking cure" near the turn of the century, but also in other popular and unpopular modernists, Wittgenstein, the Vienna positivists, Gertrude Stein, and William Carlos Williams. In one striking example, Walter Benn Michaels emphasizes the ways that Williams's poetry emphasizes the *material* aspect of language rather than its representational function: "it is the 'opacity' of Williams's words that make their 'reality' *as* words visible," he argues; he concludes that "from this standpoint, Williams's modernism is inextricably connected not exactly to American nationalism but, more precisely, to American nativism."[63] As I argue in

Chapter 4, Cole Porter pursues a similar procedure of turning words into sound that is much more discernable in musical lyrics than in poetry.

This turn to the "formal" aspects of language is also a function of – or at least imbricated in – the transformation of industrial capital into finance capital in the years around the turn of the century, which pursued the "industry" of documentation as strongly as industrial capital pursued production. As already noted, it is precisely to function in this industry of documentation that the new lower middle class streamed into American cities. Moreover, the creation of documents (rather than "things") emphasizes the sense of performativity that Austin isolates in linguistic activity. One such example of a performative speech-act is the creation of a corporation, a legal pronouncement that, in the United States, made a commercial entity a legal "person." The number of corporations in England rose from 700 in 1855 to 7,900 in 1883,[64] and trusts and cartels dominated America's "gilded age." Such growth is closely connected to the "inventions" of both the periodic table in chemistry and Schoenberg's twelve-tone music, both of which emphasized formal, systematized composition.[65] Fats Waller, in his music and performances, captures a strong sense of the music of language, which I describe in the context of the African American phenomenon of signifyin'.

A fourth aspect of cultural modernism, I believe, is *the re-enchantment of experience*. By this I mean that the great motor of modernity in the West, Enlightenment calculation, created for many a strong sense of the desacralization of experience, the reduction of quality to quantities. (This observation is the burden of much of Max Weber's sociology that Campbell attempts to supplement in his study of consumerism as well as productionism in the early modern period.) Such calculations are seen and felt in Newton's mathematical physics, Bach's well-tempered music, Jeremy Bentham's cost-effective ethics, even in Thomas Jefferson's sense that all "men" are interchangeably equal and George Eliot's sense that men and women are similarly equal. Twentieth-century modernism responded to this with a renewed emphasis on what E. M. Forster calls the "invisible" in experience, but what I prefer to call a strong sense of "anagogic" experience in which huge, incalculable, impersonal powers seem to punctuate experience.[66] In the *Merriam Webster's Dictionary*, *anagogic* is described as an "interpretation of a word, passage, or text (as of Scripture or poetry) that finds beyond the literal, allegorical, and moral sense a fourth and ultimate spiritual or mystical sense." In this way *anagogy* designates a global meaning that, like "modernism" itself, is a whole way of apprehending phenomena, understanding things or simply experiencing things, in which experience, understanding, apprehension are strangely impersonal.

This is felt in much modernist literature and music – again, Stravinsky's *Rite of Spring* is a good example – and, negatively, in the powerful passions of the "modernist" politics of Hitler, Stalin, and fundamentalists of one stripe or another. My extended example in Chapter 6 is the television recording of the performance of "Fine and Mellow" by Billie Holiday and Lester Young in 1957, their reunion after twenty years of estrangement to perform the song she wrote in the 1930s. Nat Hentoff, who co-produced this show for CBS, describes how sick Young was for this performance – he had missed several big-band solos earlier in the show – and how "somehow he managed to stand up, and then he blew the sparest, purest blues chorus I have ever heard."[67] The anagogic sense of musical modernism grows out of a peculiar – maybe ancient[68] – sense of communal life, of a common life that the individualism of Enlightenment modernity came to see as illusory, a mistake, something to be disregarded. The popular jazz of the 1930s – perhaps like music of all time, even, perhaps, like the unpopular music of the early twentieth century – offers something else. In Holiday's answer to Young's solo in 1957 she sings like the horns that, in her youth, she claimed to admire and imitate from recordings: she plays with the rhythms of the blues in song that answers Young's powerful melodious solo in a montage of sound that insists on its wholeness as well.

Behind this survey of the musical modernism of Gershwin, Porter, Waller, and Holiday are four important categories of understanding that grew up in relation to conceptions and new experiences in the context of aesthetic and cultural modernism.

1 The importance in cultural modernism of the *social nature* of tonality and counterpoint, participating in what Mikhail Baktin called the "dialogics" in twentieth-century literature as it relates to everyday experiences. This phenomenon can be seen in the music and lyrics of George and Ira Gershwin. Bakhtin was born in 1895, Gershwin in 1898.

2 The representation and provocation of *desire* in twentieth-century arts. The psychoanalyst, and self-proclaimed heir of Freud, Jacques Lacan is particularly noted for focusing on the ways in which desire *punctuates* time. Lacan's contention that desire is essentially metonymic – that it can somehow be located in the constant displacement of signifiers sliding across our experience and understanding – can be heard in Cole Porter's syncopations of both lyrics and music (as in the threes against four of the bridge of "Night and Day" and the way Billie Holiday emphasizes

this in her performance by singing consistently before the beat).[69] Lacan was born in 1901, Porter in 1893.

3 The emphasis on *linguistic play* in twentieth-century literature and culture. This is associated with almost everyone in literary modernism – and with Igor Stravinsky, Béla Bartók, Charles Ives, and even Aaron Copland in "high" musical modernism as well. But in relation to the popular music and performances of Fats Waller it is most pronounced in the context of slavery and its aftermath in the United States, including the remarkable African American linguistic practice of signifyin'. But it is also associated with musical manifestations of signifying in jazz improvisation, ensemble music, cutting contests, and the like. In *Shadow and Act* Ralph Ellison offers a definition of "signifyin'" as "meaning, in the unwritten dictionary of American Negro usage, 'rhetorical understatements.'"[70] In other words, one way of understanding Waller's lyrics and performances is not as an expression of psychology or of social interactions, but as the appropriation of language; it is writ large in the appropriation of language by Louis Armstrong's scat singing. Ellison was born in 1914; Waller in 1904; Armstrong in 1901.

4 The power of what I am calling the *anagogic* nature of certain global effects of early-twentieth-century literature and twentieth-century art and culture more generally. This is associated with particularly powerful, almost "revelatory" moments: think of Joyce's Nighttown in *Ulysses*, Woolf's ragged woman in *Mrs. Dalloway*, Heidegger's histrionics (which I touch upon in Chapter 4), Picasso's *Guernica*. As I have already noted – as history noted with a vengeance – such global histrionics may well be associated too with the violence that greeted Stravinsky, and the more terrible violence of twentieth-century politics and its great thirty years' war. But we can hear this in the way in which the performed blues of Billie Holiday's "Fine and Mellow," focusing on the most ordinary aspects of life – clothes, household items, the vicissitudes of love – emerges out of and returns into its chords and improvisation, the uncanny echo of voice and saxophone that suggests the world itself might be apprehended in sound. Stravinsky and Joyce were both born in 1882, Holiday in 1915.

As I mentioned in the Introduction, I take this catalogue from the examination of what J. Hillis Miller has called "The Search for Grounds in Literary Study," in which he argues that when literature – or the arts more generally – assumed the burden of sustaining cultural values, as it did in the time of Matthew Arnold (which is to say at the far-off beginnings of twentieth-century modernism), it focused, more or less explicitly, upon four, mutually exclusive "grounds" for literature: social, psychological, linguistic, and a last ground he describes as metaphysical or religious for which I'm using the term "anagogic." Miller suggests these categories are exhaustive – that as a framework there are no aspects of human experience, understanding, and value that are left out – and this might well be true, even if one could organize (or "constellate," as Walter Benjamin describes it)[71] a different set of "exhaustive" categories. As they are realized in the popular music of the 1930s, they are consistently performative, enacted in dialogics, metonymies of desire, improvisation and cutting contests, and anagogic musicality.

These four categories, I am arguing, help define cultural modernism: its enormous social changes, its private individual changes, its linguistic play, its sense of the sacred; transformations in religion, conduct, politics, and art, as Woolf noted. They also summarize the focus of the chapters to follow. Most powerful, I believe, are the transformations in religion or, more generally, in spirit, what I have been calling anagogic effects. I mean by this term making experience sacred by means of a new global framework in which *everything* must be reevaluated. Holiday and all these musicians at their best make music their framework. Cultural modernism itself accomplished this across the many categories of cultural life I have touched upon in this and the preceding chapter.

Each musician I study here participates in cultural modernism under all these categories as well. Thus, the multivoiced tonalities of discourse Bakhtin describes in modern literature (especially of Dostoevsky) not only situates the Gershwins' music and lyrics within the contexts of the culture of literary modernism but it also situates Holiday's singing of Porter and the way that Louis Armstrong, in his Louis Armstrong & His Orchestra band, makes Waller's New York music play with banjoed southern jazz. Or the fact that the desire Holiday syncopates (à la Lacan) in Porter's music, transforming meanings into musical sounds (as Porter does elsewhere: "do do that voodoo that you do so well!"), is felt in Gertrude Stein, T. S. Eliot, and Armstrong's and Waller's scat singing as well. Or the ways that Fats Waller's stride piano, growing out of the rent parties and cutting contests of early-twentieth-century Harlem, takes its place, along with the wit in Porter's "Night and Day" (which begins with African tom-toms) and Holiday's blues, among examples of linguistic modernism, such as literary language organizing itself in relation to dialect and "racial masquerade," as Michael North has argued in a penetrating study of the encounter of races in American modernism.[72] And finally, I hope I have suggested, in Chapter 6, the ways in which the ensemble music of Holiday creates what Stravinsky describes as the possibilities of "a reflective system between the language structure of the music and the structure of the phenomenal world,"[73] an anagogic system that rings as well in D. H. Lawrence, Wallace Stevens, William Carlos Williams, HD – and even in those other modernists, Ralph Ellison, George Gershwin, Cole Porter, Fats Waller, studied here. Each of the four musicians I examine participate in all four categories describing what might be distinctive features of literary and cultural modernism, its anagogic power, psychological insight, and participation in new and contested social and linguistic formations.

PART II

Gershwin, Porter, Waller, and Holiday

CHAPTER 3

Melting pot and meeting place: the Gershwin brothers and the arts of quotation

In important ways, it is proper to begin discussions of strategies of music and lyric composition in *Modernism and Popular Music* with the Gershwin brothers. They worked at the heart of commercial popular music in the United States in the early twentieth century, New York City, and, in the face of the racism of American society, they were the first to introduce elements of African American jazz to commercial music in the United States. In fact, Cole Porter – Protestant, from Indiana and living outside New York – felt throughout his life that the kind of popular music he was writing was significantly "outside" the work in New York, that he himself didn't fit into the popular music scene. And Fats Waller, a lifelong New Yorker, developed a music that was also "outside" the New York City mainstream of Tin Pan Alley in his stride piano of Harlem. In many ways, then, Jewish American composers and lyricists, striving to articulate in music what Irving Berlin described as "what the people want, what they understand, what hits them and hits me,"[1] accomplished situating themselves, as Charles Hamm says, "in the absolute center of American popular culture" by pursuing the "twofold strategy" of the new immigrants in the early twentieth century: "(a) trying to become 'invisible,' by modifying all obvious signs of ethnic origin (dress, language, sometimes their names and even physical appearance) in an attempt to be indistinguishable from 'mainstream' Americans; and (b) trying to make positive and visible contributions to American life and culture."[2]

Still, this kind of schematic understanding does not do justice to the rich musical life in America in the early twentieth century. In the late 1920s George Gershwin described his hopes about his music which should, I think, help to introduce the theme that gathers together the chapters of this book, the relationships among language, music, and – at least in passing – American culture after World War I. In 1929 Gershwin said:

What I'd like to do would be to write an opera of the melting pot, of New York City itself, with its blend of native and immigrant strains. This would allow for many kinds of music, black and white, Eastern and Western, and would call for a style that should achieve out of this diversity, an artistic and aesthetic unity . . .

New York is not only an American city. It is a meeting-place, a rendezvous of the nations. I'd like to catch the rhythms of these interfusing peoples, – to show them clashing and blending. I'd especially like to blend the humor of it with the tragedy of it.[3]

The manner of "clashing and blending" Gershwin describes can be found in the musical lines, harmonic structures, and lyrics of George and Ira Gershwin. The Gershwin brothers bring the art of simple melody and complex harmony together – clashing and blending – in ways that demonstrate the arts of quotation and what their Russian contemporary, Mikhail Bakhtin, calls "dialogics," in relation to sound, sense, and the larger cultural formations George is describing. Every utterance, Bakhtin writes, is a form of "responsive understanding,"[4] which, like the blended strains of post-war American culture Gershwin describes in his music, enacts the quotation – the repetition and articulation – of what comes before. Quotation repeats and transforms its object, and the Gershwins' songs – in their melodies, lyrics, and harmonies – repeat and transform the often hackneyed music of Tin Pan Alley and, perhaps more strikingly, the varied carols of city life. In an important way, Bakhtin's dialogic conception of discourse and meaning is above all *performative*: like the popular music that Richard Middleton describes, it is an enacted performance of social life, the process of "an active tendency" not simply within music, as Middleton says, but within the whole field of social and ideological meanings.[5] To the extent that the Gershwins' music is dialogue, it epitomizes and clarifies the vigor of twentieth-century popular music more generally.

CLASHING AND BLENDING

Specifically in terms of the technicalities of music, the combinations of "black and white, Eastern and Western" music Gershwin talks about articulate themselves in a repeated motif in his music, the pentatonic scale (see Figure 1). "While George wrote all his songs (except some for *Porgy and Bess*) in a major key," Deena Rosenberg notes, "writing melodies consisting largely of notes from the pentatonic scale enabled him to tinge the positive major sound with a poignant minor one, because the five notes contain both a major and a minor chord."[6]

The five-note pentatonic scale combines minor and major chords – in this instance, A minor (A-C-E) and C major (C-E-G) chords, on the scale

Figure 1 The pentatonic scale

with no accidental notes – and thus offers a strong sense of what is called the "blue" note, the minor third played against a major chord. Many musical and cultural historians argue that the blue note came into the American musical vernacular from two sources, "African-American blues and Jewish liturgical music,"[7] and Isaac Goldberg even wrote of the Gershwins' 1927 song "My One and Only," from *Funny Face*, that "it begins Yiddish and ends up black."[8] As I suggested in Chapter 2, Gershwin had a particular affinity for and, for a white person, an unusual acquaintance with African American music. "It should also be noted," Hamm writes,

> that Gershwin, more than any other composer (or critic, or historian) of his time, constantly sought out black musicians and listened to the widest possible range of black music. He knew Will Vodery, Lucky Roberts, Duke Ellington; he heard New York "stride" pianists [such as Waller] play downtown, and often visited the Cotton Club and other spots in Harlem to hear the bands of Ellington and Cab Calloway; through his friendship with Carl Van Vechten, he heard Bessie Smith and other black singers perform at social gatherings; and while in South Carolina to work on *Porgy and Bess*, he heard and even participated in rural black church singing.[9]

Moreover, he was highly respected in the black community. "Gershwin was so well known for his 'black' compositions," Jeffrey Melnick writes, "that Langston Hughes was inspired to joke that during the 1920s 'any Harlem Negro of any social importance at all would be likely to say casually: . . . "As I said to George –," referring to George Gershwin.'"[10]

Along with the blue note – which he introduced to Broadway and repeatedly plays throughout his music – Gershwin heard in African American blues the pentatonic scale which he himself used throughout his music, as he himself noted.[11] This is strikingly clear in a comparison of the pentatonic scale to some of his most famous melodies, shown in Figure 2. (I have transcribed all these songs to the same key in order to make this comparison clear.) Pentatonic scales and the blue note they express – syncopated, submerged, and repeatedly cited – repeat and transform the new languages of American urban life after World War I.

As Rosenberg notes, with the exception of two or three pieces from *Porgy and Bess*, all of the Gershwins' songs – and I should add that George and

Figure 2 Gershwin songs and the pentatonic scale

Ira composed more than seven hundred songs together during George's short life[12] – are written in major keys, yet they are almost all haunted by the blues minor. The Gershwins' great contribution to American popular music – and, indeed, to the development of the American musical theater – was their ability to incorporate the ethnic colloquialisms of blues and major/minor modalities (such as the pentatonic scale) in their melodies, lyrics, and harmonies at what Rosenberg calls the precise moment when "the new, urbanized nation – brash, insouciant, anxious, insecure" faced the question of defining itself: "rural or urban, Protestant or polyglot" (xx). The

Figure 3 "'S Wonderful," refrain; music and lyrics by George Gershwin and Ira Gershwin

Gershwins, first-generation Jews from New York, quoted and articulated the new urban polyglot of post-war America.

Perhaps the best musical example of what I am talking about is their 1927 song "'S Wonderful" (Figure 3).

Refrain

'S wonderful! 'S marvelous –
You should care for me!
'S awful nice! 'S paradise –
'S what I love to see!
You've made my life so glamorous,
You can't blame me for feeling amorous.
Oh, 'S wonderful! 'S marvelous –
That you should care for me!

Figure 3 (*cont.*)

The music of this song is remarkably elemental – as elemental as the simplicity of Beethoven's Fifth Symphony,[13] which it approaches in its architecture of repeated (minor) thirds. Both the opening verse and the main lyric are built on the repetition of thirds: minor thirds building to the major thirds in the opening; and the repetition of the same minor third – B♭/G – six times in the refrain. Moreover, the bridge of the song is built upon the repetition of seconds with the transition to the refrain – the B♭-to-G minor third again – simply a chromatic transition, C, C♭, B♭. If the verse and refrain recall the simplicity of Beethoven's Fifth, the bridge recalls the even simpler so-called melody of the Allegro of Handel's Concerto Grosso No. 7 (Op. 6), which consists of the repetition of a single

Figure 4 "'S Wonderful," verse; music and lyrics by George Gershwin and Ira Gershwin

note. The musical lines of "'S Wonderful" – especially its repetition of thirds – seem almost clichés, the simplicities of which might well explain the widespread attraction of Gershwin's melodies to jazz improvisation.

This music seems in its repetitions of thirds to repeatedly quote itself precisely because its repeated elisions of "it's" as "'s"("it's wonderful, it's marvelous, it's awfully nice," in "'S wonderful! 'S marvelous–" etc.) seem to be versions of self-quotation insofar as they seem anomalous before the truncated adverb ("awful") – and to a lesser extent before the pronoun ("what"). Ira more explicitly captures this elision pattern in the opening verse of the song (Figure 4).

Figure 4 (*cont.*)

VERSE
Don't mind telling you,
In my humble fash,
That you thrill me through
With a tender pash.
When you said you care,
'Magine my emosh;
I swore then and there
Permanent devosh.
You made all other boys seem blah;
Just you alone filled me with Aah!

With these contractions of the verse – "fashion" as "fash," "passion" as "pash," and "emotion" as "emosh" – Ira Gershwin is doing a lot of work.

First of all, he is quoting the vernacular instead of formal English, which embodies precisely the "clashing and blending" of cultures that George described in 1929. "Listening to the argot in everyday conversation," Ira wrote in the *New York Times* in 1930, "results in pay-dirt for the lyric writers."[14] Many years later he elaborated on his quotation of slang and cliché: "the literary cliché," he wrote in 1959, "is an integral part of lyric writing. The phrase that is trite and worn-out when appearing in print usually becomes, when heard fitted to an appropriate musical turn, revitalized, and seems somehow to revert to its original provocativeness."[15] Moreover, his uses of the argot and cliché repeat the high modernism of his contemporaries: both Bakhtin with his lifelong focus on the "speech genres" of discourse, and James Joyce with his lifelong focus on the efficacies of cliché. Another great modernist writer of cliché is Flannery O'Connor, who, like the Jewish Gershwins in Protestant America, was an outsider – a Catholic in Protestant Georgia. The *work* of cliché is to say something when some statement is called for ("Have a nice day!"), even though nothing much is meant. Clichés, above all, are forms of citation: they are "quoted" over and over again by rote, without much thought. In a way, they participate in formalism *without* semantics. The work of outsiders – Gershwin, O'Connor, Joyce – is to *hear* the meaning of cliché, even when nothing much is meant, to apprehend the *semantic* inhabiting its seemingly empty formalism.[16] Such an operation creates, as I noted in Chapter 2, what Aaron Fox calls "a defamiliarizing movement away from 'ordinariness,' a movement in which poeticians have discovered the basis of verbal art's social power."[17] After all, we all want to have a nice day. This is the power of even unconscious cliché: to be so familiar with interpersonal goodwill that we can give it a nickname, a shorthand expression. Moreover, this work above all – Ira suggests as much in claiming cliché for popular music – is *performance.*

RHYMES AND RHYTHMS

A second aspect of Ira's lyrics is the way they integrate themselves within the musicality and harmonies of his brother's music. This is clear in his elaboration of rhymes. His most elaborate discussion is his description of the rhyming of "I Got Rhythm" – another song, as I mentioned, organized around the pentatonic scale (Figure 5). "For over two weeks," he wrote,

> I kept fooling around with various titles and with sets of double rhymes for the trios of short two-foot lines. I'll ad-lib a dummy to show what I was at:

Figure 5 "I Got Rhythm," music and lyrics by George Gershwin and Ira Gershwin

"Roly-Poly / Eating solely / Ravioli / Better watch your diet or bust // Lunch or dinner, / You're a sinner. / Please get thinner. / Losing all that fat is a must."[18]

Ira found, however, that the series of double feminine rhymes didn't work,[19] and he abandoned this elaborate system of rhyming for non-rhyming lines.

I got rhythm,
I got music,
I got my man –
Who could ask for anything more?

I got daisies,
In green pastures,
I got my man –

Figure 5 (*cont.*)

Who could ask for anything more?

Old Man Trouble,
I don't mind him –
You won't find him
'Round my door.

I got starlight,
I got sweet dreams,
I got my man –
Who could ask for anything more –
Who could ask for anything more?

In these famous lyrics he still maintained a few audible rhymes: "more"/"door" and the feminine rhyme "mind him"/"find him."[20] But in "'S Wonderful," the final rhyme of the verse presents a more elemental sense of rhyme, rhyming phonemes rather than words, with language approaching the level of pure sound: "You made all other boys seem blah; / Just you alone filled me with Aah."

Like the uses of slang and cliché, all these forms of rhyming are instances of quotation – the quotation of sound rather than sense – that take up the worn-out and trite. Rosenberg repeatedly describes similar quotations in George's music as well as Ira's lyrics and argues that in "'S Wonderful" George quotes musical phrases from the title song of the musical in which that song appeared, *Funny Face*.[21] The particularities of musical quotation here are notable. In "their opening melodic figures," Rosenberg writes, "the falling third in ''S Wonderful' is reversed to become the rising third of 'Funny Face'" (159). Similarly, she notes that the line "We'll dance into the sunshine out of the rain" literally quotes the opening notes of W. C. Handy's "St. Louis Blues" (87); that both the words and music of "Slap That Bass" cite the words and music of "I Got Rhythm" (330); and that throughout his career George repeatedly cites himself. Perhaps the most striking example of such musical quotation is the way that "Nice Work If You Can Get It" again asks "who could ask for anything more?" in the same rhythm as "I Got Rhythm,"[22] but translates the major mode singing the tonic of the earlier song into the haunting, almost atonal dissonance of the subdominant diminished-fifth seventh of the later song, that is, the C7(♭5) in Figure 6.

More than a decade before the Gershwins wrote "Nice Work" and almost a decade before they met Schoenberg in California – Schoenberg played tennis once a week on George's courts[23] – the music critic Linton Martin noticed that George practiced "a sort of tonal jiu-jitsu. Right in

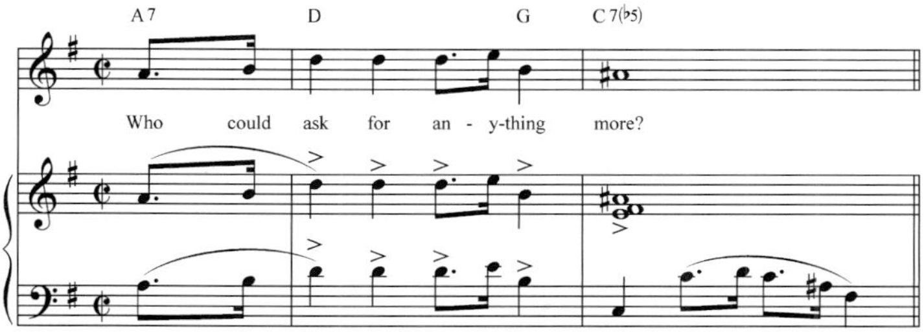

Figure 6 "Nice Work If You Can Get It," music and lyrics by George Gershwin and Ira Gershwin

the middle of a bit of bouncing jazz he will insert an echo of the whole tone scale, hitherto heard only in the ultra-modern music of symphony concerts."[24] Martin's term "echo," of course, is a term for quotation. In this, the whole of "Nice Work" alludes to the larger changes in post-war symphonic music, playing its haunting, almost atonal melody against a "chronological bass" – that is, chord progressions that contain notes that allow for a chronological scale to be played in the bass with the proper inversions – the way that "Embraceable You" and "The Man I Love" both play their *tonal* melodies against a similar "chronological bass." The example of "Nice Work" brings together both the quotation of words and the repetitious sounds of the quotations of music. Such repetitions of sound, found throughout the Gershwin songs, offer moments when sound and sense – words and music – approach one another to blend and clash and gather together the emerging America of the 1920s and 1930s. "I Got Rhythm" was written in 1930, "Nice Work" in 1937. In "'S Wonderful" – written in 1927 – the rhyme of the (more or less) semantic "blah" and the asemantic "AAH" is a graphic example of rhyming sound and sense, history and meaning, and the marking of difference within quotation. My equation of sound and sense with history and meaning is of great importance to *Modernism and Popular Music* in my larger aim at suggesting, in the popular music of the early twentieth century, the "feel" of America after the decisive victory of World War I and the emergence of the United States as an economic and cultural world power.

In any case, Ira's rhymes – existing on the level of simple sound – complicate those sounds with other systems of meaning just as George's simple melodies are complicated by the systematic transformations of those simplicities in relation to complex harmonies. In "'S Wonderful," for example, the minor thirds of the refrain are played over E♭/E♭6,

C7/B♭-diminished, and other harmonies that sound the minor third as part of, first, a minor seventh, then a diminished seventh, a tonic major, and other modalities of sound. (See Figure 3, especially bars 2–3.) Similarly, Ira juxtaposes simplicity and complexity in the lyrics. The rhymes of the refrain of "'S Wonderful" are almost the simplest imaginable in English ("me," "see," "me") while those of its bridge ("glamorous"/"amorous" and, in the second bridge I didn't quote earlier in this chapter, "clover time"/ "overtime") are polysyllabic and complex feminine rhymes. The simplest rhyme-sound in English, as Jonathan Culler and others have argued,[25] is the vocative "O" of pure sounding, rung in "'S Wonderful" in the last lines of the refrain ("Oh, 'S wonderful! 'S marvelous –") and rung again within the almost equally basic "No, no!" of the Gershwins' "They Can't Take That Away from Me." What such simple rhymes do, as A. J. Greimas argues in linguistic terms in discussing the power of poetry, is to create the impression of "the shortening of the distance between the signifier and the signified" so that "poetic language, while remaining part of language, seeks to reachieve the 'primal cry', and thus" results in an "illusory signification of a 'deep meaning'" within the language of verse.[26]

If the simple rhymes of the refrain of "'S Wonderful" bear the weight of the power of poetry – its "primal cry" – then the complex rhymes of its bridge bear a very different burden. Ira himself describes some of the most complex rhymes he ever wrote as being in "Embraceable You," its four- and five-syllable rhymes of "embraceable you"/"irreplaceable you" and "silk and laceable you"; "tipsy in me"/"gypsy in me"; and what he calls "a trick four-syllable one" in "glorify love"/"'encore!' if I love."[27] Such complex rhymes are elaborations of feminine rhymes in these cases, in which the last syllables are direct repetitions of sounds while an earlier syllable offers the combination of similarity and difference of usual rhymes. The tendency of such feminine rhymes, especially in Gershwin, is to create the worldliness that George described in his comments to Goldberg with which I began this chapter, the diversity and "rhythms of interfusing peoples" he describes in New York.

In Chapter 4, I examine the direct repetition of rhyming in Cole Porter as a transformation of *rime riche*, the phenomenon in medieval and Renaissance poetry (in English and other languages) that rhymed homonyms such as the "stair" of a house and the "stare" of a gaze or "well" as an adjective and "well" as a noun. Porter, as I argue, simply repeats the same word as a "rhyme" rather than its homonym. In this, he is participating in the practice of such modernist poets as Eliot and Yeats – *European* modernist poets, or at least heirs to the symbolist movement – in whose work such rhyming forgoes the medieval practice of rhyming different meanings by means of the same sound in order to rhyme signs as a whole, both their meaning and their sound. Especially in the case of Yeats, such rhyming of words with themselves participates in the attempt of the symbolist poets of the late nineteenth century in France to create a metaphysics of meaning, the rhyming of "natural" and "supernatural" meanings that I will describe in Porter's music. This is very different from rhyming the "natural" and the "artificial" that I described in semantic formalism in the Introduction. It is also very different from William Carlos Williams's attempt to emphasize and recover the material "reality" of words that I mentioned in Chapter 2. Both Williams's and Yeats's senses of poetry are "post-symbolist" sensibilities, but Williams's focus on the worldliness of language is much more akin to that of George and Ira Gershwin than is Yeats's, which is closer to that of Porter. Porter often utilizes this modernist (that is, non-homonymic) *rime riche* while the Gershwins, as far as I know, never do. In "But Not for Me," for instance, the Gershwins present a traditional *rime riche* by rhyming the "not" of the song's title and repeated verses and "knot," something that is found in very few of their contemporaries: "When ev'ry happy plot / Ends with a marriage knot– / And there's no knot for me." In addition, they create elaborate feminine rhymes such as those Ira describes in "Embraceable You."

In a way that I hope becomes clear, it is the non-reduction of feminine rhymes to *rime riche* that situates their songs as worldly in the "natural" realm of memory rather than the "supernatural" realm of desire to which, as I note in Chapter 4, Porter – and modernist poets such as Yeats – aspire. In this way they are much more akin to Williams than to Eliot. In his *Autobiography* Williams calls *The Waste Land* "the great catastrophe to our letters" by halting, "under the blast of Eliot's genius," the "drive that was gathering headway upon the theme of a rediscovery of a primary impetus, the elementary principle of all art, in the local conditions."[28] "Critically Eliot," he said, "returned us to the classroom just at the moment when I felt that we were on the point of an escape to matters much closer to the essence of a new art form itself – rooted in the locality" (174). Williams emphasizes the *local* nature of art, the "local" life of popular music as opposed to the "absolute" of so-called classical music I described in chapters 1 and 2, the "museum art" of its concert hall (and the classroom) that is *marked off* from ongoing activities in the local life of its listeners. It is the local nature of art, rather than seeming supernatural powers in Eliot (and Porter), that mark the Gershwins' affinity with Williams. It is characteristic – and touching – that directly after describing *The Waste Land* as "the great catastrophe"

Williams uses more than half of his chapter entitled "The Waste Land" to describe the ways that immigrant patients materially helped him in his work of "giving birth" (148) to their children. In a way, the Gershwins' rhymes are much more complex than those of Porter or Yeats: they aspire to the complications of modern American society, just as Williams does, that take in the "dialogue" between listener and composer, the joint work of patient and physician in "giving birth" – in the powerfully *performative* sense of art I described in the Introduction.

In this context, it is clear that the simple musical lines and complex harmonies of the Gershwins are another version of "complex" rhyming. Such complexity, I think, is best exemplified in Ira's so-called "trick" rhyme in "Embraceable You," "But hang it – / Come on, let's glorify love! / Ding dang it! / You'll shout 'Encore!' if I love."[29] In these lines the argot of "hang it," "Ding dang it!", and the very different idiom of "encore!" clash together in a kind of discourse of quotation that doesn't resolve itself in primal passions. It is as if the social phenomenon of a discursive genre – what Bakhtin calls the "speech genres" of our shared social lives – never allows for the apprehension of a level of experience that transcends the *differences* of native and immigrant strains, black music and white music, Eastern and Western modalities, embodied in the repeated pentatonic scale of Gershwin's musical lines and the distinct major/minor scales of his harmonies. It never allows music to be conceived outside of performance and outside of montage. Just as George does in the music, in his lyrics Ira emphasizes the diversity – the clashing and blending – implicit in rhymes and in quotation more generally when he repeats a line but alters its meaning, e.g., "no knot for me" in "But not for me."[30] This aspect of rhyme – its combinations of similarity and differences – is homologous with what Rosenberg calls the "Gershwin trademark [of] starting a song with a striking melodic fragment and then repeating it with a different and unexpected harmony underneath" (45).

RETICENT MUSIC

A third aspect of Ira's lyrics, which ties together all these elements in both the music and the lyrics of the songs of the Gershwin brothers, is the indirection of his meanings, what Rosenberg calls a structure of "indirection-then-revelation"[31] and what Ira himself called "the left field or circuitous approach to the subject preponderant in Songdom":[32] by *this* circumlocution, Ira means the preponderant subject of "love." If, as I have noted, the Gershwins' music rarely resolves itself in the "primal passions" of what Culler calls the apostrophic "image of voice, . . . the pure O of undifferentiated voicing,"[33] this is underlined in the truncation of passion itself in "'S Wonderful," the articulation of "passion" in the refrain simply as "pash." There is a remarkable reticence throughout the lyrics – and indeed throughout the music – of the Gershwins. The declaration of love, for instance, is rare indeed: Bess sings "I Loves You, Porgy," and in "Bess, You Is My Woman Now" both Porgy and Bess declare each will "keep dis vow," but throughout the great love songs – "But Not for Me," "Embraceable You," "A Foggy Day," "I Can't Get Started," and many others – love is unspoken, usually something imagined for the future (as in "The Man I Love" and "Someone to Watch Over Me"), something overlooked ("How Long Has This been Going On?"), or some object in the world that can be lost or found ("Love Is Here to Stay," "Nice Work If You can Get It").

The reticence of the Gershwins takes the forms of the periphrastic wordiness of repeated quotations and the repetitions of musical fragments over and again, like Ira's disquisition on "songdom" in order not to say the word "love" or the repetitions of the pentatonic scale throughout George's music in order to bring together major and minor, Western and Eastern, black and white, music. In such periphrastic wordiness – as in their feminine rhymes – they participate in the "rhythmic decomposition" of the aesthetics of popular music I discuss in the Introduction. That is, for the Gershwins (unlike Cole Porter, for instance) the objectification of love is not its mystical and all-but-silent assertion – Greimas's "primal cry" and Culler's "pure voice" – but a form of loquacious indirection, a way of *situating* feeling on the level of objects in a cluttered and noisy world by verbalizing feeling in words that have already been spoken. My favorite of these indirections is from the verse of "Someone to Watch Over Me," where the singer declares, circuitously, "I'd like to add his initial to my monogram."[34] The declaration of love by describing the addition of a letter to a monogram may well be the extreme "literalization" of quotation, a version of Williams's "materialization." In the same way that a repeated cliché transforms meaning into a rote word or phrase ("Have a nice day!"), so this indirect declaration of love transforms meaning into inscription reduced not to words but to letters standing for words.

My second favorite example is the periphrastics of "But Not for Me."

VERSE

Old Man Sunshine – listen, you!
Never tell me Dreams Come True!
Just try it –
And I'll start a riot.

Beatrice Fairfax – don't you dare
Ever tell me he will care;
    I'm certain
  It's the Final Curtain.
  I never want to hear
  From any cheer-
  Ful Pollyannas,
Who tell you Fate
Supplies a Mate –
It's all bananas!

REFRAIN
They're writing songs of love,
  But not for me;
A lucky star's above,
  But not for me.

With Love to Lead the Way,
I've found more Clouds of Gray,
Than any Russian play
Could guarantee.[35]

This song is almost entirely made up of quotations, with the singer spelling out her situation in the words of Old Man Sunshine, and of Beatrice Fairfax, in songwriters "writing songs of love, / But not for me," in allusions to the grimnesses of Russian plays, and, in the final refrain, with the generic conventions of "ev'ry happy plot / Ends with the marriage knot – / And there's no knot for me."[36] Moreover, the song also "quotes" the argot of slang, describing the end of love as "the Final Curtain" (spelled out, like any monogram, with capital letters), the advice of cheerful Pollyannas as "all bananas," and confusion as being "all at sea." The song is from *Girl Crazy*, and the singer, Molly Gray, is a country postmistress from a small town in the American West invaded, so to speak, by sophisticated New Yorkers: a version of George's "Eastern and Western" music. Still, if these are my favorite examples of loquacious indirection, the Gershwins' favorite example, I think, was *Porgy and Bess*, clashing quotations from the Gullah dialect of black rural Carolina in the context of the harmonies of New York jazz to bring together urban and rural idioms sounded throughout the post-World War I movement of rural people to America's cities.

In their music the Gershwins follow what Walter Benjamin, another powerful contemporary, calls "the art of quoting without quotation marks."[37] The use of such quotation, as Rosenberg notes, raises "the question of voice in Ira's lyrics, and lyrics more generally." "Who is speaking in ['But Not for Me']?," Rosenberg asks.

> Surely not a postmistress in some woebegone Western town. And yet she *is* speaking, but through Ira's words, set to music. Characteristically, Ira's approach to voice – and Lorenz Hart's, and Yip Harburg's, and Howard Dietz's, and Cole Porter's – was to effectively express the emotions peculiar to a given character in their own language of theater song lyrics.[38]

What Rosenberg is describing is Bakhtin's sense of "speech genres," the available vocabularies and modes of speech we have with which to express ourselves. "The category of speech genres," Bakhtin says, "should include short rejoinders of daily dialogue . . . , everyday narration, writing (in all its various forms)."[39] Bakhtin argues that speech genres create a horizon of experience for particular generations and for literary discourse, including representations of cliché; they also, I am arguing here, create such a horizon of experience for the "literary discourse" of the lyrics and music of song. Above all, such speech genres are "dialogical": they are not simple one-way movements of communication but a process of performance like – and *in* – popular music itself, a *local* speech situation in which "the listener becomes the speaker" (68). (In the concert hall, the listener rarely becomes the speaker. The *Rite of Spring* riot is an exceptional case.)

In their local enactments, speech genres entail two kinds of performance I've already suggested inhabit popular music: both the seeming word-for-word recitation of particular texts/song, such as Billie Holiday's performance of "They Can't Take That Away from Me" I discuss in Chapter 6; and, in addition, the jazz improvisations based on the harmonies of Gershwin's song, such as the different takes on "I Got Rhythm" I mentioned in Chapter 2.[40] In "Discourse in the Novel" Bakhtin explicitly describes these two modes of performance. "When verbal disciplines are taught in school," he writes,

> two basic modes are recognized for the appropriation and transmission – simultaneously – of another's words (a text, a rule, a model): "reciting by heart" and "retelling in one's own words." The latter mode poses on a small scale the task implicit in all prose stylistics: retelling a text in one's own words is to a certain extent a double-voiced narration of another's words, for indeed "one's own words" must not completely dilute the quality that makes another's words unique; a retelling in one's own words should have a mixed character, able when necessary to reproduce the style and expressions of the transmitted text.[41]

In this passage Bakhtin is articulating not only the stylistic opposition between Eliot's citations and Joyce's retellings in *The Waste Land* and

Ulysses or Holiday and Waller performing Gershwin. He is articulating also George and Ira's own procedures, the "dialogics" of discourse in which discourse is always and only to be understood as historically and socially situated *enunciated* discourse. That is, language – and music, I would add – always materially embodies in the speaker's (composer's/performers') own words the social forms and genres of discourse, and, moreover, such a sense of language, as Bakhtin says here, always has a double-voiced, mixed character.[42] That both "reciting by heart" and "retelling in one's own words" are "double-voiced" also suggests why both singing Tin Pan Alley standards and improvising on them are versions of "jazz."

In *Marxism and the Philosophy of Language*, Bakhtin (writing with or under the name of V. N. Voloshinov) offers a formal description of this mixed character of speech in "free indirect discourse," the ability of an author to quote without quotations marks. "Free indirect discourse" – Bakhtin calls it "quasi-direct discourse"[43] – is distinguished from "direct discourse" (e.g., "I've found more clouds of gray than any Russian play could guarantee," Mary said) and from "indirect discourse" (e.g., Mary said she found more clouds of gray than a Russian play could guarantee). In free indirect discourse it is not altogether clear whether something is being quoted and is attributable to a particular person or character or not. When Joyce begins his story "The Dead" with the sentence: "Lily, the caretaker's daughter, was literally swept off her feet," it is not clear whether the sentence is Lily's indirect discourse (rendering, indirectly, "I was literally swept off my feet," said Lily) or the narrator's description of what happened. The problem here is that the word "literally" is a figurative and colloquial expression more likely to be Lily's than some omniscient narrator's while, at the same time, Lily wouldn't describe herself as "the caretaker's daughter" while she was telling a story.[44] Of course, the phenomenon of a transcendental "omniscient narrator," like the absolute "transcendental" music of the "classical" tradition, is precisely what Joyce, Gershwin, and Williams replace by their *performative* discourses enacted in relation to what Williams calls "the local conditions."[45] As both Joyce and Ira Gershwin might suggest, the use of clichés, like the "speech genres" Bakhtin describes, always suggests "free indirect discourse" insofar as clichés and speech genres are expressions that do not fully belong to – or fully express – the speaker.

As Hugh Kenner has suggested, the great master of free indirect discourse in our language is James Joyce, the Gershwins' contemporary.[46] But the great master of the free, "indirect" discourse in the musical theater is George Gershwin himself. This is especially clear in his repeated uses of the pentatonic scale against the traditional major and minor scales of

Enlightenment modernity. "In my songs and in my pieces for symphony orchestra," George told Isaac Goldberg, "I've made plentiful use of the five-note scale."[47] This scale allows the combinations – the clashing and blending – of major and minor modes and the combination of African American blues and Jewish liturgical music, the Western and Eastern musics George mentioned in 1929. In bringing together, in the pentatonic music of his songs, these cultures excluded from the "Age of Europe" I mentioned in Chapter 1 – the Jewish and African diasporas – Gershwin is pursuing the kind of "dialogism" that Bakhtin described in the 1920s and 1930s. "*Any true understanding,*" Bakhtin wrote in 1929, "*is dialogic in nature.* Understanding is to utterance as one line of a dialogue is to the next."[48] "Any utterance," he says earlier in *Marxism and the Philosophy of Language*, "– the finished, written utterance not excepted . . . carries on the work of its predecessors, polemicizing with them, expecting active, responsive understanding, and anticipating such understanding in return" (172).

The two modes of repetition I am describing, performance and improvisation, are brought together in the quotation without quotation marks of free indirect discourse which blurs the distinction between quotation and narration. In the 1920s such dialogism can be seen in T. S. Eliot's *The Waste Land*, with its unmarked citation of other poets, in James Joyce's *Ulysses*, with its retellings of the stories of Ulysses, Hamlet, Don Giovanni in dialects of early-twentieth-century Dublin, and even in Williams's short stories, which constantly eschew quotation marks.[49] For Bakhtin, the free indirect discourse of "quasi-direct speech" is meaningful discourse that always materially embodies in the speaker's own words (even when those words are quoted) the social *historical* forms and genres of discourse. Such a sense of language, as he says, always has a double-voiced, mixed character that allows the other's words to resonate in discourse. The Gershwin songs – both music and lyrics – pursue *this* art of quotation which, like the addition of a letter to a monogram, accumulates meaning by accumulating the signs of a discourse. This art exhibits the elements of the aesthetics of popular music I described in the Introduction: the "wholeness" (of completed statements – even clichés, which are essentially *whole* phrases), the "rhythmic decomposition" of rhyming parts, and the resulting "montage" of double-voiced discourse.

QUOTATION WITHOUT QUOTATION MARKS

The complications of the kind of quotation which Benjamin describes in his phrase "quotation without quotation marks" are most clear, I think, in

Figure 7 "They Can't Take That Away From Me," music and lyrics by George Gershwin and Ira Gershwin

the last musical example I want to offer in this chapter, the Gershwins' late song "They Can't Take That Away from Me" (1937) written ten years after "'S Wonderful" (Figure 7).

> VERSE
> Our romance won't end on a sorrowful note,
> Though by tomorrow you're gone.
> The song is ended, but as the songwriter wrote,
> The melody lingers on.
> They may take you from me,

Figure 7 (*cont.*)

I'll miss your fond caress.
But though they take you from me,
I'll still possess:

REFRAIN

The way you wear your hat,
The way you sip your tea,
The mem'ry of all that –
No, no! They can't take that away from me!

The way your smile just beams,
The way you sing off key,
The way you haunt my dreams,

Figure 7 (*cont.*)

No, no! They can't take that away from me!

We may never, never meet again
On the bumpy road to love,
Still I'll always, always keep
The mem'ry of –

The way you hold your knife,
The way we danced till three,
The way you've changed my life –
No, no! They can't take that away from me!
No! They can't take that away from me

Figure 7 (*cont.*)

This song is *about* quotation; it offers another form of what I am calling the literalization of quotation where the singer quotes gestures of the beloved as "things" – small citations – that, like the substantified "love" in "Love Is Here to Stay," cannot be lost even in a world of impermanence: the way the beloved wears a hat, sips tea, smiles, sings, eats are all cited in the course of the song. (More generally, it epitomizes popular music in its future life of being repeatedly sung, and in Chapter 6 I discuss Billie Holiday's performance of this song as one such instance of the repetitions of popular music.) Within its internal citations of the beloved's gestures,

Figure 7 (*cont.*)

moreover, the singer offers indirect declarations about the way his or her dreams are haunted, their dancing together, "the way you changed my life." The rhyming of "knife" and "life" also rhymes the discourses of citation and declaration – it clashes and blends the subjects of discourse – in one of Ira's most powerful circuitous indirections. In an important way, the song builds to this declaration which, like the all-night dancing, ties lover and beloved together in language, fact, and memory.

The relationship between repetition and quotation is, of course, very close, and the lyrics as well as the music quote themselves throughout. This is most striking in the title, which is repeated four times in the seventeen lines of the refrain; it is also clear in the repeated "The way you . . . " repeatedly sung on the tonic. But such repetition can also be seen in the "never, never" and "always, always" of the bridge and in the repeated "No, no!" of the refrain, with the whole song ending with the (almost) word-for-word repetition of the refrain's last line in an extra, seventeenth, line. (Alec Wilder uncharacteristically calls "the arresting nature of the *b* flat over 'No!' in the thirty-second measure . . . a masterpiece, as are the quarter and half notes of the ending, achieving a calm, pastoral resolution in the face of the lyric's refusal to be separated from all those loving qualities.")[50]

Here repetition becomes quotation. Both this extra line and the song's "No, no!" – like the repeated interjection "Oh" in "'S Wonderful" – underline the curiosity of quotation, the way it both repeats and changes what it articulates. In this song, the first two "No, no!"s are sung on the sixth (with "they" also sung on the sixth: "No, no! They") only rising to the tonic on "can't"; in the last instance of the repeated "no," it is sung on the tonic itself, descending, as in all the cases, to the tonic an octave lower. "They Can't Take That Away from Me" is remarkable in Gershwin's music in its insistence on the tonic: no other refrain begins, as this one does, with the insistent repetition of the tonic note, in this case five times. In draft it was three times, but Ira suggested the further repetition and also the syncopation.[51] But even in the verse, the sustained note sung on a "sorrowful note" is the first instance of the tonic E♭ in a song that rings the tonic more than fifty times. Singing "sorrowful note" – which, for the Gershwins, is the minor third or the blue note – on the tonic is another instance of what I might call an inverse quotation, like the reversed falling and rising thirds of "'S Wonderful" and "Funny Face," which quotes a structure or relationship rather than a word or sound. The "songwriter" mentioned in the Verse is Irving Berlin.

What this song suggests about the relationship between repetition and quotation – and, perhaps, about the relationship between the sense and sounds of song and the blendings and clashings of cultural discourses – is striking. Quotation is repetition – just as the rhymes of this and other songs are both repetition and quotation. Thus the bridge of "They Can't Take That Away from Me" has the only non-rhyming lines of the song: "We may never, never **meet** again / . . . Still, I'll always, always **keep**"; yet these lines "rhyme" in the syntax ("never, never meet"/"always, always keep") and rhyme also in the soundings of "meet" and "keep," a syncopated half-rhyme that allows the words "The mem'ry of" of the third line of the refrain to be remembered through their repetition and transformation in the bridge.

In *The Logic of Sense* Gilles Deleuze discusses the workings of what he calls "fundamental repetition." "Psychoanalysis, it is true," he writes, "taught us that we are ill from repetition, but it also taught us that we are healed through repetition."[52] "One theme runs through the entire work of [the artist and philosopher, Pierre] Klossowski," he goes on to say, namely:

> the opposition between exchange and true repetition. For exchange implies only resemblance, even if the resemblance is extreme. Exactness is its criterion, along with the equivalence of exchanged products. This is the false repetition which causes our illness. True repetition, on the other hand, appears as a singular

> behavior that we display in relation to that which cannot be exchanged, replaced, or substituted – like a poem that is repeated on the condition that no word may be changed . . . True repetition addresses something singular, unchangeable, and different, without "identity." Instead of exchanging the similar and identifying the Same, *it authenticates the different.* (288–89)

The banal music of Tin Pan Alley exchanges the similar and identifies the Same. The Gershwins achieve the high possibility of modernist popular music by authenticating the different by means of the creation of the feeling of wholeness through rhythmic decomposition and montage – in "They Can't Take that Away," the montage of attributes of the beloved that conveys, indirectly, commitment and love. The difference between false and true repetition, Deleuze suggests, is the difference between the too-quick assimilation of phenomena to pre-existing conditions – to make the local case *simply* an example of the general case, as I mentioned in Chapter 1 – and the ability to achieve repetition without assimilation, to authenticate the varied worldly discourses and dialogues that Bakhtin and Joyce, as well as George and Ira Gershwin, describe as clashing and blending in the world after World War I. Such repetition is the work of the Gershwins' music, whether it be the love songs I have discussed, their slang, or even the ringing of Jewish immigrant music and indigenous African American music together in George's pentatonic scales.

Moreover, as Deleuze suggests in his reference to poetry, this "fundamental" repetition is achieved by means of the power and authentication of quotation. This is why Deleuze goes on to argue that "in language – at the heart of language – the mind grasps the body, and the gestures of the body, as the object of a fundamental repetition. Difference gives things to be seen and multiplies bodies; but it is repetition which offers things to be spoken, authenticates the multiple, and makes of it a spiritual event" (289). "They Can't Take That Away from Me" grasps in its montage "the gestures of the body" as things to be spoken, to be quoted: the way you wear your hat and sip tea and hold your knife, the way you smile, the way, finally, those quoted gestures are so woven into my life that my life repeats them endlessly, the same, different, *authenticating* difference. This, perhaps, is even one definition of love: the authentication of difference. Rosenberg describes the America the Gershwins confronted and articulated in the 1920s as "the new, urbanized nation – brash, insouciant, anxious, insecure – at the precise moment that the question of the nation's character – rural or urban, Protestant or polyglot – was the central issue in American life, politics, culture."[53] Such a world,

I am suggesting, called for the reinvention of love in terms of dialogue, quotation, and their singular, fundamental repetition in new American song.

"What's going on here?" you might say. "We just want to hear about Gershwin." But to hear about Gershwin is to listen to him, to listen to Billie Holiday as we will do in Chapter 6, singing his song – quoting him – in a way that underlines what Deleuze only barely suggests: that when we don't change the words of a poem we still can – in fact, we cannot help but – change its rhythms, the montage of its tones, the wholenesses of its harmonies. This, after all, is at the heart of what is "popular" in popular music: the ways that such music *belongs* to performers as well as composers – performers "quoting" its songs – and to those who listen and now and then, doing something else in their everyday lives, hum them back. Such quotation authenticates difference just as the Gershwins' music authenticates New York in the blendings and clashings in the heady years after World War I. It is the appearance of singular behaviors of love in which – as in the collaborations of George and Ira Gershwin – the complexities of dialogue, of words and music, of melody and harmony, can achieve, as George said, an American meeting place.

CHAPTER 4

"What is this thing called love?": Cole Porter and the rhythms of desire

In the preceding chapter I examined the relationship between music and the social languages of the post-World War I American metropolis in the popular songs of George and Ira Gershwin. The very focus on the collaboration of these brothers underlines, I hope, the sense of the *public* and popular nature of the American musical theater. In this chapter, I examine the *private* nature of that music in describing the relationship between music and desire in Cole Porter. Such privacies, I will suggest, are no less "popular" than public music: indeed, they help delineate the felt sense of self and subjectivity which a population (and a generation) share; they create what Raymond Williams called "the felt sense of the quality of life at a particular place and time: a sense of the ways in which the particular activities [of life] combined into a way of thinking and feeling,"[1] what he repeatedly describes as a "structure of feeling." Cultural modernism itself can be understood in terms of such a structure of feeling as well as historical occurrences and social formations. Desire itself, I am arguing, is such a "structure of feeling," and therefore it is strangely impersonal, emerging in performance, oddly "popular."[2] Whether its formation – its "structure" – is historically specific as Williams suggests is difficult to determine precisely because we are inhabited by it, constantly performing it, which makes our desire – and our pleasure – seem simply "natural" and simply part of being human. In any case, a version of desire that is associated with the music of Porter, which I examine in this chapter, can help us understand the formation of desire and the shape of pleasure in cultural modernism. The relationship between music and desire has often been asserted, yet the intricacies of this relationship are subtle and complicated. In this chapter, I examine the musical line, structure, and lyrics in Porter just as I examined the melody, structure, and lyrics of the Gershwins' songs in the preceding chapter. Here, however, I am attempting to tease out wellsprings of desire in the rhythms and semiotics of language and sound, an attempt to sketch or point to the relation of *things* – objects, somatic functions, the speaking body – to discourse rather than to the "dialogics" of the speech genres, clichés, and repetitions of social life I examined in Chapter 3.

MATTER AND MEANING IN MUSICAL RHYTHMS

Many years ago, the anthropologist and philosopher Claude Lévi-Strauss argued that the power of music resides in the manner in which music brings together or juxtaposes – what I describe in this chapter as the manner in which music "syncopates" (using the term both figuratively and literally) – the physiological or "natural" rhythms of our bodies and the semiotic or "cultural" rhythms of our understanding.[3] Lévi-Strauss's extended description of the emotional – which is to say the seemingly *private* – power of music is relevant to my discussion of syncopation as well as to the use of the rhetorical figure of "metonymy" as a figure for desire. "The musical emotion," Lévi-Strauss argues,

> springs precisely from the fact that at each moment the composer withholds or adds more or less than the listener anticipates on the basis of a pattern that he thinks he can guess, but that he is incapable of wholly divining because of his subjection to a dual periodicity: that of his respiratory system, which is determined by his individual nature, and that of the scale, which is determined by his training. If the composer withholds more than we anticipate, we experience a delicious falling sensation; we feel we have been torn from a stable point on the musical ladder and thrust into the void, but only because the support that is waiting for us was not in the expected place. When the composer withholds less, the opposite occurs: he forces us to perform gymnastic exercises more skillful than our own. Sometimes he moves us, sometimes he forces us to make the movement ourselves, but it always exceeds what we would have thought ourselves capable of achieving alone.[4] (17)

In this passage, Lévi-Strauss is describing the power of music precisely in terms of syncopations, the "clashing and blending" Gershwin describes in the social world of New York now understood in relation to the structure and perception of music. Such syncopations are not altogether arbitrary: rather, they are the juncture of sensation and semiotics.

Syncopation itself is related to what musicology describes as "polyrhythm," which Robert Jourdain defines as "the use of different meters among simultaneous musical lines."[5] Syncopation, Jourdain notes, is "a mere hint of a second [rhythm,]"

> in which beats are accentuated apart from the regular metrical pattern. Accentuations away from beats are found in all music. We tend to call music "syncopated" when the offbeats are so regular that the listener begins to anticipate them. In essence, the syncopated beats form a second rhythmic line countering the first,

a ghost of true polyrhythm. In Western music syncopation is nowhere so pronounced as in the broken rhythms of ragtime – "time in tatters." (129)

Thus syncopation enacts the "dual periodicity" that Lévi-Strauss describes, yet it does so in entirely musical terms that absorb, so to speak, the opposition between nature and culture Lévi-Strauss presents into the formal description of art (an opposition that reiterates the one between the natural and the artificial I mentioned in the Introduction in relation to semantic formalism).

It is a question whether or not such *absorption* is a working description of art in general or just the particular arts of the twentieth century. Stephen Greenblatt, speaking of Shakespeare, imagines that such absorption characterizes art in general in arguing that in "contrast [with ordinary texts,] most of which are virtually incomprehensible when they are removed from their immediate surroundings," "works of art . . . contain directly or by implication much of [their cultural] situation within themselves, and it is this sustained absorption that enables many literary works to survive the collapse of the conditions that led to their production."[6] In any case, in his juxtaposition of culture and nature Lévi-Strauss is describing what I call in this chapter the relationship between discourse and things, the relationship between meaning and matter, the "cultural" semiotics and the "natural" physiology, that music presents. This relationship, as I mentioned in Chapter 1, constantly fascinated Enlightenment modernity, particularly in its focus on transcendental form (hence my term "semantic formalism"). Lévi-Strauss argues for the special status of music in creating such a relationship by comparing music to painting. "Painting," he writes,

through the instrumentality of culture, gives intellectual organization to a form of nature which it was already aware of as a sense pattern. Music follows exactly the opposite course: culture is already present in it, but in the form of sense experience, even before it organizes it intellectually by means of nature. It is because the field of operation of music is cultural that music comes into being, free from those representational links that keep painting in a state of subjection to the world of sense experience and its organization in the form of objects.[7]

Within this passage, Lévi-Strauss is describing music as a phenomenon in which culture already informs "sense experience" so that the opposition between nature and culture *feels* confused, and cultural phenomena – meaning, intellectual organizations, feelings themselves – are apprehended as *things*. For this reason, as I hope to show, in this passage from Lévi-Strauss the term "desire" or "pleasure" could fruitfully be substituted for music. *Culture is already present in desire – and in pleasure – in the form of sense experience; and because the field of operation of desire (pleasure) is cultural, it is not organized in the form of objects (of desire or pleasure), even as it is represented and apprehended that way.*

This formulation, I think, supports Colin Campbell's contention that "pleasure . . . is not an intrinsic property of any object but is a type of reaction which humans commonly have when encountering certain stimuli";[8] pleasure, he continues, "is inseparable from our paying attention to it" (62). It is because of the objectlessness of desire, I believe, that Jacques Lacan situates desire between the physiological "need" that can be satisfied by objects and things in the world and the semiotics of "demand" that articulates contrary-to-fact assertion. Desire and pleasure both create the feeling that particular objects and things, on the verge of being "organized . . . by means of nature," will satisfy them. The syncopated opposition between phenomenological "organization" and semiotic "representation" is clear in the lyrics, music, and structures of Porter's songs. But it is also clear, as I suggested in the Introduction, in the achieved aesthetics of popular music more generally. The syncopations of the natural and the artificial manifest themselves alternatively in rhythmic decompositions, montage, and the dialectics of felt wholeness.

The great modernist poet – and Cole Porter's almost exact contemporary – T. S. Eliot noted that his poems began as complicated rhythms which only later shape themselves into sense. Another of Porter's contemporaries, the psychoanalyst Jacques Lacan, similarly argued throughout his career that desire is "metonymic" in its elements. "Metonymy" in rhetoric is the substitution of an associated element – usually a worldly element or "thing" – for that element itself: to say "the White House announced last night" is to substitute the building the announcer is in for the person who makes the announcement. What metonymy does is *displace* its referent: in the case of the White House announcement, it displaces the speaker – the subject of the message – with the physical location, a "thing." More generally, linguistics distinguishes between the meaning and the vehicle of meaning, the "signified" of a message (what it means) and its "signifier" (the sentence or word or sound that signifies the message's meaning). Lacan suggests that desire can somehow be located in the constant displacement of signifiers sliding across our experience and understanding that *suggest* without precisely delineating meaning (the signified). Such displacement provokes the more or less objectless affect of desire even while it anchors desire to things that feel like its object. In other words, desire *works itself out* in the interplay – the juxpositions or syncopations – of sense and meaning, of the two meanings of "sense" as sensation and significance I mentioned earlier. Thus, in these three areas – of delineated meaning, of elemental (bodily) impulses, and of structures of interplay – we can discern the contours of desire that play across the sounds and meanings of Porter's modernist music. That Lacan's master, Sigmund Freud, articulated his science of desire during the second Industrial Revolution of the early twentieth century is, as I hope I suggested in Chapter 2, no accident.

The fact that Porter's music, lyrics, and melodies – like the music, lyrics, and melodies of the Gershwins – compose a version of the "modernist" American culture of the early twentieth century is of the utmost importance for my argument. In his work, the project of the lyric of high modernism – international cosmopolitan modernism, as found in the poetry of Williams or Eliot, Stevens or H.D. – that attempts to isolate and provoke what I like to call "free-floating" affect, free-floating desire, is most clearly discernable. It is so because the rhythms of Porter's lyrics are apprehensible on levels of both sensation and meaning – levels of phenomenological organization and semiotic representation – in ways that are more difficult to distinguish in more purely verbal forms of lyric poetry. Moreover, Porter's music allows us to see more clearly than otherwise the appropriateness of Lacan as a major interpreter of modernist desire and modernist poetry. The Lacanian account of the work of desire chimes so remarkably well with the lyric energy in Porter's work – especially in relation to what both describe as desire apprehended as a "thing" – that in focusing on his songs we can discern the larger outlines of the *private* lyric project of high modernism just as the Gershwins reveal its *public* project. And also Porter – unlike Yeats, Eliot, and Rilke (but not necessarily Stevens and Williams in America) – brings to the lyrics of desire an enormous degree of fun. As I noted in the Introduction, Simon Frith argues that popular music suggests "the ideal of cultural experience is *fun*; pop provides routinized pleasures, more intense than the everyday but bound into its rhythms, and legitimized emotional gratification, a play of desire and discipline."[9] The very popularity of popular music makes its pleasures more pronounced – or at least closer to the surface – than those of the high modernist arts.

THE METONYMICS OF DESIRE

In "I Love Paris" (1953), Porter describes his love for Paris "ev'ry moment of the year" – "in the springtime," "in the fall," "in the winter when it drizzles / . . . in the summer when it sizzles" – all "Because my love is near."[10] In this song, as in many others, Porter's verses, his rhymes, and, indeed, his music – that is, the elements of language, sound, and musical structure – describe metonymic patterns of displacement: he displaces his beloved with Paris – a place like, but very different from, the White House – and loves *that*. In "I Love Paris," the feminine rhyme of "drizzles" and "sizzles" – a kind of rhyming Porter repeats throughout his lyrics in a manner different from Ira Gershwin's use of feminine rhyme – emphasizes the metonymics of rhyme altogether, the displacement of rhyme to the first syllable and the quiet assertion of rhyming a word with itself to the unaccented syllable. As I noted in Chapter 3, *rime riche* describes rhyming in medieval and early modern poetry that rhymed homonyms such as "not" and "knot" or "well" (adjective) and "well" (noun). In modern poets such as Eliot and Yeats – and in Porter's feminine (and sometimes direct) rhymes – such rhyming forgoes the semantics of rhyming differences of meaning (signifieds) in favor of rhyming signs as a whole: rather than emphasizing the similarities and differences of meanings (the heat and humidity of "sizzles" and "drizzles") – emphasizing, that is, the clashing and blending of meanings – Porter's feminine rhymes aim to create a single sensation-meaning. Such a single effect is the rhyming of sense experiences (the sounds of words) that have already been shaped, as Lévi-Strauss might say, by cultural forms. In other words, his feminine rhymes seem more like the rhyming of a word with itself – a modernist version of *rime riche* – just as, we shall see, W. B. Yeats rhymes the word "face" with "face."

Such rhyming, not quite the traditional *rime riche* – especially in the case of Yeats's end rhymes rather than Eliot's internal repetitions of sounds – participates in the symbolist attempt in the late nineteenth century to create a metaphysics of meaning, the rhyming of "natural" and "supernatural" signification I describe later in relation to Yeats, that is akin to, yet slightly different from, the "rich" rhymings, in medieval and Renaissance poetry, of different meanings despite the similarities of sound. (In the modernists, including Porter, the emphasis is on the rhyming of sound. Again, this will become clearer in the discussion of Porter and Yeats later in this chapter.) This also allows us to understand the full import of Walter Pater's late-Victorian assertion – which greatly influenced Yeats, Eliot, and other modernist poets in Britain and America – that "poetry aspires to the condition of music." Porter differs from the Gershwins in his use of feminine rhyme to emphasize the repetition of sound rather than the clashing and blending of meaning.

In any case, the large and small metonymic displacements – beloved/Paris; the juxtaposition of "sizzle" and "drizzle" that displaces differences of summer and winter with a single place – describe the international nature of Porter's work. This is clear from Richard Rogers's remark that early in his career Porter thought that the road to success in a profession dominated by Jewish composers such as Jerome Kern, Irving Berlin, and the Gershwin brothers was to "write Jewish tunes." Rogers thought that one needed only to hum Cole Porter melodies – his examples were "Night and Day," "Begin the Beguine," "Love for Sale," and "I Love Paris" – and one would hear "minor-key melodies [that] are unmistakably eastern Mediterranean."[11] Throughout his life, Porter himself repeatedly claimed exotic origins for his songs based upon his life-long world travels: "Night and Day," he claimed, originated in Morocco, "Begin the Beguine" in Kalabahai, "You're the Top" in a flatboat as he floated down the Rhine, "What Is This Thing Called Love?" in Marrakesh – though Porter's biographer, I should add, suggests that Porter is not quite honest in these accounts (143).

But more than his sophisticated internationalism, the metonymic displacements emphasize the rhythms of desire that inhabit his songs and music. In "Ev'ry Time We Say Goodbye" (1944) Porter makes the syncopated relationship between minor and major key in his lyrics an explicit theme in the song: "how strange," he writes, "The change / From major to minor." In this song – as in much of his work – Porter creates a complicated relationship between sense and meaning by displacing harmonies among words, sounds, and music (Figure 8). "Ev'ry Time We Say Goodbye,"[12] for instance, is globally governed by the alternation of major and minor – the opening melody alternates relative major and minor, E♭, Cm, E♭, Cm, E♭, Fm7, B♭7 – where the minor chords are consistently marked by syncopated rhythms, culminating in the last verses, "There's no love-song finer / But how strange / The change / From major to minor" (206), which transforms an A♭ to A♭m.[13] Such syncopations of sense and meaning – I examine them most closely in Porter's 1934 song "I Get a Kick Out of You" – allow us to apprehend repetition as new beginnings. In such syncopations we can see most closely the functioning of what Shoshana Felman calls the "scandal" of the speaking body,[14] the power of language and semiotics in the service of desire.

The rhythms of desire have commanded a great deal of attention in recent years, in large part because of the rereading of Freud in relation to the psychoanalytic work of Lacan that I have already alluded to. Lacan argues that Freud teaches us that desire is governed by metonymic relationships of meaning. In rhetoric "metonym" as a figure of speech is often associated with the figure of "synecdoche." In 1956, Roman Jakobson published a very influential essay that argued that the rhetorical figures of both "metonymy" and "synecdoche" should be opposed to "metaphor." Synecdoche is a figure that substitutes a part for the whole or the whole for the part. The phrase

Figure 8 "Ev'ry Time We Say Goodbye," music and lyrics by Cole Porter

"all hands on deck" is synecdochical in this sense: it offers the part of the sailors, their "hands," as a figurative substitution for the whole of each person. Similarly, when in "All of You" (1955), Porter describes his love in terms of "The eyes, the arms, the mouth of you, / The east, west, north, and the south of you,"[15] he is using the parts to stand for the whole of his beloved. Metonymy, as I have already mentioned, is a related rhetorical figure that substitutes contiguities (as opposed to parts) for a term: to describe the king as the "crown," the President as "the White House" each is metonymic, as is loving Paris because your "love is near." In this distinction, synecdoche is hierarchical in that one part – the "hand," the "heart" – is taken to be most important, the articulation of the very *essence* of a phenomenon that was the goal of Enlightenment modernity. Synecdoche is able to subsume the parts to the whole and (more rarely) vice versa. Such hierarchy is significantly different from the dialectical conception of the aesthetic wholeness that Adorno describes, where parts and wholes are reciprocally constitutive, as I noted in the

Introduction. Metonymy, on the other hand, is non-hierarchic (that is, it is "paratactic") in that more or less accidental attributes are chosen, more or less arbitrarily, to stand for the whole. It is a figure that might be associated with the "shattering of belief" which Jean-François Lyotard describes, a kind of *decomposition* that Adorno also mentions. Moreover, it, above all, describes the modernist *montage* Adorno observes, juxtapositions of seemingly non-essentially related elements.[16]

In Porter, the compass points in "All of You" – "The east, west, north, and the south of you" – erase or confuse the distinction between synecdoche and metonymy by suggesting parts can also be conceived as spatial contiguities. This example describes the confusion of semiotics and things, culture and nature, the artificial and the natural. It confuses the paratactic and accidental relationships of metonymy (which, because they are paratactic, are therefore artificial rather than natural) with the hierarchic *essential* relationships of synecdoche (which "naturally" conform to the "law" of the existence of a particular phenomenon). Moreover, it suggests the ways that syncopation – a defining example of rhythmic decomposition – is allied with metonymy rather than synecdoche insofar as it juxtaposes rhythms that are not part of one another. The same metonymic relationship can be seen in the manner in which language confuses itself and stutters in its juxtaposition of abstract meanings and seeming reference. Charles Sanders Peirce – another "modernist" figure – notes this aspect of language and semiotics when he distinguishes from one another the "symbolic" function of language and its "indexical" or referential function.[17]

In any case, in his famous essay "Two Aspects of Language and Two Types of Aphasic Disturbances," Jakobson describes two kinds of aphasia – a medical condition, usually attributed to brain damage, resulting in the dysfunction or loss of language – as falling into the general inability or problem of being able to substitute one word for another (a "similarity" disorder affecting the ability to name synonyms) and the general inability or problem of creating syntactically correct sentences (a "contiguity" disorder affecting the combination of parts of a sentence). These disorders, he says, embody the opposition between metaphor and metonymy. Together, metaphor and metonymy enact two aspects of language, selection and combination, which Jakobson aligns with the "paradigmatic" and "syntagmatic" axes of language and with the two "generalizable" aphasic conditions suffered by people with brain damage I have mentioned: the inability to recognize substitutable words ("similarity disorder") and the inability to recognize associative phrases such as "knife and fork" ("contiguity disorder").[18] "Metonymy," in his discussion, emphasizes spatial extension, and he opposes it to the rhetorical figure "metaphor," which offers global or instantaneous linguistic substitution from which both space and time are excluded. A more striking way to describe this is to note that metonymies entail the accidents of physical attributes in ways that metaphors do not: the metonymies of language are the locus of *things* in discourse; "culture" is already present in metonymy but, as Lévi-Strauss says, "in the form of sense experience."[19]

"Metaphor," in fact, is what linguists call an "unmarked" term: it both refers to the opposite of metonymy, a figure of speech based upon global substitution rather than a (metonymic) figure based upon the substitution of a contingent attribute such as color or clothing for the object of figuration, *and* it also refers to the general category of substitution altogether, which includes metonymic substitution. "Metaphor," then, like unmarked terms more generally, allows easy translation from the particular case to the general case; it allows for the translation of physical phenomena – the "things" of the world – into meaning.[20] One simple example of metaphor (as opposed to metonymy) is to call one's love a "rose," or, as in Porter's song "I'm a Gigolo" (1929), to describe oneself as "a flower that blooms in the winter," "a baby," "a pet," "a gigolo."[21] In these examples, we can see that metaphor is unmarked by specificities of information. Thus, the ways in which the singer is "a flower that blooms in the winter" are not specified, while metonymy specifically notes the significance of figuration: Paris, for instance, is marked by the physical presence of the beloved that renders its weather of little consequence.

As well as describing these categories in relation to linguistic structure and abnormal language performance, Jakobson also aligns the opposition of metaphor and metonymy with the "condensation" and "displacements" of meanings Freud describes in dream work.[22] Following Jakobson in rereading Freudian psychoanalysis, Lacan emphasizes the temporal as well as the spatial extensions of metonymic figures and argues that desire is metonymic insofar as it repeatedly pursues what it cannot achieve. "Metonymy," Lacan writes, "is . . . the effect made possible by the fact that there is no signification that does not refer to another signification, and in which their common denominator is produced, namely the little meaning (frequently confused with the insignificant), the little meaning, I say, that proves to lie at the basis of the desire."[23] In this passage, Lacan is arguing that metonymy is circular, like pursuing dictionary definitions which, leading from one definition to another, finally returns us to the words we began with, and the endless, circular pursuit of meaning is not simply an insignificant on and on and on, but *enacts* "the little meaning" lying "at the basis of desire." For Lacan, desire is metonymic precisely in the multitudinousness of its articulations rather than the absoluteness of its meaning. (In this, desire is like pleasure in Campbell's discussion that I examined in the Introduction in relation to the aesthetics of popular music.) Desire inhabits the accidental world of time and space, the arbitrariness of signifiers referring to other signifiers with no seeming resting place. And it does so because, like popular music and like pleasure, it must be *performed* to exist at all.

In other words, metonymy inhabits the ambiguous borderline between sense and meaning, things and discourse. Thus Lacan describes what has been called the "Freudian slip" – the slip of the tongue, but also the "breaks" in the hesitations and stutterings of language, and especially emotionally charged language – as

> Impediment, failure, split. In a spoken or a written sentence something stumbles. Freud is attracted by these phenomena, and it is there that he seeks the unconscious. There something other demands to be realized – which appears as intentional, of course, but of a strange temporality.[24]

Such stumbling is like the triple forte screech of the saxophone that Keil mentions,[25] a seeming impediment and failure that strangely seems meaningful. More generally, I am arguing, it is a manifestation of syncopation, and as such it is local and temporally metonymic, the rhythms of desire that give rise to "the little meaning," which is a "meaning" the signifier of which is the relentless pursuit of signifiers across things. The saxophonist's screech is both meaningfully metonymic – the "climax" of his solo – and simply accidental. In this, metonymy never fully or self-evidently "signifies" – it never results in, even momentarily, an anchored meaning – even while it does provoke responses to its fruitless pursuit: free-floating anxiety, a haunting sense of something missing, restless desire, and, as with the saxophone, an accident that in also seeming essential provokes pleasure. Such metonymic gestures all constantly seem to verge on meaning. Lacan attempts to describe this ambiguous operation in an important essay, aptly entitled "The Freudian Thing."[26]

MUSICAL METONYMIES

An extreme example of the restlessness of metonymy is Porter's song, "It's De-Lovely" (1936), which can help us to understand the spatial and, indeed, the temporal nature of metonymy. In that song the repeated line, "It's delightful, it's delicious, it's de-lovely,"[27] defines the song's title's neologism simply by the contiguity of the syllable /de/ of the adjectives.[28] At the end of the first refrain this line is "exploded" into a longer list of adjectives beginning with /de/: "it's delightful, it's delicious, / It's delectable, it's delirious, / It's dilemma, it's delimit, it's deluxe, it's de-lovely." In the second refrain this "explosion" is no longer of real adjectives beginning with /de/ but rather with parallels to the word "divine" – that is, with the sounds /de/ + /v/. Porter writes: "It's divine, dear, it's diveen, dear, / It's de-wunderbar, it's de victory, / It's de vallop, it's de vinner, it's de voiks, it's de-lovely." Porter, here and elsewhere, is shifting the focus from the signifieds of language to the signifiers, in this case to the morphemic/phonemic sounds rather than to the meaning. The displacement from major to minor, as the lyrics in "Ev'ry Time We Say Goodbye" note, enacts a similar change in focus, by directing attention from the meaning of the words to the qualities of the sounds. And when, at the end of the verses of "What Is This Thing Called Love?" (1929), the implicit mode of C minor is displaced by C major, Porter is making the formal signifiers of music do the work of the semantics of his lyrics in that the simple change of musical modality becomes a vehicle of meaning.

Such work is the work of desire, a wanting that can never be satisfied, a constitutive inability to articulate desire that, for Lacan, enacts the "primal repression" in Freud's sense of the word. Lacan presents a topology – a systematic mapping – of biological "need," linguistic "demand," and "desire" playing between them. "Desire," he writes, "is neither the appetite for satisfaction ["need"], nor the demand for love, but the difference that results from the subtraction of the first from the second, the phenomenon of their splitting."[29] In this split, he asserts, "the power of pure loss emerges" (287). Moreover, the difference between need and demand – he describes this as "that which is . . . alienated in needs" – "constitutes," he writes, a "primal repression," "an inability . . . to be articulated in demand, but it re-appears in something it gives rise to that presents itself in man as desire" (286). This translation of Lacan, Jane Gallop has argued, uses the term "re-appears," "a sense of a return, of desire as a return of the proto-repressed. But in the original text," she goes on, "it is not a return; the only appearance of the primary repressed (which cannot appear as such) is its appearance as desire. Born of an alienation, primal repression cannot appear any place, cannot have its own place, cannot have a home."[30] In this analysis the "something" of desire is a curious kind of "thing" – it is "strange," a "funny thing," a "kick," "mysterious," a "thrill," "just one of those things," to use phrases that recur in Porter's lyrics – that above all is homeless, uncanny, neither here nor there.

Lacan argues that desire is metonymic because, in its "splitting" it is marked by temporal displacement as well as the spatial homelessness that Porter pursued in his endless international travels. I'm calling this a temporal as well as a spatial displacement because such metonymic discourses are above all temporal, creating what Jacques Derrida calls, in a musical figure, "intervallic" time different from the regularities of comprehensible historic time in its "type, rhythm, mode of inscription."[31] The discourse of music, as opposed to semantics, emphasizes this temporality in its *tempos* of music and language, its syncopations of sound and sense. The lyric poetry of high modernism does this as well, confronting the somatic, bodily nature of the signifier (the time and place of utterance and, above all, the "occasion" or "need" for utterance) with the semantics of significance (the transcendental "demand") in order to provoke desire. In *The Birth of Tragedy from the Spirit of Music*, Nietzsche emphasizes the relationship between lyric temporalities and the "spirit" of tragedy in what he calls "the wing-beat of longing that accompanies the highest delight."[32] In this way, the strange "something" of desire Porter describes is also temporal activity, the process of performance, the wing-beat of longing: "the beat beat beat of the tom tom" he sings in "Night and Day" (1932),[33] or the fact, as he says elsewhere, that "You do something to me, / Something that simply mystifies me" (94).

Metonymy multiplies discourses: it replaces *necessity* such as a "head" with the accidents of contingencies, such as a golden headband or places one finds oneself, that create possibilities of endless substitutions, endlessly new beginnings. Nietzsche describes this "intervallic" temporality under the figure of Demeter, "sunk in eternal sorrow, who *rejoices* again for the first time when told that she may *once more* give birth to Dionysus."[34] Wallace Stevens captures a sense of the temporality of desire that seems to add "a little meaning" to blank repetition:

> This warmth is for lovers at last accomplishing
> Their love, this beginning, not resuming, this
> Booming and booming of the new-come bee.[35]

In apprehending repetition as beginning – "again for the first time," "this beginning, not resuming" – metonymic desire emphasizes intervals, syncopation, and morphemic and conceptual rhyme in ways that multiply the occasions for discourse, the dizzying repetitions of popular music that Adorno took as a sign of its failure. The apprehension of repetition as beginning distinguishes this metonymic discourse of desire from the remembered, social repetitions of the Gershwins' rhymes.

In "Philosophy as a Kind of Writing" Richard Rorty argues that "writing always leads to more writing, and more, and still more – just as history does not lead to Absolute Knowledge or the Final Struggle, but to more history, and more, and still more."[36] Porter's music is a kind of writing in this metonymic sense, leading on to more and still more. The example of "It's De-Lovely" makes this clear, where sounds lead to explosive lists of neologisms to which one can always imagine adding more. But Porter's ubiquitous use of proper names in his lyrics crowds them with contemporaries in a similar fashion. The *locus classicus* of this procedure is "You're the Top" (1934) – Wilder calls it "probably the greatest of all the Porter 'list' songs"[37] – inhabited, as it is, by Richard Strauss, Shakespeare, Mickey Mouse, Vincent Youmans, Mahatma Gandhi, Greta Garbo, Bishop Manning, Irene Bordoni, Eugene O'Neill, Jimmy Durante, Mrs. Astor, among others.[38] But this is a repeated procedure in Porter's lyrics. "Anything Goes" (1935) is another powerful example, naming Ned McLean, Rockefeller, Max Gordon, the Vanderbilts and Whitneys, Sam Goldwin, Anna Sten, Lady Mendl, and Franklin Roosevelt. And "A Picture of Me without You" (1935) names Henry Ford, H. G. Wells, "Av'rill" Harriman, Huey Long, Ogden Nash, Father Couglin, Billy Sunday, and many others (134). Such paratactic lists expand the world in both time and space, "rhyming" figures in a manner that confuses beginnings and repetition. It follows the outlines of the metonymic internationalism of European high modernism that Eliot expresses in *The Waste Land* – "Jerusalem Athens Alexandria / Vienna London / Unreal" – though Eliot does so without Porter's fun, and also without naming the Gershwins' (and Waller's) New York City.[39] (Porter and Billie Holiday, unlike Eliot, were frequent visitors to New York.) Such lists are thoroughly metonymic precisely in the fact that something can *always* be added to them, such as the international city of New York Eliot doesn't seem able to acknowledge in his work (or the fact, as I suggested in the Acknowledgments, that my brother and I grew up there). It is as if, in leaving America, Eliot couldn't imagine its originary as well as repetitious significance; as if, in opposing and equating memory and desire, he couldn't imagine the ways desire apprehends repetition as beginning (or misapprehends it in the Lacanian "misrecognition" [*méconnaissance*] that governs "objectification").[40]

That is, if metonymy multiplies discourses, it also confuses them. As in the metonymy of "I've Got You Under My Skin" (1936), it marks and erases difference: "I've got you deep in the heart of me, / So deep in my heart, you're really a part of me, / I've got you under my skin."[41] The curious rhythms of desire confuse synecdoche and metonymy, the "nature" and "culture" in Lévi-Strauss's description or the figures of home and homelessness I've been using in relation to the spacious desire of the globe-trotting Porter. More than anything else, I believe, such rhythms of desire give Porter's music its power and pleasure. In "I Get a Kick Out of You," for example, Porter enacts the rhythms of desire as a species of syncopation by defining the "kick" of seeing the beloved's face – the combination of recognition and surprise – against the boredom of alcohol, drugs, and air flight.

> My story is much too sad to be told,
> But practically ev'rything leaves me totally cold.
> The only exception I know is the case
> When I'm out on a quiet spree
> Fighting vainly the old ennui
> And I suddenly turn and see your fabulous face.
>
> I get no kick from champagne.
> Mere alcohol doesn't thrill me at all,
> So tell me why should it be true
> That I get a kick out of you.
> Some get a kick from cocaine.
>
> I'm sure that if I took even one sniff
> That would bore me terrific'ly too
> Yet I get a kick out of you.
>
> I get a kick ev'ry time I see
> You're standing there before me.
> I get a kick though it's clear to me
> You obviously don't adore me.
>
> I get no kick in a plane.
> Flying too high with some guy in the sky
> Is my idea of nothing to do,
> Yet I get a kick out of you. (122)

When Porter first wrote this song, he named Mrs. Lindbergh in the last section, but the kidnapping of the Lindbergh child – a "contingency" with a vengeance – led him to rewrite those verses and transform its proper names to generic names. Originally, he wrote:

> I get no kick in a plane.
> I shouldn't care for those nights in the air
> That the fair Mrs. Lindbergh goes through
> But I get a kick out of you.

Figure 9 "I Get a Kick Out Of You," refrain; music and lyrics by Cole Porter

Such a transformation repeats the musical transformation from the specificities of minor to the general unmarked major Porter effects at the end of "I Get a Kick Out of You" and, as I shall argue, at the end of "What Is This Thing Called Love?"

In "I Get a Kick Out of You," Porter defines desire against boredom – ennui, total coldness, nothing to do, or simply going through the motions. The rhythms of the song are interesting, precisely in the ways they syncopate going through the motions (Figure 9). (Wilder notes, however, that "unless it is very carefully sung" – that is, unless one is particularly careful *not* to simply go through the motions – its syncopated melody "will turn into a waltz.")[42] The structure of the refrain follows a regular 16-bar construction, the chord progression E♭–Cm–Fm7–B♭7 found in such standard tunes as Jerome Kern's "Blue Moon" or "Can't Help Lovin' Dat Man."[43] But Porter syncopates the chord progression by beginning a conventional series in the middle, and displacing the C minor chord to G minor, the minor related to the tonic E♭, so that the chords progress Fm7–B♭7–E♭–Gm, ending the 16-bar riff on G minor, except for the end where the song sustains the E♭ major.

Similarly, the song syncopates the musical line. It plays 3/2 triplets against the song's two-beat measures in 5 of the 16 bars of the refrain (hence Wilder's fear that the melody will turn into a waltz); it starts the last musical phrase on the last beat of the twelfth bar rather than in the thirteenth bar; and it transforms the rhythm of the bridge to the almost waltzlike quality of its sustained notes (Figure 10).

The lyrics are syncopated in their rhymes as well. In addition to the repeated, internal rhymes – "alcohol"/ "all"; "if" / "sniff"; "high" / "sky" (and "care" / "air" of the Lindbergh version) – in two of the three verses Porter adds an additional internal rhyme based on syllables not words: /rif/ of "terrific'ly," and /ai/ of "idea." He also had added the "*fair* Mrs. Lindbergh" rhyming with "care" and "air," but the earlier discarded version lacked the wit of rendering the contingencies of sound (in syllables) into the necessities of meaning (in words). My favorite of these is the semantics of /rif/, which allows Porter to import a musical term ("riff") sounded in *terrific'ly*'s syllable. But my point is that the song syncopates lyrics as well as musical line and musical structure in order to achieve a rhythm of desire. Even "kick" does this, by equating, metonymically, the "thrill" of champagne, cocaine, and flying with the different kind of "thrill" of encountering the face of the beloved, the thrill of desire.

THE METONYMIC THING

Porter's lyrics are crowded with such faces. "It's All Right with Me" (1953) begins with face, there the synecdoches of smile (rhyming with "style") and lips (rhyming with "chips"), which all lead to a "strange" attraction.[44] Similarly, in "I Concentrate on You" (1940) "Whenever skies look grey to me / And trouble begins to brew," the singer concentrates on the smile and the light in the eyes of the beloved (159). Perhaps the strongest example,

Figure 10 "I Get a Kick Out Of You," bridge; music and lyrics by Cole Porter

though, is "You Do Something to Me" (1929). This song is occasioned by the shock of recognition of such a face. "I was mighty blue," it begins the verse,

> Thought my life was through,
> Till the heavens opened,
> And I gazed at you.
> Won't you tell me dear,
> Why, when you appear,
> Something happens to me
> And the strangest feeling goes through me? (94)

The "strange feeling" is the feeling of desire, marked here in the contingency – the emphasis on morphemic sound rather than completed meaning – that the feminine rhyme of "to me" and "through me" rhymes internally with the earlier "blue," "through," "you." The rhyming of a word with itself – the "*rime riche*" of "through" and "through" – marks the uncanniness of the seeming metonymic contingencies of rhyme displaced by absolute metaphorical identity.

Yeats, Porter's older contemporary, is the great master of the modernist *rime riche* in English. Yeats displays such mastery not only in his early poetry, such as "He Wishes for the Cloths of Heaven" (1899), which aims at transcendental revelation, repeating the rhyme words "cloths" three times in five lines, "light" also three times in five lines (including "the dark cloths / Of night and light and the half-light"), and "dreams" three times in three lines in order to "rhyme" supernatural "cloth" and natural "dream."[45] More significantly he displays it in his powerful short poem "A Deep-Sworn Vow" (1919), which rhymes "face" and "face" in such a way that, in Porter's words, "the heavens opened":

> Others because you did not keep
> That deep-sworn vow have been friends of mine;
> Yet always when I look death in the face,
> When I clamber to the heights of sleep,
> Or when I grow excited with wine,
> Suddenly I meet your face. (152)

Sharon Cameron discusses "the too-close bond between the two lines: 'Yet always when I look death in the face . . . Suddenly I meet your face."[46] The rhyming of the face of death and the face of the beloved – what Cameron describes as the way that "meaning remains affixed to an image's value as it breaks through the mundane reality, enlightening reality with terror" (217) – enacts, I believe, the eruption of "the power of pure loss" that Lacan associates with desire within the contingencies of everyday life.[47] The modernist version of *rime riche* is not simply the quotation I examined in relation to the Gershwins. (Moreover, the fact that Louis Armstrong *cannot* rhyme "face" with "case," as I mentioned in Chapter 2 and will more closely examine in Chapter 5, underlines the difference between social language and the language of desire.) Rather, emphasizing the more ordinary metonymies of rhyme altogether, Yeats's rhyme adds "something" to nothing – it adds a "little meaning" to blank repetition – by confronting the mundane "need" of sound with the transcendental "demand" of meaning. In this operation of rhyming, a "thing" becomes a signifier not in order to signify something else, but to create the illusion of "meaning" itself. As Lévi-Strauss says of music, "culture" is already present in this thing "in the form of sense experience."[48] The face of the beloved is such a "thing" that enlightens reality with somatic signification, with the terror of desire. Desire, for Yeats, is always marked by supernatural terror. For Porter it is marked by syncopations of meaning, fascinating rhythms – and, as I suggested of popular music more generally, with shared pity rather than isolating terror.

Thus, in "You Do Something to Me" the seeming contingency of a face occasioning the absolute and non-contingent opening of heaven gives rise to the "little meaning" of Lacan's metonymic desire so that the haunting of its homelessness can be felt and, perhaps, discerned. The philosopher Emmanuel Levinas traces in such a face a meaning that

> means from the very start in a way that goes beyond those plastic forms which forever try to cover the face like a mask of their presence to perception. But always the face shows through these forms. Prior to any particular expression and beneath all particular expressions, which cover over and protect with an immediately adopted face or countenance, there is the nakedness and destitution of the expression as such . . . From the beginning there is a face to face steadfast in its exposure to invisible death, to a mysterious forsakenness.[49]

It is "natural" for humans – and, to a lesser extent, primates in general – to recognize and respond to faces: we possess particular neurons that respond solely to faces, what neurologists have described as "face-responsive [neuronal] cells."[50] Yet Levinas – and Porter, for that matter – takes this "natural" phenomenon and overlays it or syncopates it with cultural meaning: for Levinas, the face to be faced is exposed to the mysterious forsakenness of a world in which things by themselves do not signify, but stand naked and destitute. Yet such exposure – like the confrontations of needs and demands or recognition and surprise – also provokes a "little meaning"; it provokes desire. That is, the rhythm of desire, as "I Get a Kick Out of You" suggests, is closely tied to the immanence and contingency of the beloved's face and to apprehended patterns of sound, and beat, and meanings, that play in the difference between boredom and inebriation and danger. Such rhythm presents endless metonymic displacement: proper names such as Lindbergh can be endlessly attached to the play of desire, just as changing tempos and changing places can – and just as new performances (Ethel Merman, Billie Holiday) can. That is, such rhythm presents the displacement of a sudden recognition of a "fabulous face" in the face of the "old ennui" or heaven opening with strange feelings occasioned by a gaze.

Figure 11 "What Is This Thing Called Love?", music and lyrics by Cole Porter

And when face signifies itself, in the supernaturalism of the *rime riche* of signification folded back upon itself, repetition seems a new beginning. Such folding back is the syncopation of desire – the syncopation of signification – in which meaning seems to inhabit a worldly "thing" so absolutely that it becomes the touchstone of value, an object of desire.

Porter explores the "mysterious forsakenness" of such a face in a song like "What Is This Thing Called Love?" (1929) and even, perhaps with less overt "mystery," in "Just One of Those Things" (1935). "What Is This Thing Called Loved?" is one of Porter's most mysterious and haunting songs. It is based on the rhythms of a chant Porter claims to have heard in Marrakesh and is dominated by the implicit mode of C minor, but it repeatedly resolves itself into C major, displacing its implicit C7–Fm, G7–Cm repetitions with C7–Fm, G7–G augmented–C major. This resolution is most pronounced at the end of the song (Figure 11), with the octave C and the question "I ask the Lord in Heaven above, / What is this thing called love?"[51]

The displacement of minor by major is especially emphasized in the 1955 arrangement by Nelson Riddle, sung by Frank Sinatra. In this arrangement the repeated motif of the clarinet makes the resolution of each verse seem minor rather than major, until the displacement of C minor by C major takes place after Sinatra finishes the ballad, as if the resolution in C major is beyond the lyrical question of the song, repressed, so to speak, in the subject's experience. The displacement of minor by major – Porter uses this in "It Was Just One of Those Things" (Dm/F), "I Get a Kick Out of You" (Gm/E♭), and more starkly and ironically in "My Heart Belongs to Daddy" (1938; Cm/C) – effects a sense of desire as that "something" Lacan talks about just beyond the reach of apprehension. Such desire, like Porter himself, is almost graspable but inhabiting homelessness.[52]

METONYMIC MODERNISM

Six years after Porter wrote "What Is This Thing Called Love?" – in the year he published "Just One of Those Things"– Martin Heidegger offered a series of lectures he published many years later under the title *What Is a Thing?* "It now becomes clear," Heidegger wrote in 1935,

> that we understand the term "thing" in both a narrower and a broader sense. The *narrower* or limited meaning of "thing" is that which can be touched, reached, or seen, i.e., what is present-at-hand (*das Vorhandene*). In the *wider* meaning of the term, the "thing" is every affair or transaction, something that is in this or that condition, the things that happen in the world – occurrences, events. Finally, there is still another use of this word in the *widest* possible sense . . . With respect to this, Kant speaks of the "thing-in-itself" (*Ding an sich*) . . . that which is *not* approachable through experience as are the rocks, plants, and animals.[53]

Such a "thing" is not approachable through experience, yet as Heidegger says it is "'something' . . . which is not nothing," like the "little meaning" Lacan describes embedded within or at the basis of desire. Heidegger likens this to poetry: "Why, for example," he writes, "has the treatment and interpretation of the poets for years been so dreary in our higher schools? Answer: Because the teachers do not know the difference between a thing and a poem; because they treat poems as things" (52). Heidegger is describing the lyric poems of modernism which are not "things" because they are inhabited by desire that is unable to settle in any particular spot – or in any particular object, proper name, adjective, musical or rhythmic structure. Instead, modernist desire *moves* from place to place, word to word, sound to sound, metonymically: as Porter says in "You Do Something to Me" (1929) – another song that attempts, metonymically, to articulate a "thing" – "Do do that voodoo that you do so well"[54] in words transformed to sounds in three bars that, as Jourdain notes, uses "different meters among

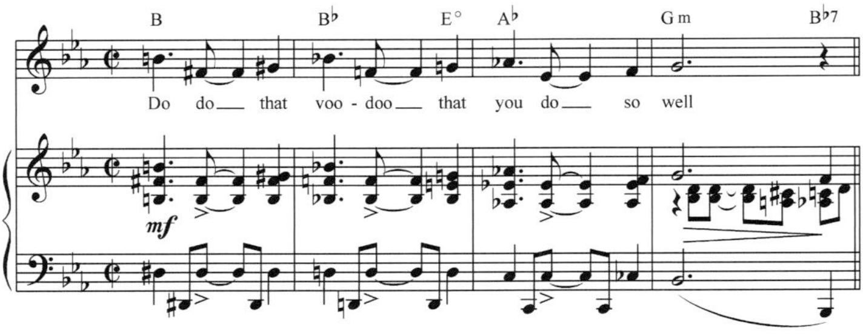

Figure 12 "You Do Something To Me," music and lyrics by Cole Porter

simultaneous musical lines,"[55] here 3/8, 3/8, 2/8 played against the 4/4 of the song's rhythm (Figure 12).

Such syncopation is the time of desire, its "kick," its "mystery"; it is the very metonymic desire that Lacan points to but cannot explain: "It is precisely because desire is articulated," he writes, "that it is not articulable."[56] Such desire inhabits in terror and exhilaration both high modernist lyrics and the popular music of Cole Porter. Like a moment of recognizing a face, it seems to add "something" to nothing: the musical semantics of "riff" in the middle of "terrific," the rich rhyming of "Do do" and "voodoo" and "you do," the stutter of "Yes my heart belongs to Daddy, / Da-da, da-da-da, da-da-da, dad!",[57] or the simple and touching metonymy "You'd be so nice to come home to" (1943; 188). In Porter, I suspect, this element of desire possesses William Carlos Williams's "location" insofar as it is always *performed*, like desire itself, so that in their homelessness his music and lyrics are always necessarily moving around, metonymically, from place to place. That is, in Porter's music the element of desire is constantly enacted, constantly pursued. The pleasures of his wit are the rhythms of his pursuit of desire that is also inhabited by desire; and the poignancies of his music – its longings – arise from the desire that plays, elusively, between his lyrical meanings and patterns of sounds. The syncopations of Porter's music provoke an apprehension of things as "real," not symbolic; they provoke a felt apprehension of the discontinuity of the real and the symbolic. Such discontinuity – the "breaks" of performed musics – forms the basis of the elusive "little meaning" of desire and allows us to see a little more clearly both the project of the modernist lyric in which he participated and the possibilities of desire enacted within the pleasures of popular music.

CHAPTER 5

Signifying music: Fats Waller and the time of jazz

If the Gershwin brothers brought to the songs of the musical theater the clashing and blending of post-War American culture in New York in the 1920s and 1930s, and if Cole Porter, born in Indiana and living high in many places throughout the world during the Depression, articulated the rhythms of desire in his songs, then the music of Thomas Wright Waller – Fats Waller – combined the musical energies of the Gershwins and of Porter in his notable performances of popular music. Yet he did so in a manner very different from his white contemporaries. First of all, unlike the Gershwins and Porter, he *performed* his music, both as a remarkably talented musician – an important developer of the "stride" piano – and as a singer and entertainer of some note. (He was the first black performer to be broadcast nationwide on mainstream white radio in the 1930s.) Second, like the Gershwins, he was from New York – he grew up in Harlem – yet his New York was so different from the Lower East Side and Tin Pan Alley of George and Ira Gershwin that we could reasonably assume that his situation in relation to the musical establishment in New York City was closer to that of the outsider Porter than that of the Gershwins. Finally, the combination of lyrics and music in his songs, like the Gershwins', borrowed from and participated in the colloquialisms and argot of his day in music which, like theirs, was a public discourse. But like Porter, the lyrics, songs, and above all the personal performances of his music also articulated deep-felt private feelings, not so much the abstraction of desire and its rhythms, but the far more destructive public rhythms of racism and discrimination. Listen to the "calling out" of all their names: "Cole Porter" rings with possession, rich, Anglo-Saxon, a Yale man. "George Gershwin"/"Ira Gershwin" – born as Jacob Gershowitz and Isadore Gershowitz in Brooklyn, New York, to Ukrainian Jewish immigrant parents – ring as first-generation immigrants in a city of immigrants, with George writing rhapsodies and concertos, as well as popular music, and harkening to Europe; and with Ira living out his life in Hollywood after his brother's death. "Fats Waller" rings with its nickname as name, a name imposed on him and marking, with its common adjective, first and foremost his body rather than himself.

SIGNIFYIN'

In this chapter I want to discuss the work of Fats Waller in relation to music, language, and culture as I did the Gershwins and Porter. More specifically, I examine the ways in which Waller's stride piano rhythmically decomposes the tempo of the ragtime it grew out of; the ways his vaudeville patter creates a montagelike counterpoint to the melodic and lyric time of his songs; the ways his Harlem music helps define an epoch of community life and racial relationships in the United States; and, finally, the way all of these aspects of his work participate in what Henry Louis Gates, Jr., and others have described as African American traditions of "signifyin'." These aspects of Waller's music articulate themselves within the categories of rhythmic decomposition, montage, and wholeness with which I described the aesthetics of popular music in the Introduction. Taken as a whole, the language of Waller's music, above all, combines the gathering up of the *public* life of discourse and dialogics as I described it in the Gershwins and the representation and provocation of the *private* life of the rhythms of feeling as I described it in Porter. "The black rhetorical tropes, subsumed under Signifyin(g)," Gates writes, "would include marking, loud talking, specifying, testifying, calling out (of one's name), sounding, rapping, and playing the dozens, and so on"; the subject doing the signifying, the "Signifying Monkey," "dwells at the margins of discourse, ever punning, ever troping, ever embodying the ambiguities of language."[1] Such signifying, as Gates says, is "the slave's trope, the trope of tropes," in that it performs "the ironic reversal of a received racist image of the black as simianlike, the Signifying Monkey" (52). If the Gershwins sing of people and persons and Porter of impersonal energies of the self – energies of desire – then Waller's signifying, as the discourse of an oppressed people, combines the public person and the private, invisible non-person in its "ironic reversal," as Gates says, of the transformation of the impersonal language of racism into the personal language of recognized selfhood.

That is, the music of Waller is both communal and individual, and it achieves this combination in the ironies of "signifyin'." More generally, the black trope of "signifying" achieves this ironic reversal – in its many forms of understatement, overstatement, specifying, loud talk, riffing – by its simple apprehensions of meaning as performance, as improvisation, as both individual and communal. Claudia Mitchell-Kernan examines "the

Black concept of *signifying*" in a language and an analysis very much like those of Mikhail Bakhtin, noting of signifying, as I noted earlier of popular music, that standard – and "transcendental" – dictionary definitions do not govern its performances.

> The Black concept of *signifying* incorporates essentially a folk notion that dictionary entries for words are not always sufficient for interpreting meanings or messages . . . A particular utterance may be an insult in one context and not another. What pretends to be informative may intend to be persuasive. The hearer is thus constrained to attend to all potential meaning carrying symbolic systems in speech events . . .[2]

Such signifying, as Gates notes, takes many forms, negative and positive. Quite often, as Mitchell-Kernan notes, it is conveyed in the language of insult, put-down, in performances of "cutting contests" of one sort of another. But in other instances, it can be seen in "black jazz musicians who perform each other's standards . . ., not to critique these but to engage in refiguration as an act of homage" (xxvii). In others, we can see "the (political, semantic) confrontation between two parallel discursive universes: the black American linguistic circle and the white" (45). In others, Gates describes signifying as a kind of "(re)naming ritual" (46).[3] And in others we can see, as Roger Abrahams suggests, "the propensity to talk around a subject, never quite coming to the point," we can hear the "making fun of a person or situation," or we encounter the very *technical* ability of "speaking with the hands and eyes . . . [that] encompasses a whole complex of expressions and gestures."[4]

All these instances, however, are not quite as separate and distinguishable as this catalogue suggests, and in them all what takes place is both "invisible" and "visible," as irony is both invisible and visible, right there in interpersonal discourse. Jacques Derrida describes this subtle and complicated process in relation to psychoanalysis where translation takes place, he argues, "from one language into itself with the 'same' words suddenly changing their sense, overflowing with sense or exceeding it altogether, and nevertheless impassive, imperturbable, identical to themselves, allowing you still to read in the new code of this anasemic translation what belonged to the other word, the same one, before psychoanalysis."[5] Two languages, two discourses seem to take place at once: in *signifying*, meaning and performance are joined together. It is important to note that Gates himself explains that Freudian psychoanalysis has "informed [his] reading of Signifyin(g)" throughout his discussion.[6] "While the insult aspect of the Monkey's discourse is important to the tales," he writes,

> linguists have often failed to recognize that insult is not at all central to the nature of Signifyin(g); it is merely one mode of a rhetorical strategy that has several other modes . . . For Signifyin(g) . . . [is] analogous to Freud's notion of how the unconscious relates to the conscious. The black vernacular trope of Signifyin(g) exists on this vertical axis, wherein the materiality of the signifier (the use of words as things, in Freud's terms of the discourse of the unconscious) not only ceases to be disguised but comes to bear prominently as the dominant mode of discourse. (58)

In this discussion, Gates is describing the ways in which signifyin(g) – like Derrida's "anasemic translation," a seeming neologism which means both another translation and no translation at all – seems to accomplish two things at the same time, the public discourse of insult where words mean what they mean and the private expression of psychological energies where words provoke or "perform" affect. Above all, Gates says, the Signifying Monkey "is not only a master of technique . . . , he *is* technique, or style, or the literariness of literary language . . . In this sense, one does not signify something; one signifies in *some* way" (54).

Such a process of what could be called "assertion" or "performance" rather than "saying" is, as Gates says, the trope of oppression, "the slave's trope, the trope of tropes," insofar as it asserts freedom, dignity, community, and authority in the face of – and in the very language of – a social situation that transforms people to "dictionary-entry" meanings of interchangeable (and for that reason "invisible") commodities. "What did/do black people signify," Gates asks, faintly echoing Ralph Ellison's figure of the "invisible man," "in a society in which they were intentionally introduced as the subjugated, as the enslaved cipher?" (47). One thing they did and do, he argues throughout his book *The Signifying Monkey*, is "to signify," to perform and assert human *reference* (which points, referentially, to a human being existing in the world) by using the "same" words that erase humanity from particular, historical people by means of the non-specifying meanings of epithets.[7] The very timely (and *semantic*) assertions of seemingly impersonal (and *formal*) technique, I will argue, are especially pronounced (if I can use this metaphor) in music.

SIGNIFYIN' WALLER

We can hear all these varied apprehensions of "signifyin'" in the music, language, and specific Harlem-style performances of Fats Waller. I want to begin my discussion – begin our hearing – with two jazzlike homages to him, that of his contemporary and fellow musician from New Orleans,

Louis Armstrong – whose career, as I noted in Chapter 2, took off with a performance of Waller's "Ain't Misbehavin'" – and that of a slightly younger man from Oklahoma and Harlem, Ralph Ellison. Waller recorded hundreds of songs before he died at the age of 39 in 1943. Many of these songs he wrote himself – often with Andy Razaf (really Andreamentena Razafinkeriefo), whose own story is remarkable. But, as I mentioned already, he never recorded one of his most famous songs, "Black and Blue." Louis Armstrong recorded it in 1929 soon after Waller wrote it, and Ralph Ellison virtually begins *Invisible Man* with a discussion of this song and Armstrong's recording. "Now I have one radio-phonograph," the narrator of *Invisible Man* says;

> I plan to have five. There is a certain acoustical deadness in my hole, and when I have music I want to *feel* its vibration, not only with my ear but with my whole body. I'd like to hear five recordings of Louis Armstrong playing and singing "What Did I do to Be so Black and Blue" – all at the same time. Sometimes now I listen to Louis while I have my favorite dessert of vanilla ice cream and sloe gin. I pour the red liquid over the white mound, watching it glisten and the vapor rising as Louis bends that military instrument into a beam of lyrical sound. Perhaps I like Louis Armstrong because he's made poetry out of being invisible. I think it must be because he's unaware that he *is* invisible. And my own grasp of invisibility aids me to understand his music. Once when I asked for a cigarette, some jokers gave me a reefer, which I lighted when I got home and sat listening to my phonograph. It was a strange evening. Invisibility, let me explain, gives one a slightly different sense of time, you're never quite on the beat. Sometimes you're ahead and sometimes behind. Instead of the swift and imperceptible flowing of time, you are aware of its nodes, those points where time stands still or from which it leaps ahead. And you slip into the breaks and look around. That's what you hear vaguely in Louis' music.[8]

Armstrong's great 1929 recording of "Black and Blue" is available on a CD called *Satch Plays Fats*.[9] Before I turn to Armstrong's performance, I want to say something about this CD. It is a reissue of an album of Armstrong playing Waller songs that was recorded and released in 1955, entitled, as the present CD is, *Satch Plays Fats*. The earlier record offered new versions of Armstrong playing and singing Waller, more or less in a 1950s style "in which," as Charles Hamm says of the posthumous recordings of Gershwin's songs, big band "arrangements and conducting style impose a neo-Romantic, 1950s ethic on the music, robbing it of all vitality and rhythmic life."[10] The earlier record did not include the 1929 recording Ellison mentions (or any of the early versions of Armstrong playing Waller). The recent CD takes the title of the original 1955 record, *Satch Plays*

Figure 13 "(What Did I Do To Be So) Black and Blue," music by Harry Brooks and Fats Waller

Fats, and it adds in its re-release all of Armstrong's recordings of Waller tunes, including the 1929 recording of "Black and Blue," performed by Louis Armstrong & His Orchestra, that includes a banjo and tuba, New Orleans style. (The 1955 version has neither, and it opens and runs with a pronounced bass playing against piano and then Armstrong, in a kind of sultry nightclub rendition. It ends with a stock close, dominant-seventh to tonic.)

It is also instructive, I think, to consider the nicknames of the title of the 1955 record and the 2000 reissue in relation to the signifyin' Gates describes and the "invisibility" Ellison describes. In *Shadow and Act* Ellison makes clear the relationship between "invisibility" and signifyin' in a discussion of racism, the function of which, he says, "was to veil the humanity of Negroes thus reduced to a sign, and to repress the white audience's awareness of its moral identification with its own acts and with the human ambiguities pushed behind the mask."[11] Armstrong's designation, "Satch" or "Satchmo" – as fully nonsense sounds as any that Armstrong and Waller wove into scat singing – comes from the nickname Satchelmouth, "thanks," George Avakian says in the liner notes to the CD (and to the original record), "to the generous size of his mouth." Waller's designation or nickname, "Fats," comes from the fact that he weighed almost three hundred pounds on his 5-feet 11-inch frame. In these nicknames, as in Waller's song, "invisibility" is accomplished by replacing human reference by synecdochical part – corpulence, the size of the mouth, or, as Waller's "Black and Blue" says, "My only sin/Is in my skin." In each instance, humanity is reduced to signs of physicality in a manner that erases all senses of person, that reduces person to "thing." In addition, another form of "invisibility," which I have already hinted at, is the fact that Waller never recorded this song, which is one of the few early standards that explicitly addresses race relations.[12]

The music of the song Louis Armstrong recorded in 1929 is given in Figure 13.

Cold empty bed,
springs hard as lead,
feel like old Ned,
wish I was dead
All my life thru –
I've been so black and blue.

Even the mouse,
ran from my house
They laugh at you
and scorn ya too
What did I do (babe) –
to be so black and blue?

Ohh – I'm white, inside,
that don't help my case,
'Cause I can't hide
what is in my face –

How will it end?
ain't got a friend,
My only sin,
is in my skin
What did I do –
to be so black and blue?

The title itself is signifyin': it takes the colloquial phrase "black and blue" – a three-word metonymic phrase that functions almost like a single word (like the "knife and fork" mentioned in Chapter 4) – and unpacks its signifiers so that its color terms, *black* and *blue*, come to signify /Negro/ and /unhappy/ even while – in a kind of *anasemic translation* – these terms mean the "same" thing that *black and blue* always means, "bruised," "beat up." In this way, as Derrida says, "the 'same' words suddenly [change] their sense, overflowing with sense or exceeding it altogether, and nevertheless impassive, imperturbable, identical to themselves."[13]

David Yaffe gives a wonderful description of the 1929 recording that the narrator of *Invisible Man* talks about. "The 1929 recording," he writes,

> shows how lyricism emerges from repression in more than the obvious way; it's there in the conflict between the artist's freedom and the song's rhythmic and thematic straitjacket. The track opens with a sentimental, rhythmically literal riff on celesta, played by Gene Anderson, which is batted away by Armstrong's brass, bluesy attack. Then he recapitulates Anderson's simple 5–1–2–3/6–1–2–4 minor phrase, a simple progression from an A minor to D minor, whose sentimental theme he subsequently dismantled with a blaring, dissenting high E atop a D-major chord. What follows is a series of mixed allusions, including additional blues variations, a trumpet onomatopoeia of a marching band's snare-drum's "rat-a-tat-tat," and a parody of a bugle call, as if he were waking us up from a dirge. Armstrong's phrasing on trumpet and voice is supple, but what continues to astound is the contrast between his rhythmic variation and his rhythm section's relative stiffness . . . The metronomic quarter notes plonked out on Mancy Carr's banjo stand in dramatic contrast to Armstrong's graceful swing.[14]

The contrast between Armstrong's improvisations and the rhythm section's stiffness is a distinctive mark of the New York stride piano playing I discuss in a moment, and even this early recording incorporates Waller's New York style with Armstrong's New Orleans music.[15]

Armstrong's voice in the 1929 recording is, as Yaffe says, "supple"; however, at a crucial moment he cannot quite allow himself to rhyme "case" and "face" in the bridge lines. Instead, he offers scat singing that pushes words to nonsense – reduces words to enacted sound rather than sign – as it creates a point where time stands still and the song virtually halts.[16] The song itself ends this way, with the unaccompanied alto sax moving down and then Armstrong's unaccompanied solo moving up near the heights of the trumpet's range in a way that, as Ellison says, bends the military instrument into a beam of lyrical sound.[17] Such scat singing achieves (or at least pushes towards) making sound a visible gesture, as in the "beam of lyrical sound" Ellison describes, by means of the apparent decomposing of meaning into physical qualities, signified by a signifier that suggests without designating a referent. In 1928, a year before recording this song, Armstrong recorded a remarkable scat version of Waller's "Squeeze Me,"[18] scat singing against chords sung by the rest of his band with only the banjo accompanying them. (Here again the recording captures the power of the stride piano, its mosaic counterpoint – its montage – of rhythms.) Twice Armstrong scat-sings unaccompanied lines that imitate the unaccompanied trumpet solos he plays a moment later. In "Squeeze Me" as well as in "Black and Blue," Armstrong's scat singing makes musical technique *visible* in its powerful performance. Such a musical performative gesture is analogous to the transformation of epithet – "Fats," "Satch" – into name, and, as I notice in a moment, it is a major aspect of Waller's repeated signifying counterpoint of speech and song in his performances of his own and others' music.

Here, though, I want to return to the way the rhythm section works in Armstrong's recording, the oom-pah of the tuba, the strumming banjo, and even the broken chords or arpeggios of the celesta-piano's introduction. The refrain of "Black and Blue" itself, unlike any other of Waller's songs I know, is built around arpeggios: an inverted A-minor chord, a D-minor beginning on the third, A-minor again, D-seventh, and then a C-major (which *sounds* syncopated even though its rhythm is the same as the broken chords of the earlier measures), G-seventh, resolving on C-major even though the song *feels* fully minor. (See Figure 13.) The arrangement, in this 1929 recording, of single-note (tuba) bass octaves below the banjo chords and the rolling opening up or "arpeggiation" of chordal configurations characterizes the great transformation of ragtime piano music into improvisational jazz that took place in the 1920s in Harlem with the creation of the stride piano. Needless to say, other kinds of improvisational music were being developed out of the blues and ensemble music in other places in the early century – we heard them (and still hear them) in the Gershwins' and Porter's songs. But unlike New Orleans, St. Louis, Chicago, and – as Ellison insists – Oklahoma City, in New York the twelve-bar blues didn't become a staple of jazz or popular music in the early twentieth century, perhaps because the cosmopolitan nature of modernism, as I suggest in the Introduction, precluded to some extent the rural travelling music of southern blues.

THE STRIDE PIANO

A center of New York jazz – very different from the Tin Pan Alley where Gershwin began his career playing the piano to sell sheet music and where Porter hoped to be a success – was Harlem. The Harlem piano music of the twenties has come to be called that of the "stride piano." This technique, Paul Machlin has noted, "whose roots lie in the formal gestures of ragtime composition, centers on a basic left-hand pattern" in which a fundamental pitch "deep in the bass range of the piano" is played on the strong, 1 and 3, beats of a four-beat measure, while the chords filling out the harmony, are "played in the tenor or mid-range of the piano on weak beats." In this way, Machlin says, "the left hand is continually shifting its position, 'striding' back and forth over the left half of the keyboard."[19] The great difference between stride and ragtime is the range of the bass of the stride piano, the fact, as Machlin says, that "a stride pianist will often roll [the weak-beat] chords" – this is what I meant by "arpeggiate" them from bottom to top – and that "in stride, these chords often incorporate sevenths, ninths, blue notes, or other unexpected pitches only distantly related to the particular harmony in question" (8–9). But, the most important chief difference between ragtime and stride, I think, is that stride calls for improvisation while ragtime is a strict musical form that demands its composition be followed "exactly as noted by the composer" (9). Waller's biographer, Joel Vance, notes that "the greatness of stride was that it did not compromise the songs played for the sake of the style. Ragtime and boogie-woogie were locked into themselves and forced material to fit in their molds. Stride was open, free, generous, flexible. It could be barrelhouse or sophisticated, violent or tender. As such, it was perfectly suited to Waller's personality. He could swing like mad when he wanted to – and he often wanted to – but took full advantage of the lyrical possibilities of stride."[20]

"Stride originated to a large extent," Machlin points out, "in the social milieu of Harlem's informal nightlife – specifically, at rent parties (or rent socials, as they were sometimes called). Needy tenants would organize these gatherings in order to generate the capital necessary to pay a landlord another month's rent."[21] Moreover, Machlin concludes,

> since rent parties often lasted through the night and well into the morning, the pianist's musical imagination was taxed to its fullest. In order to keep the music

fresh and vital, and to keep the dancers' energy from flagging, improvisation became a practical as well as aesthetic necessity.[22] (9–10)

Quite often, these socials would involve multiple pianists and "cutting contests" where different musicians would compete with one another. James P. Johnson, who is often said to have been the first to develop the stride piano and with whom Waller studied, first introduced him to rent parties in the early 1920s (11, 12). By the middle of the decade Johnson and Waller, along with Willie "the Lion" Smith, were considered the great masters of the technical virtuosity of stride piano, and George Gershwin often went uptown "to listen and learn" from them.[23]

Vance notes that "Gershwin's admiration for Johnson, Smith, and Waller was not based on any feelings of inferiority as a keyboardist . . . What attracted Gershwin to the Harlem trio . . . was that they did exactly what he did. They were not, in his estimation, any more 'jazz' players than he was, though they used syncopation and jazz technique. Gershwin was thrilled and delighted by Johnson, Smith, and Waller because they were melodists of extraordinary caliber, because their compositions were concertos of variations on a theme, and because in performance these variations were presented in *concert* form . . . The Harlem trio and Gershwin were modern American composers who had arrived at the same musical conclusions independently" (41).[24] Machlin offers a more detailed analysis of the variations and theme of Waller's work that Vance mentions by focusing on the "artfully constructed melody of 'Ain't Misbehavin'." "What we take for granted as merely a pretty tune," he writes,

is actually a carefully crafted melodic line, logical and organic in its use of a motivic cell. In fact, this type of melody is characteristic of Waller's approach to the composition of a line. His predilection for short gestures that accumulate, as opposed to a long flowing line, derives from his training in stride, which stresses the need for maintaining a readily available vocabulary of short right-hand gestures for use in improvisation. Pieces as diverse as 'Honeysuckle Rose,' 'Rusty Pail,' and '(What did I do to Be So) Black and Blue?' all share this characteristic. (28)

The short gestures that accumulate in stride piano build into the aesthetics of rhythmic decomposition, montage, and wholeness I discuss in the Introduction. "Ain't Misbehavin'" can be decomposed into "short right-hand gestures for use in improvisation"; it confronts and is *signifyin'* Gershwin's "The Man I Love" (as I mentioned in Chapter 3); and, at the same time, it achieves wholeness in its "crafted melodic line [that is] logical and organic in its use of a motivic cell."

In a tune like Waller's early composition "The Minor Drag," the stride piano sounds clearly.[25] When Waller recorded this song in 1929 – with piano, trumpet, trombone, clarinet/tenor, and banjo – its producer, the banjoist and band organizer Eddie Condon (who plays the banjo in this recording), glanced "nervously at the assembled executives. Waller sat at the piano. The recording engineer gave the signal to start, and the quintet charged into the first tune at a boiling pace." Condon had wondered about the absence of a drummer and a bassist, but [he later wrote] "when I heard Waller's left hand I knew we didn't need them."[26] This song, according to Vance, was composed "on the spot" (48), though the executives of the Victor Talking Machine Company praised the band for exhibiting "the virtues of well-rehearsed bands." Afterwards, their staff confused this song with another and released it as "The Minor Drag" even though Waller had entitled it "Harlem Fuss" (49).

As Condon mentions, this song needs no drum or bass because of Waller's stride left hand. Waller was said to have enormous hands, which helped accommodate his striding: one blind man mentioned that shaking hands with him was like grabbing a bunch of bananas. The drag moves down from clarinet to trumpet to trombone then to Waller's powerful piano solo syncopating his left and right hands. The remarkable transition from minor to major in the middle of Waller's solo – all while the bass is solidly anchoring the improvisation (as it does with the winds) – allowed the Victor people to claim the title wasn't altogether "off." More to the point, this transition from minor to major – very different from Porter's use of that transition to produce a sense of hidden meaning behind apparent sound – creates one of the temporal nodes that Ellison notices in Armstrong's music, a moment of standing still that suddenly leaps ahead. The final refrain plays out the stride in the brass: first with the trumpet and trombone singing the stride chords against the saxophone's improvisation, then the trombone alone playing a one-note stride "roll" (so to speak) against the sax solo.

The jazz pianist Dick Wellstood nicely describes the energy of the stride piano in his liner notes to the Donald Lambert album, *Harlem Stride Classics*. He begins by arguing that the "conventional wisdom" connecting stride to the oom-pah bass of "classic rag" is "mistaken, as usual. Franz Liszt [whom Waller loved], Scott Joplin, Jelly Roll Morton, Earl Hines, Teddy Wilson, Erroll Garner, and Pauline Alpert," Lambert writes, "all monger a good many Oom-pahs and, whatever their other many virtues, none of them play stride." Stride, he says,

> requires a certain characteristic rhythmic articulation, for the nature of which I can only refer you to recordings by such as Eubie Blake, Luckey Robert, James P. Johnson, Fats Waller . . . [all of whom accent] the first and third beats. This [is] perfect. A straight four is too confining; a simple two [that is, emphasizing the second and fourth beats] makes you seasick. At any rate, the characteristic rhythms of stride are provided by the right hand, not the left . . . By pulling and tugging at the rhythms of the left, the right hand provides the swing.
>
> Now, if the right hand is to be able to do this, the left hand must be, not only quasi-metronomic, but also totally in charge. The propulsion, what the musicians nowadays call the "time," must always be in the left hand.[27]

With the time in the left hand, the right hand is free to improvise; when "the time switches to the right hand," Wellstood concludes, "the left hand [is left] merely to wag [and] the momentum [the "swing"] goes out the window."[28] Throughout Waller's work there are many moments of the strong "anchor," as I have called it, of the stride bass.

IMPROVISATIONS

The anchor of the stride technique, I am suggesting, offers great possibilities for the improvisations of the rent parties and the jam sessions that came to characterize the Harlem flowering of jazz in the 1920s and 1930s. It might well be argued that the advent of what is called jazz, at least in part, is marked by the *institution* of improvisation into music.[29] To conceive of stride performance as an institution is to emphasize the technical (and more or less impersonal) side of its performance, and such virtuosity is clearly a powerful – and joyful – aspect of Waller's music. But technique is always more than simply an impersonal tool handed down from generation to generation, like the common meanings of words such as "fat" or "satchel." Talking about the odd and sometimes embarrassing meaning of his own "borrowed" name, Ralph Waldo Ellison, in the context of the historical fact that "we bear, as Negroes, names originally possessed by those who owned our enslaved grandparents,"[30] Ellison describes the strong sense of technique: "I mean to remind you," he writes, "that fictional techniques are not a mere set of objective tools, but something much more intimate: a way of feeling, of seeing and of expressing one's sense of life. And the process of *acquiring* technique is a process of modifying one's responses, of learning to see and feel, to hear and observe, to evoke and evaluate the images of memory and of summoning up and directing the imagination"

(164). In this passage focused on the formality of technique, he is narrating the concept of semantic formalism.

In his thoughtful survey *Jazz in American Culture*, Peter Townsend describes four "aspects" of jazz in an attempt to define "jazz as music": "repertoire, improvisation, rhythm and individual technique"; he calls these aspects "the stable elements in any consensus as to [the] musical definition" of jazz.[31] Repertoire, improvisation, and rhythm encompass the elements of wholeness, montage, and rhythmic decomposition. But the fact that he describes the fourth aspect of jazz, technique, as "individual" is important, because it is, of course, an individual acquirement that Ellison includes in his catalogue of jazz attributes: "the technical mastery, the tonal authenticity, the authority and the fecundity of imagination of such men as Hawkins, Young, Goodman, Tatum, Teagarden, Ellington and Waller."[32] But such technique, as Ellison also suggests, balances community and individualism in a manner that is analogous to the way that, I am suggesting, *signifyin'* balances community and individualism. I should reiterate that these descriptions of technique display the quality I described as "semantic formalism" in the Introduction, the combination of the natural and the artificial: "technique" is a formal skill, yet it is also a vehicle for the meanings, the responses, learning, observing, evaluating – the very means of "seeing and expressing one's sense of life" Ellison describes (164). "Technique," I am suggesting, is like a name, or even analogous to scat singing insofar as it presents itself as contentless – without "semantics" (as a proper name is or seems solely referential, without any general meaning) – yet may be taken up to transform dull noise into beams of lyrical sound. Waller taught himself to become the master of the difficult piano technique of stride, a technique he learned from Johnson and Smith and from simply living in Harlem. And he helped to institutionalize it and institutionalize, more generally, improvisation into the popular music and lyrics of his time as improvisation modified his feeling, judgment and imagination. Such systematic improvisation, as we shall see, distinguishes him – and Billie Holiday in the following chapter – from Gershwin and Porter as composers of popular music, but it also joins him to them insofar as Gershwin and Porter *wrote* improvisation into their scores as they reimagined or "jazzed," as Alfred Appel, Jr., has said, the ordinary music of Tin Pan Alley and gave it "new life,"[33] just as Waller and Holiday do in their performances.

The institution of jazz, in Waller's Harlem, grew into jam sessions in private homes and, later, in more public places. Townsend describes some of the economic and social factors that helped to institutionalize improvisational music in Harlem and elsewhere in the 1920s. Discussing the necessity for "a sufficient critical mass of working musicians, audiences and places to play in" – criteria which emphasize the *urban* nature of this popular music – he notes that this "culture took root typically in black entertainment districts, away from but within reach of mainstream entertainment outlets. In these districts rents and running costs were lower, and night clubs and cabarets could be set up quickly and cheaply. The main centres from the 1920s through the 1940s were Harlem in New York, the South Side of Chicago, and a small but influential section of Kansas City."[34] An important element of what I am calling the "institution" of improvisation was the "competitive interaction" of its "cutting sessions," the way that its performers, as Jacqui Malone says of black dance in America, "inspired each other and pushed the evolution of their art forms along through improvisation, competition and hard work."[35] Such "competitive interaction," Malone argues, is "the driving force that keeps African American dance, music and song in the avant garde worldwide. We see it, for example, in the jam sessions of jazz musicians, cutting sessions of tap dancers, challenge matches of break dancers, colorful parades of black social aid and pleasure clubs, and the 'sing-offs' of blues shouters of the twenties, gospel quartets of the thirties and forties, and doowop vocalists of the fifties" (5). Ellison describes "the delicate balance struck between strong individual personality and the group during those early jam sessions" which were, he says, "a marvel of social organization" in terms of the individual musicians' "will to achieve the most eloquent expression of idea-emotions through the technical mastery of their instruments . . . and this give and take, the subtle rhythmical shaping and blending of idea, tone and imagination demanded of group improvisation."[36] Such a balance is present in signifyin' as well: the way in which the imposed, more-or-less-dehumanizing name – "Fats," "Satch," even "Filthy" in an early nickname for Waller or the term Gates traces, "the signifying monkey" – can, in the referenced interplay of individual and community, turn into positive designation: human reference rather than timeless meaning, a visible "beam" of sound.[37]

Having grown up with the rent parties of the twenties, Waller was a master at cutting contests and jam sessions. In fact, his 1935 recording of "I Got Rhythm" is one of the few records of such a cutting contest.[38] There, in the context of a big band, Waller "duels" with his protégé Hank Duncan. By this time, Gershwin's 1930 song was such a jazz standard – Townsend mentions that it "has been improvised on in some form by every jazz musician who played a note since the song was published . . . [and] is the base for innumerable other tunes, including at least eight written by

Charlie Parker" – that Waller doesn't even have to present a "straight" version of it when he sings it at the beginning of this recording.[39] In fact, he begins simply with a stride riff – which is repeated later by bass and brass.

Moreover, in this performance Waller improvises on the music and lyrics, singing consistently behind the beat, even pushing the second refrain towards scat singing in which the "daisies way over there in green pastures" and "a great big girl" slur almost into sound and run down the tempo and the scale. Such lyric improvisation approaching scat is a form of signifyin', what Ellison describes in an essay about Charlie Parker as a "'signifying riff' or melodic naming of a recurring human situation, . . . played to satirize some betrayal of faith or loss of love observed from the bandstand."[40] Here Waller is gently mocking Gershwin (Ira this time), speeding up the furious tempo of the band, challenging Duncan and himself.

Waller also offers in this song other forms of signifying, what Morroe Berger has called "his own mock pretensions or exaggerated jive talk"[41] outside the music – the signifyin' of his patter in his speaking-singing with the trombone. There he sings/speaks

"Swing it on up with jazz"
"Jazz, jazz"
"aha," "yeah, yeah"

as verbal and then simply phonic-scat counterpoint to the trombone solo. More impressively, he improvises talk against Duncan's and his own piano solos. As Duncan plays, he and other members of the band offer running – "cutting" – commentary.

Ah, that's brother Duncan – he's getting smart too. [Duncan's piano chorus.]
Look at that cat striding over there – look's like he's tryin' to get something from me.
– Come on Fats.
Looks like he's tryin' to get something *from* me.
– Show him how to swing, Hanky!
Aw, I ain't gonna have that. Oh I got him some.
He's mine. *He's mine*. Hang loose. [Waller begins to play his chorus, the stride piano against Gershwin's chords.] Ha. Ha. Well *all right*. [At the end of the chorus he bangs the piano keys with his arms, ends the riff, and the band takes up the music.]

In a moment I'll talk about this punctuation of music with contest, word, and voice – and the temporality of this punctuation – in relation to the music, language, and culture of jazz.

But here I want to examine it in relation to the institution of the cutting contest of rent and jam sessions. In the fifth chorus, Paul Machlin has argued,

> this version of "I Got Rhythm" becomes a historical document of some significance. For the dialogue between Waller and the members of the band that ensues during Duncan's solo makes clear that a friendly but serious competition is taking place between Duncan and Waller. Given the spirit of competitiveness that flourished among the first generation of stride pianists, what we witness in these two solo choruses is nothing less than a miniature old-fashioned cutting contest, fueled by Waller's boisterous challenges and mock-injured pride.[42]

In this solo (beginning at 1:47 of the *Very Best of Fats Waller* cut), Duncan plays a strong stride bass in the refrain and powerful arpeggios in the bridge (that are reminiscent of the scored bridge of "Ain't Misbehavin'," which, as I have said, was signifyin' Gershwin). Against his repetition of the final refrain when a member of the band says "Show him how to swing, Hanky!", Waller yells, "Aw, I ain't gonna have that. Aw, I got him some – he belongs to me! He's *mine*!"[43] Then Waller's solo begins with his shouting, "Cut loose."

Just as Waller's singing is behind the beat, so his solo is ahead of the beat, making us aware of what Ellison calls time's leaping ahead and the heady acrobatics of not-quite-achieved anticipations that Claude Lévi-Strauss described. Waller plays the bridge in time, but comes out of it running against the beat – we might call this signifyin' the beat – until he slams his arm against the keys twice. But in the last refrain, the stride bass holds onto the beat to such a degree that the wind solos are purely its rhythmic counterpoint and the clarinet sings sustained notes and then breaks it up with dotted repetitions that literally "cut" the stride. Here is signifying with a vengeance, loud talking, calling out, *specifying*: Waller is playing against but also with Duncan, and improvisatory competition, as Malone and Ellison say, seems to balance and embody a community of values just as individual technique can balance and embody community. Here is decomposition, montage, and wholeness.

PUNCTUATED IMPROVISATIONS

"Playing against and with" might well be a good definition of jazz improvisation, and certainly it is a good definition of Waller's jazz, which plays with and against both his own tunes and others' tunes. Here I've offered Armstrong playing Waller ("Black and Blue"), Waller playing Waller ("The Minor Drag"), and Waller playing Gershwin ("I Got Rhythm"). I will end this chapter with Waller singing Waller, signifyin' his own music the way he signifies Duncan's and Gershwin's: by breaking up their time. (Surely his movement towards scat by slushing Gershwin's "daisies way over there in green pastures" rivals Armstrong's defacing of his "face" in "Black and Blue.") In a recording of a radio broadcast in 1936 of his early song "I'm Crazy 'Bout My Baby" – this performance can be found on *The Definitive Fats Waller* – Waller introduces his song with a musical fanfare that has little to do with the song, and then he says: "And now, ladies and gentlemen, when I latch on here I have to express *e-vry-thing* – you know, I feel so effervescent I've gotta do a set eulogizing – you get it? – so listen here." In this introduction, Waller's alliterative verbal patter – "ladies"/"latch"; "express"/ "everything"/ "effervescent"; "eulogize"/ "you got it" – is notably marked by the deepening tone of voice in "everything," just as, in the song he deepens and slurs the tones of "baby" (as he did Gershwin's "daisies": at one point he even pronounces "baby" as "maybe").

Morroe Berger has noted Waller's "unusual ability" – a *gestural* ability – "to amuse and to convey feelings by slightly changing the pronunciation of consonants and vowels."[44] This tonal gesture emphasizes the signifier at the expense of signification and, like the referential assertions of a name like "Satch" rather than "satchel" or "satchelmouth," it does so by making performative power rather than constative meaning essential, to return to J. L. Austin's terms. Ellison, an aspiring musician, points out the same thing when he describes how *The Waste Land* "seized my mind . . . by its power to move me while eluding my understanding."[45] In this, Ellison is emphasizing *potential* meaning, in the sense of its power, rather than the "literal" meanings of understanding. (Eliot's poem was, in fact, born in music-hall music, and is one of the great pieces of signifying jive talk in our canon. Still, Eliot himself rarely exhibits in his "serious" poetry – unlike other high modernist authors – the "ideal cultural experience [of] *fun*," its "routinized pleasures, more intense than the everyday but bound into its rhythms, and legitimized emotional gratification, a play of desire and discipline" that Simon Frith sees in the popular arts.[46] It is as if, like Adorno, he emphasizes "truth" at the expense of "pleasure.") In Waller's introduction, the playful-sounding words are "effervescent" and "eulogize," and it is no accident, I think, that "I'm Crazy 'Bout My Baby" begins with a figure for "effervescent," "walking on air" (Figure 14):

I'm walking on air
for I left all my blue days behind;
I've learned how to care,
and there's love, really love, on my mind.

Figure 14 "I'm Crazy 'Bout My Baby (And My Baby's Crazy 'Bout Me)," music by Thomas "Fats" Waller; lyrics by Alexander Hill

In the signifying patter of his introduction, Waller is literalizing figurative language: "effervescent," as Machlin suggests, may well be "a reference to the effects of some intoxicating substance" even while "Alex Hill, the lyricist, certainly intended this phrase as a metaphor for happiness."[47] The substitution of a large word for a simpler one is one of the techniques Waller picked up from vaudeville, and it runs parallel to – it might well signify on – Ellison's own definition of "signifying" as "meaning, in the unwritten dictionary of American Negro usage, 'rhetorical understatements.'"[48] In his exaggerations, Waller punctuates the lyrics in what Berger describes as his satirical response to the vapidity of the popular lyrics he was forced to record for Victor (1973). Thus, at the end of the song when he replaces short words with long words, he signifies on his own song, almost talking the last verse and replacing the lyrics, "I'm crazy 'bout my baby / and my baby's crazy about me," with "I'm exasperated by the offspring and the offspring's exasperated by me." By replacing the colloquial "baby" with literal – and I might say *technical* – "offspring" and "crazy" with "exasperated," Waller is literalizing (through their exaggeration) the clichés of thinking of a lover as a baby and love itself as madness. Waller's literalization of cliché is very different from Ira Gershwin's quotation of cliché: his performance comes much closer to that of Flannery O'Connor.[49] Another exaggerating punctuation of the lyrics can be seen in the rhythmic repetitions and variations of the words of the bridge he performs – "Parson, get that book out, / Ready in your hand, / Keep a steady lookout, / You can understand"[50] – which, in their progressive syllabic and syncopated elaborations perhaps present, as Machlin suggests, "an oblique commentary on the parson's inability to hold the book 'steady in his hand.'"[51] Such punctuation, by the way, is directly analogous to the technical elaborations and improvisations, of both notes and chords, of the stride piano.

I am using the term "punctuation" with a meaning that is close to Roland Barthes's term *punctum*, by which he designates the temporal node of haunting mortality he perceives in photography which "rises from the scene, shoots out of it like an arrow, and pierces me."[52] Barthes's example is a haunting one: "In 1865," he writes,

> young Lewis Payne tried to assassinate Secretary of State W. H. Seward. Alexander Gardner photographed him in his cell, where he was waiting to be hanged. The photograph is handsome, as is the boy: that is the *studium*. But the *punctum* is: *he is going to die*. I read at the same time: *This will be* and *this has been*; I observe with horror an anterior future of which death is the stake. By giving me the absolute past of the post (aorist), the photograph tells me death in the future. What *pricks* me is the discovery of this equivalence. In front of the photograph of my mother as a child, I tell myself: she is going to die: I shudder, like Winnicott's psychotic patience, *over a catastrophe which has already occurred*. Whether or not the subject is already dead, every photograph is this catastrophe. (96)

The "equivalence" Barthes describes is precisely the action of signifyin'. That is, with his *punctuation*, Waller is performing the opposite of the reductive invisibility Ellison describes in Armstrong and in his novel that makes physical substances unselfconsciously significatory, as in calling Waller "Fats" or Armstrong "Satch" or any African American person invisibly "colored." In the verbal patter commenting on his songs as well as the lyrical-musical patter riffing on the songs, Waller is achieving more than the "effective and penetrating" satire that Machlin describes (though he is certainly doing this). He is also *signifying* his song, as he did Gershwin's and many lesser songs (he even begins "Two Sleepy People" as "Two Sloppy People"),[53] as he did Duncan and his stride teacher James P. Johnson, as he did ragtime with his stride piano. To articulate "baby" as "offspring" is to make reference visible in a particular performative gesture.

Berger offers a fine examination of the kinds of signifying Waller performs. "His favorite targets," Berger writes,

> were crooners, popular tenors, Broadway or Hollywood musical leading men, and occasionally even an operatic style. He sang sweetly, harshly, in falsettos, whispering, shouting, imploring, disbelieving, flattering, insulting, condescending, praising, exhorting, and warning. He went so far as to make fun of the blues in a tune he wrote, 'B Flat Blues,' which he introduced by demolishing the many fake imitators of that genre (if only they had been listening and could recognize what was being done to them). He starts with a deep, impressive voice, as if he were an M. C. 'Lads and lassies, we bring you the B Flat Blues, the woozy-woozy bluesy-*woozy* woozy blues. Here 'tis, take it easy, now. Get in the groovie and make a movie.' The only music that he played without ever mocking it was the spiritual, which he recorded beautifully but infrequently on the organ.[54] (7–8)

I suspect that, if he could, he would have played "Black and Blue" without mockery as well; this might explain why he never recorded it. Berger also notes that Waller "was a master of the scat vocal" and "one of the earliest jazz singers to engage in the bantering vocal duet, recording one with Jack Teagarden as early as 1931" (10).

Waller's signifying performance – what we might call his "bodily music" – is illuminated by another remark of Ellison's. In his essay "Change the Joke and Slip the Yoke," Ellison takes up Armstrong again in ways that encompasses Waller as performer. (Waller was Armstrong's contemporary although he died many decades before Armstrong did.) Ellison is discussing the trickster in literature who, he quotes a friend and literary critic arguing, "represents a personification of the body." (Is this personification like the name "Fats"? like "Satchelmouth"?) Such bodily representations, Ellison suggests, can be used to other effects, apprehended in terms of potential as well as literal meaning. Ellison's friend Stanley Hyman, he writes,

> would have found in Louis Armstrong a much better example of the trickster, his medium being music rather than words and pantomime. Armstrong's clownish license and intoxicating powers are almost Elizabethan; he takes liberties with kings, queens and presidents; emphasizes the physicality of his music with sweat, spittle and facial contortions; [and] he performs the magical feat of making romantic melody issue from a throat of gravel . . .[55]

In doing these things – all of which Waller does as well – Ellison suggests, Armstrong makes body and sound referentially human and, in the manner he describes "Black and Blue" in *Invisible Man*, timely in their performance. The signifying entertainments of both Armstrong and Waller are not the acts "of a concealment in darkness in the Anglo-Saxon connotation of the word," Ellison describes later, "but that of a voice issuing its little wisdom out of the substance of its own inwardness – after having undergone a transformation from ranter to writer" (71). Such transformation is above all a matter of technique in its replacement of ranting with writing. In another essay from *Shadow and Act* – an essay entitled "The Golden Age, Time Past" that creates a "node" of time in the jam sessions at Minton's Playhouse in Harlem – Ellison notes that we should not "overlook the despair which must have swept Minton's before the technical mastery, the tonal authenticity, the authority and the fecundity of imagination of such men as Hawkins, Young, Goodman, Tatum, Teagarden, Ellington and Waller" (209). There is technical mastery that realizes itself in the signifying practices of improvisation.

Waller's technical mastery, tonal authority, and fecundity of imagination embodied themselves, tricksterlike, in the manner in which his stride piano embodies, referentially, the meaning of the competitive and communal interactions of his Harlem culture, the meaning of the competitive and evolutionary interactions of improvisational music, and the significations, human and satirical, of the clichés of popular songs. Such "technical mastery," like the emphasis on the referential signifier in signifyin', which is very different from the emphasis on the physical in racism, is the motor of competitive and communal interactions: it allows for "individual techniques" of the marvel of social organization Ellison describes in jazz's jam sessions. "Louis Armstrong," Berger argues,

> respected these songs in the sense that he played and sang them seriously, cutting their sugariness with his own deep emotional approach that always seems too good for them . . . But Fats Waller went at this music differently. Although he improvised on it superbly, he couldn't resist making fun of the lifeless lyrics when he came to the vocal choruses. His ingenuity in demolishing the pathetic pretensions of these verses constitutes an art form in itself.[56]

That form is that of signifying, the art that gathers up in nodes of punctuated time rhythms, conversation, and culture – rhythm, montage, and wholeness – and makes them apprehensible and visible in song.

CHAPTER 6

Music without composition: Billie Holiday and ensemble performance

> I don't think I'm singing. I feel like I am playing a horn. I try to improvise like Les Young, like Louis Armstrong, or someone else I admire.
>
> Billie Holiday[1]

In the preceding chapters, I have discussed the popular music of the Gershwins, of Cole Porter, of Fats Waller. In doing this, I have focused on the relationships among music, language, and culture – and, particularly, on social, psychological, and linguistic aspects of the modernist culture of America between the two world wars. George and Ira Gershwin's parents were recent immigrants to America when Ira (Isadore) was born in December 1896 (the family was living on the lower east side of Manhattan) and George (Jakob) in September 1898 (the family was living in Brooklyn); the Gershwins lived a secularized life in America, and they were never poor. Cole Porter was born in Peru, Indiana, to a wealthy family in 1891; he attended Yale and served in World War I. Thomas Waller was born on 134th Street in New York in 1904, in the heart of Harlem, of parents who had married in Virginia and moved to New York to raise their family; Waller's father, Edward Martin Waller, worked in a stable and, before Waller's birth, became a deacon in the Abyssinian Baptist Church, where his wife Adeline – Waller's mother – sang in the choir and played the piano and organ for services. All of these people had beginnings very different from that of Eleanora Fagan – later known as Billie Holiday – who was born in Philadelphia in 1915 to a young, unmarried woman of twenty, Sadie Harris, and spent her childhood, in and out of her mother's care, in Baltimore. Growing up, she worked in brothels, both as a servant and, in her teens, as a prostitute, and sang at clubs for tips. She and her mother moved to New York, and in 1933, when she was eighteen, John Hammond – "the farsighted millionaire who had left Yale to pursue his interests in jazz and leftist politics" – heard her singing from table to table at Monette's in

Harlem.[2] "When I first heard Billie sing at Monette Moore's," he remembered years later, "I heard something that was completely new and fresh – the phrasing, the sound of an instrumentalist."[3]

Unlike the other musicians I have discussed – even Waller – Billie Holiday was essentially a performer, and, more than this – and even more than the Gershwin brothers – an *ensemble* performer. In his autobiography, thinking about the great talent he was able to assemble (he introduced Holiday to Benny Goodman, Teddy Wilson, Lester Young, Ben Webster, Roy Eldridge), Hammond noted, "It astonishes me, as I look back, at how casually we were able to assemble such all-star groups. It wasn't that we didn't know how great they were. We did. It simply was a Golden Age; America was overflowing with a dozen truly superlative performers on every instrument."[4] If, in the preceding chapters, I have focused on the relationship between music and language, Billie Holiday *realizes* the music she sang and recorded – the songs of the Gershwins repeatedly, Porter occasionally, Waller on rare, late occasions – in terms of the relationship between music-and-language and its articulation in rhythm and tone. Music comes to life in Holiday's performances – the very *language structure* of music, in Igor Stravinsky's description, comes to life – in ways that gather up the musical modernism of America between the world wars.

PERFORMING MUSIC

In his analysis of the recordings of Billie Holiday, the great historian of jazz Gunther Schuller offers this remarkable description of her work in the late 1930s. He notes how her songs were recorded without rehearsal or even pre-recording meetings among the performers, without an agreed-upon game plan, without the designation of someone to be the final arbiter of musical decisions, without written or even simply planned arrangements. "But, of course," he writes,

> [John] Hammond didn't want arrangements for Billie – a laudable and correct premise, but not without its risks. With almost no preparation, quickly fashioned head arrangements, no composing (even in the Ellingtonian sense), no absolute leader in an essentially collective-ensemble approach: given these conditions, it is a miracle that performances have stylistic integrity as often as they do. In retrospect those risks were worth taking.[5]

Holiday and her ensembles – the Teddy Wilson recordings, those under the name of the "Billie Holiday Orchestra," even her early work with Benny Goodman, her stint with the big-band Count Basie Orchestra, and the remarkable late performance of "Fine and Mellow" produced for CBS in 1957 – seemed to constellate music without composition in the manner that physical, biological, and cultural phenomena seem to "self-organize" without a central organizing agency.

Needless to say, Schuller's account of the lack of central control is powerfully – and to large degree properly – countered by Farah Jasmine Griffin's study of the "myths" of Billie Holiday, where she traces the manner in which Holiday controls and organizes her music, and argues throughout that the myth of untutored talent is simply not true.[6] Examining surreptitious recordings of a rehearsal between Holiday and her accompanist, Jimmy Rowles, Griffin notes that Holiday speaks in "a voice that is street-smart yet loving, at times vulnerable and self-doubting and most often in control – clapping out rhythms, setting the key, directing the other musicians, as leader, collaborator and peer" (85). Still, even Griffin quotes Rowles's comment that "When Lady made those 78s with Teddy Wilson, she was just a vocalist. The records were issued under Teddy's name, and she only sang a chorus. But on the records we made together she was the artist – even though she just acted like one of the guys."[7] And Robert O'Meally – who also persuasively argues for Holiday's artistic control of her work – notes that "the first great Billie Holiday period ["the early years of her recording at Columbia, from 1935 to 1939," he notes] was her jam session/after-hours period, when she did not attend lessons or rehearsals per se; rather, *she lived in terms of the music at all times*."[8] O'Meally goes on to quote Teddy Wilson's detailed description of going over music with Holiday in order for her to "get it into her ear": Holiday's "ear was phenomenal," Wilson writes, "but she had to get a song into her ear so she could do her own style on it" (111). When the pianist Bobby Henderson first met Holiday – she was sixteen, singing at Basement Brownie's in Harlem – even "before hearing Holiday sing a note, Henderson could tell from this encounter that she was not just another singer. She had stood back and listened while he had told his story on the keyboard. He had used a well-known tune as his vehicle, but she had spotted his personal variation on it. She was listening to the music in precisely the same way a hip instrumentalist would. As the saying of the day went, 'She had *ears*'" (24).

My point here about Holiday's music, however, is that the issues of "control" and "intention" – and even propriety and proprietariness – are all somewhat besides the point in discussing musical performance (and, to some degree, popular music more generally),[9] and in this chapter I examine Holiday's performances against the paradigmatic governance of music by composer, conductor, or even key. Very often Holiday sang in the odd – off-the-beaten-track – key of G♭. G♭, Salim Washington has noted, is a very difficult key for people who learn music by reading rather than by ear. "This opposition between literacy and orality," Washington notes, "is significant . . . because those who learn to play by reading music invariably learn from a paradigm which contains no sharps or flats: the key of C. Those who learn to play by ear, depending upon the instrument, do not necessarily (and most certainly not invariably) learn from a paradigm key."[10] Citing this passage, Farah Jasmine Griffin quotes pianist Jimmy Rowles as saying that Holiday "used to come up with some awful keys – six flats unfurnished" (89). This need to avoid a paradigmatic key led the great master of musical formalism, Johann Sebastian Bach, to promote the great Enlightenment compromise of Western music, the well-tempered keyboard that I discussed in Chapter 1.[11] But Holiday pursued the democracy of communal music outside the mechanical formalism of a keyboard machine, in the semantic formalism of her music and song.

That is, what I examine in this chapter are the *meanings* that arise or emerge from her performances – performances which might aptly be described in the words of John Holland (a prominent researcher in artificial intelligence) as "emergent behavior that occurs without direction by a central executive."[12] Such performances produce or embody what I am calling "semantic formalism," experienced meanings that emerge out of configurations (or "constellations") of phenomena and are therefore not *fully* governed by specific, individual intentions. The idea of semantic formalism, as I noted earlier, is closely related to Igor Stravinsky's description of the possibilities of "a reflective system between the language structure of the music and the structure of the phenomenal world."[13] Stravinsky's use of the terms "reflection" and "structure" suggests in both the cases of art and of experience that art does more than simply reveal the "structures" implicit in experience; it also organizes that experience as well – momentarily and locally configuring and answering experience.[14] The term "structure" also suggests the formalism of – and, consequently, an important element of non-intentionality within – this procedure. Such a reflective system between the "language structure" of experience or knowledge and "the structure of the phenomenal world" is a version of what Bakhtin calls the "answerability" of art to culture. It is the *formality* of these meanings – functioning like musical forms: twelve-bar blues, thirty-two-bar ballads as well as the late Beethoven quartets Stravinsky is discussing – that positions them, like Holiday's ensemble music, as not entirely intentional, "with almost no preparation, . . . no composing (even in the Ellingtonian sense), no absolute leader."[15] Daniel Albright contends that Stravinsky's observation asserts "the deep equivalence of the natural and the artificial,"[16] so that the form of the organizing principle of "the language structure of the music" Stravinsky describes neither precedes nor comes after the phenomena it organizes. Instead, both form and phenomenal meaning arise together and thereby "reflect" one another. This is true of other "modernist" formal systems of the turn of the twentieth century such as the periodic table, the innovative notation system of mathematics Einstein developed for the Special Theory of Relativity, even the poetic structures of an imagist poem. Enlightenment modernity developed hierarchies of law and phenomenon, system and "fact" – whether it claimed the phenomenal acoustical physics preceded the order of keys or that the formal tonic governed phenomenal melodies – but in the new twentieth century, as Mary Poovey has shown,[17] across a host of disciplines the hierarchy between system and fact gave rise to the kind of "reflective" relationship Stravinky is describing.

The nature of the semantic formalism I am unfolding is particularly clear in the relationship between words and music in Holiday's performances. The fact that Holiday listened to music "the same way a hip instrumentalist would" suggests that the semantic *meaning* of the texts she hears and sings, while not totally disregarded, takes its place within – is comprehended as a reflection of – the larger configuration of phenomena as *musical*.[18] Thus, Schuller notes that "the primary creative impulse in [Holiday's] singing came not from the printed page and the priority of the text, as with most orthodox singers, but from a basically instrumental conception into which text and original melodic line were subsumed. Other singers would *perform* or *render* a song, [Holiday] would *create* one." "On the whole," he goes on,

> she resolved the problem of not letting the words (by often less-than-first-rate lyricists) interfere with her singing by instrumentalizing the material at hand, and by alchemizing words and music into a new alloy in which the parts were no longer separable.[19]

Schuller's odd metaphor, "alchemizing" words, points to the anagogic nature of this phenomenon which I discuss later in this chapter. One version of this "alchemizing" that I examined in relation to Cole Porter in Chapter 4 is the transformation of words to sound. Scat singing seems a clear example of this, yet Schuller makes clear that scat never quite abandons its *semantic* content, even when it presses to do so: "the voice," he writes, "is not only the most personal of instruments, but it deals of necessity with texts (or – in scat-singing – with syllables that nevertheless have abstract verbal associations)" (528). Scat, then, is a form of decomposition that also creates *musical* meanings.

Holiday rarely (if ever) performed scat, yet her songs absorb ("alchem-ize"?) meaning into music. In his comparison of Holiday and Bing Crosby singing "I'll Be Seeing You" in 1944, David Brackett contrasts Crosby with Holiday. Crosby renders the lyrics as "a type of song about generalized loss that was common and popular during World War II . . . 'I'll Be Seeing You' fits comfortably into this category and, indeed, Crosby was closely associated with entertaining the troops during the war."[20] "In Billie Holiday's performance" – a recording of this performance is available on Commodore CCD 7001 – on the other hand, Brackett points out,

> we no longer hear the qualities with which Crosby's audience identified; it does not matter any more that the song was recorded during the war; indeed, the specific details of the song – the "park across the way," "the children's carousel," "the chestnut tree" – all seem somewhat ludicrous in the new context . . . Holiday's performance, in contrast to the generic reassurance provided by Crosby, vitiates the banality of much of the song's lyrics: the clichés "every lovely summer's day" and "every thing that's bright and gay" are withered by the sadness of Holiday's voice: we cannot believe that this singer will experience another "lovely summer's day"; the vocal flip on "lovely" both accentuates the word and produces a distancing effect by emphasizing its sonic materiality. (61–62)

When Brackett describes the "sadness" of her voice – and Schuller writes in similar but more developed terms of "the ultimate anguished meaning" of her singing – they are flirting with a sense of Holiday's singing as essentially expressive.[21] What is more important to emphasize, however, is the manner in which she *musically* "vitiates" banality and cliché by transforming words into music and into musical meanings, the "alchemy" of semantic formalism.

That is, the emphasis on the "sonic materiality" of her singing – and, I might add, of much modernist art, in literature, painting, architecture, which also emphasizes the materiality of its meanings – allows its "semantic formalism" (or "reflection" or "co-presence" or "alchemy" – words stutter here) to be felt as real and as "reality" itself that has less to do with "sadness" and "anguish" than a realized wholeness articulated through the montage of rhythmic decomposition. In an analysis I have already alluded to, Walter Benn Michaels argues that this combination of materiality and meaning, in the repeated "versions" of the *sounds* /ing/, /and/, /all/ of William Carlos Williams's "Spring and All," makes "their 'reality' *as* words visible" – which is to say creates the semantic effect of "reality" in his poetry.[22] In Holiday, I am arguing, this phenomenon is clearer, *audible*, so that we are confronted with a semantic effect that seems to grow out of – or simply inhabit – the material sound itself. Surely this is what Brackett means by "the sadness of Holiday's voice" and Schuller means by "the mood of utter loneliness" that arises from her ensemble performance of Ellington's "Solitude." Sounds *perform* such meaning that is felt but cannot be located in any particular element of their soundings. Such a performance, as Steven Mithen argues, is "gestural."[23]

Such more or less "non-intentional" meanings – they are not *simply* unintentional – are repeatedly enacted in the powerful musical performances of Holiday, who, after all, *performed* the works of Gershwin, Porter, and Waller I have discussed throughout *Modernism and Popular Music*. More particularly, they can be discerned, as Schuller and Brackett point out, within the tonal and especially the rhythmic qualities of her performances taken as a whole. And they are, I am arguing, both the source and the power of Holiday's musical art. Unlike the seemingly more intentional work of the best of the composers she sang – the planned, organized, and above all "New York" meanings of the Gershwin brothers; the private rhythms, rhyming, and desires of Cole Porter; and even the remarkable striding scat of Fats Waller – Holiday's music creates its meanings within the aesthetics of the constellated ensembles of performed (and, in this sense, "popular") music. Her ensemble music is not exactly improvised, as is Waller's;[24] it does not fully push towards the translation of words into sounds, meanings into rhythms, as do the haunting musics of Porter; nor does it attempt – or single-mindedly attempt – to represent and participate in the world in which it exists, as do the songs and lyrics of the Gershwins.

MUSIC AND THE QUALITY OF RHYTHM

An important aspect of the performance of popular music, as Middleton notes – and an important aspect of Billie Holiday's performances – is the quality of rhythm.[25] As O'Meally says, "more than any other aspect of her singing, musicians and other close listeners have singled out Holiday's unfailing rhythm as the beautiful base upon which her distinctively sculpted songs were placed." O'Meally goes on to quote Bobby Tucker – "one of the best in a long line of Holiday's excellent piano collaborators" – asserting that Holiday "was the easiest singer I ever played for" and that "she had the greatest conception of a beat I ever heard."[26] "As a keeper of the time," O'Meally concludes, "she was as surefooted as a drummer or rhythm guitar player" (38).[27] Holiday rarely in her career worked with big bands – Schuller's observation which I quoted on page 156 is about her small ensemble work, which constitutes the huge bulk of her performances and recordings – but early in her career she did sing with the Count Basie Orchestra, notably in recordings of Gershwin's "They Can't Take that Away from Me," which I mentioned in Chapter 3 in relation to quotation.[28] Of course, all lyric singing is a kind of "quotation," but what is striking in Holiday's singing of Gershwin is the beat and rhythm of quotation. "As a rhythm singer," O'Meally writes, "she was just right for Basie's rhythm machine, wherein Basie (as Ralph Ellison has observed) would use the whole band as if it were a drum."[29]

In Holiday's recording of "They Can't Take that Away from Me" – the 1937 recording is a radio "aircheck" rather than a studio recording, a performance that is widely available, e.g., *Love Songs Billie Holiday* – Holiday's rhythm is as steady as O'Meally describes it, yet it is performed constantly behind the beat. Stuart Nicholson describes "her secure, behind-the-beat rewriting of 'They Can't Take That Away From Me'" as "so contagious that it lingers in the memory long after the record has stopped."[30] Such rhythmic "rewriting" is remarkable in this recording: the bridge is constantly behind Basie's band culminating in the last line of the bridge, "Still I'll always, always keep / The mem'ry of–," that seems to change the time signature of the lyrics altogether so that, while still as strict as a "metronome" and against Basie's time which is also strict as a metronome, she almost sounds like she is talking against the orchestra's different beat. What Humphrey Lyttelton said of her performance of "I'll Get By" can be said of this performance of "They Can't Take that Away from Me":

> the art of this exaggeratedly 'laid back' phrasing, distinguishing it from mere affectation, is that the listener should not detect the point at which the performer catches up with the regular metre. The listener who expects Billie to re-orientate herself by clinging, if only for a few bars, to the beat must wait, in this instance, for ever. Like a child striding out to avoid stepping on the lines between paving-stones, she picks her way through the entire vocal chorus without once stepping fairly and squarely on the beat.[31]

The performance of the Gershwin song, like that of "I'll Get By," is a clear example of what Gilles Deleuze describes as the "singular behavior" of "true repetition"[32] I cited in Chapter 3, and just as the Gershwins' song, as I mentioned earlier, grasps the "gestures of the body" as things to be possessed and quoted, so Holiday "gestures" with her voice, halfway between singing and discourse, in the ensemble of the Count Basie Orchestra performance.

As already mentioned, however, the bulk of Holiday's recorded performances were in small ensembles, and such performances epitomize

Holiday's "collective-ensemble approach" that Schuller describes.[33] Stuart Nicholson, Holiday's biographer, offers a specific example of this. The recording date of January 1937, he notes, "was the most musically intimate of all Billie's sessions to date, the optimum environment for her great talent and those of the soloists who surrounded her. Gone was the rhetorical bombast of a Jonah Jones [Basie's drummer] or the exuberance of a Roy Eldridge; now Billie was supported by musicians who were acutely aware of what she was trying to achieve and were uniquely qualified to help her realize it. [Benny] Goodman, [Lester] Young and [Buck] Clayton [again, Basie's trumpet player], accustomed to the grander gestures required in big band solo work, would revel in the atmosphere of free exchange in [Teddy] Wilson's relaxed musical democracy."[34] Bruce Crowther and Mike Pinfold describe this phenomenon in the special relationship between Holiday and the saxophonist Lester Young, with whom she recorded music from 1937 to 1941. "The musical partnership of Holiday and Young was remarkable . . . Their bond was of minds, hearts and emotions. There have been many such relationships in jazz, but they have been between two instrumentalists: Louis Armstrong with Earl Hines and with Jack Teagarden, Dizzy Gillespie and Charlie Parker, Goodman and Wilson . . . etc. There are few, if any, comparable blendings of singer and instrumentalist . . . Individually, Holiday and Young were unique; together, they comfortably subordinated themselves to the partnership and miraculously retained their individuality; and as a pair they were similarly unique in the annals of jazz."[35]

The partnership of Holiday and Young can be heard in another Gershwin song, the 1939 recording of "The Man I Love." (This recording is widely available, for example on *Love Songs Billie Holiday*.) Gershwin's song, as I mentioned in Chapter 3, is remarkable in its counterpoint of tonal melody and what I call the "chronological bass." In this recording, what is striking is the contrast between Holiday's chorus and Lester Young's solo: the difference between Holiday's consistent delayed singing – singing off the beat – and Young's consistent use of the beat. "Listening to Young's solos with [Holiday]," Nicholson writes, "one is immediately struck by their restraint, one of the hallmarks of his style. He always sounded unhurried and there is never the crowded feeling of gratuitous virtuosity . . . His solos always seemed conceived as a whole, minor architectonic miracles where nothing could be added or subtracted without destroying the symmetry of the whole."[36] Against the wholeness and strictness of Young's solo, Holiday's choruses – both before and after the solo – constantly off the beat, delayed, seemingly at cross purposes with the strict rhythms of the song, perform rhythmic decomposition, just as she did with the Count Basie Orchestra.

The quality of rhythm is crucial for ensemble performance and for Holiday's power. "Rhythm," the cognitive psychologist Merlin Donald has noted, "is a uniquely human attribute; no other creature spontaneously tracks and imitates rhythms in the ways humans do, without training. Rhythmic ability is supramodal; that is, once a rhythm is established, it may be played out with any motor modality, including the hands, feet, head, mouth, or the whole body."[37] Elsewhere he says rhythm "is a fuzzy skill, where the Gestalt, or overall pattern, dictates the shape of the action."[38] The overall pattern here of this song, as it is in much of Holiday's early ensemble work, is that of call and answer – perhaps reminiscent of the African "ring shout" Griffin describes[39] – where Holiday answers Gershwin's bass with her rhythmically "delayed" discourse that both sings and opposes song with an almost talking language.

The interplay of song and speech organizes the *meaning* here:[40] it is the formality – and formalism – of a specific binary opposition, but insofar as it gathers itself up in the ensemble of this music, it is what Angela Davis calls (in a little different context) a "noncontradictory opposition."[41] If the genius of song is the powerful relationship it offers between the performative "force" of music and the constative "meanings" of language, Holiday makes this opposition work in both the lyric–music opposition in Gershwin and the vocal–instrument opposition in the ensemble. That is, in her performances Holiday renders language and its formal properties as a kind of music and, at the same time, renders the formalities of music into powerful meanings: this is her "reflective" art, the felt immediacy of her song that Brackett, Schuller, and many others note. "Never much of a scat singer . . . ," O'Meally argues,

> Holiday used her impeccable diction to make herself into a great interpreter, often really a subtle destroyer and then rebuilder, of her songs' lyrics. To magnificent effect, she delivered her songs on a visceral as well as an intellectual level. Every note was an idea, and every idea was a comment on (if not an outright complement to) the given song's meaning as expressed in its lyrics. In the best Holiday material, all the ideas fit together to create a wonderful musical unity: melody sustained mood, emotion sustained quality of voice.[42]

The means of this success, however, was not simply the counterpoint of words and music, as seen in the great composers of popular music in the thirties.

Rather, Holiday's music was of a piece, so to speak, just as her ensemble work was of a piece. Schuller describes it this way: "it was her hornlike approach to singing that so endeared her to musicians and that allowed her to fit so seamlessly into an overall performance."[43] Perhaps a better description is Davis's more general account of the blues as the construction of "seemingly antagonistic relationships as *noncontradictory oppositions*."[44] Her example – one that fits Holiday precisely – is "a female narrator in a women's blues song who represents herself as entirely subservient to male desire might simultaneously express autonomous desire and a refusal to allow her mistreating lover to drive her to psychic despair" (xv). But another example – that fits *this* argument – is a singer who represents herself or some impersonal situation in words and simultaneously articulates representations in the musical sounds – tones, phrasings, rhythms – of those words. Billie Holiday, Davis argues, "can be said to have drawn upon a cultural tradition rooted in West African histories in which the communicative power of speech is grounded in and enhanced by its 'musical' structure, and in which the communicative power of music is grounded in and enhanced by its relation to speech" (174).

Davis's description of Holiday's remarkable performances can be more clearly discerned in terms of the possible relationships between music and lyric enacted by her contemporary composers: the Gershwin brothers *collaboratively* organize words and music; Porter does it by himself; and Waller takes the words and music of others – sometimes even his own music, lyricked, so to speak, by Andy Razaf – and comments verbally on those other words and music. Holiday, on the other hand, rarely distorts the lyrics in her song – she is universally praised for the clarity of her diction – and, as already noted, she rarely, if ever, scat-sings. Instead she plays with and, I might say, "re-composes," the *form* of her music, melody above all but, notably in "The Man I Love," melody that emphasizes rhythm, to create meaningful formalism that is subtly "reflective" of "phenomenal meaning." This is Stravinsky's description of Beethoven and of music in general I mentioned earlier: the creation in music of a "language structure" of its own that "reflects" the structure of experience.[45] In her singing, the words and lyrics, remarkably, recede, not exactly into the background, but into *accompaniment* through their "noncontradictory" rhythmic counterpoint: thus, in the Basie recording of "They Can't Take That Away from Me," Holiday sings strict – though off-the-beat – lyrics while the clarinet counterpoints her "rhythm-section" singing with a jazz riff. In the 1937 recording of "Easy Living" – available, again, on *Love Songs*

Billie Holiday – first Buster Bailey improvises on the clarinet, Teddy Wilson on the piano, Lester Young on the tenor sax, then Holiday sings straight offbeat lyrics closely with Wilson in the rhythm section as Buck Clayton improvises on the trumpet.

INSTRUMENTALIZING MUSIC: THE QUALITY OF TONE

Holiday's singing supplements its rhythms with the quality of its sound. Lyttelton captures, I think, a good sense of the quality of her voice. Unlike Bessie Smith's voice, which was, he notes, "projected in conventional, if self-taught fashion, from the depths of the diaphragm," Holiday's voice "resembled Louis Armstrong's in the way that it seemed to emerge, somewhat the worse for wear, after battling its way through a jungle of tangled obstruction in the area of the throat."[46] Thus, he notes that there were those, early in her career, who claimed "that she had no voice – or, to put it more colourfully in a phrase attributed to, among others, the established star Ethel Waters – that she sang 'as if her shoes were too tight'" (199). But again, perhaps Schuller's description that I've already discussed of the "alchemicalization" of Holiday's sound, which she accomplishes "by instrumentalizing the material at hand, and by alchemizing words and music into a new alloy,"[47] might be a better place to begin examining the quality of tone than Ethel Waters's description. Schuller's metaphors – "instrumentalizing," "alloy," "alchemizing" – all point to the way that the form and the felt meaning of her performances – their semantic formalism as I am describing it – situates her within the play of formal organization and phenomenal experience found across disciplines of science, art, and understanding in the early twentieth century.

This aspect of Holiday's music can lend itself to a more precise description that I can present here in relation to tone just as I presented it earlier in relation to language. To sound technical for a moment, let me turn to a strict, "formal" definition of music. In the *Encyclopedic Dictionary of the Sciences of Language* Oswald Ducrot and Tzvetan Todorov argue that "music is a code [in that] all the elements of a composition (pitches, intensities, tones) are interrelated, but they do not signify."[48] That is, they suggest that music is the "second articulation" of a semiotic system of organized, material parts (its sound) as opposed to the "first articulation" of meanings (53). In other words, in this structuralist account music is – like mathematics and much mathematical science – seemingly a formal system without meaning, a "non-semantic formalism." The fact that brilliant achievements in music, as in mathematics and chess, have, as many have observed, been produced by people before adolescence – that is to say, before significant or extensive life experiences – seems to corroborate this formal definition of music. (It is notable, however, that lyrical popular music, like poetry itself, cannot boast such pre-adolescent achievements. Even when there are child stars, it is hard to disentangle them from the ensemble production of popular music.)

Still, others might argue, as Merlin Donald has argued, that simply because music does not involve "symbolic" or "referential" language does not mean it fails to convey meaning or that it fails to "signify."[49] Describing human cognitive activities – including, he says, "non-literate, or naive, musical invention like much of early jazz, or most sports, and of the most ancient human crafts like pottery and weaving, which are learned, to this day, largely without language"[50] – Donald argues that there is a human capacity for "mimetic skill or mimesis" (168) which can help us understand the evolution of language and consciousness. ("Rhythm," he says, "is, in a sense, the quintessential mimetic skill" [186].) That is, he argues that, if we translate Darwin into "modern terms," we can see that "Darwin was suggesting that the first aspect of voice control to evolve was prosody, not phonetics. Prosody is basically the background modulation of the voice during speech; it forms an 'envelope' of emphasis and emotion around words, and its exaggeration is the basis of chanting and song" (38).[51]

Donald goes on to argue that the "mimetic stage" of human development – including within it prosody that pre-exists phonetics – allows for a functional stage of evolutionary development that can be understood as a precursor to symbolic language and that still is found, vestigially, in human behavior (e.g., laughter, facial expressions, etc.).[52] Furthermore, the mimetic can be "taken up"– that is, "instrumentalized" with the aim of creating a "new alloy" – by symbolic systems. "Most modern art forms," he writes, "even those that depend heavily on oral or written language are cognitive hybrids. Opera and theatre are good examples, where the prosodic aspects of acting and singing, the facial expressions and gestures, and the interrelationships between principals are mimetic, whereas the lyrics and script are linguistic in content."[53] His discussion also allows us to understand the precise meanings of Schuller's metaphors: that by "*instrumentalizing* the material at hand, and by *alchemizing* words and music into a new *alloy* in which the parts were no longer separable"[54] Holiday is incorporating prosody within (or along with) the phonetics of her material, in a fashion similar to the absorption of meaning into music I mentioned earlier. (It is, perhaps, their focus on such "prosody" rather than on personal expressiveness that leads Brackett and Schuller to talk about the withering "sadness of Holiday's voice" and "its ultimate anguished meaning.") Schuller's metaphors almost suggest the elements of the aesthetics of popular music I described in the Introduction: rhythmic decomposition, montage, and wholeness.

Of course, this is what song – and *music* – always does. All singing powerfully emphasizes sound against sense. This is the work of the aesthetics of popular music. The Gershwins, as I have noted, accomplish this by *crossing* different formal musical and linguistic modalities in the clashing and blendings of their montages; Cole Porter *writes this out* in lyrics like "It's De-Lovely," examined in Chapter 4, which positions phonemes (/de/) to sound seemingly without a semantic content in his rhythmic decompositions; Fats Waller *performs* this in his signifying of music and lyrics in the sense of wholeness that emerges from his contest and banter. But more clearly than these composers, Holiday accomplishes the aesthetics of popular music by emphasizing, in her ensemble performance, the mimetic "interrelationship between principals" that Donald describes. This, I believe, is the meaning of Schuller's metaphor of her "instrumentalizing" singing: Holiday imbues – in the formality of a seemingly repeatable semiotic procedure – the meanings of language with an instrument of music. In her ensemble singing she offers a powerful aesthetic example of what Donald has called the phenomenon of "human cognitive communities" and Stanley Cavell calls "a living community."[55] Discussing the evolutionary development of language through the stage of mimetic development – here he is particularly talking about humans' unique sense of rhythm – Donald notes that "all previous [non-human] brains had been designed to fend for themselves, not to form cognitive networks with other brains. Mimesis reversed that tendency, started a distributed cognitive process, and triggered a series of cultural revolutions" (274).

If Donald is describing the "history" of Holiday's ensemble music on an evolutionary scale, Angela Davis has described this "history" more locally, as the "vocalization" of music in Holiday that grows out of what Davis calls "the African-American music tradition." "Initially," she writes,

> slave music was made by the unaccompanied human voice, because the primary musical instrument associated with various West African cultures – the drum – was banned by the slave owners, who knew that clandestine communication could be transmitted by its rhythms. The musicalization of speech arose as both aesthetic impulse and political impulse, incorporating African customs and expressing emancipatory yearnings. Through field hollers and work songs, black people communicated to one another a sense of membership in a community that challenged

their collective identity as slaves. They created a language whose meanings were indecipherable to everyone who was not privy to the required codes.[56]

The "musicalization of speech"– its "vocalization," its "instrumentalization"– complements nicely what the philosopher of music Victor Zuckerkandl describes as the essentially living and human nature of musical tones. "Only life can produce tones. Living beings, out of themselves, add tone to the physical world that confronts them; it is the gift of life to nonliving nature."[57]

Zuckerkandl distinguishes tones from sound precisely in terms of their form. A tone possesses a "dynamic quality" – he calls this "the properly musical quality of tones" (21) – that exists as part of a "musical whole," an ensemble. "The tune-deaf person," he writes, "is deaf precisely to the dynamic quality of a tone, to the quality that accrues to a tone in the context of a melody, as part of a musical whole" (20). As such, both tone and melody "have no counterpart in physical nature" (23); they are (though he doesn't use this language) formal, relational – "informational" – entities. He makes this "formal" definition clear when he asserts that "the musical difference between the two tones is, strictly speaking, not a difference of pitch but of position in the tonal system" (34). Zuckerkandl adds that "every tone of a melody, as it sounds, directly announces at what place in the system we find ourselves with it. Hearing music does not mean hearing tones, but hearing, in the tones and through them, the places where they sound in the seven-tone system." And then he adds a note to this assertion: "experiments with animals reveal the extent to which musical tone is not mere tone, an acoustical phenomenon. Conditioned reflexes, which are otherwise infallibly produced when a certain tone sounds, are not produced when the tone appears in the context of a melody" (35).

If, as I have suggested, "They Can't Take That Away from Me" and "The Man I Love" present what I might fancifully call the "speechification" of music in Holiday's rhythmically delayed singing, then a late example of her singing, again with Lester Young, might offer a final example of her ensemble music. This late song, "Fine and Mellow," recorded for the 1957 CBS special *The Sound of Jazz*, is a rare blues in her recordings (Figure 15).[58]

> My man don't love me
> Treats me oh so mean
> My man he don't love me
> Treats me awfully
> He's the lowest man
> That I've ever seen

Figure 15 "Fine and Mellow," words and music by Billie Holiday

He wears high trimmed pants
Stripes are really yellow
He wears high trimmed pants
Stripes are really yellow
But when he starts in to love me
He's so fine and mellow

Love will make you drink and gamble
Make you stay out all night long
Love will make you drink and gamble
Make you stay out all night long

Love will make you do things
That you know is wrong

But if you treat me right baby
I'll stay home everyday
But if you treat me right baby
I'll stay home everyday
But you're so mean to me baby
I know you're gonna drive me away

Love is just like the faucet
It turns off and on
Love is just like the faucet
It turns off and on
Sometimes when you think it's on baby
It has turned off and gone.

In fact, one of the distinguishing features of Holiday's music is that her almost constant vehicles were Tin Pan Alley tunes, most often undistinguished songs, though she also recorded performances of Gershwin, Porter, and Waller.[59] But the blues is a particularly good example for what I am describing in Holiday because it grows out of a tradition, as Davis argues, of the communal articulations of music. Moreover, this late performance is particularly important because it has commanded the attention of many who appreciate Holiday from Schuller to Nat Hentoff (who co-produced the TV special for CBS) to Farah Jasmine Griffin (who ends her study of Holiday with a coda focused upon this performance). In any case what Holiday accomplishes in her song is the gathering up of emotive, gestural phenomena embodied – assembled, ensembled in Zuckerkandl's "tone" – into a meaning system. What I am describing here as "semantic formalism" is an abstract way of expressing what Mikhail Bakhtin calls the "answerability" of discourse.[60] His term is particularly apt in relation to this performance of "Fine and Mellow": as in a jam session, one performer after another answers her or his predecessor and the music itself. Particularly striking here, I think, is the way that Lester Young answers Ben Webster, the way that he replays melody against what can only be called Webster's riffing on the blues chords. That is, Webster's music is unsingable – unless it is scat-sung – while Young offers a new melody that is very different from the blues "jazzing" that precedes him in that one can imagine lyricking and singing it.

In fact, Young does sing it in the same way that Holiday performs and realizes the "sonic materiality" of sadness in Brackett's description of her performance of "I'll Be Seeing You." Nat Hentoff describes how sick Young was for this performance – he had missed several big-band solos earlier in the show – and how "somehow he managed to stand up, and then he blew the sparest, purest blues chorus I have ever heard."[61] Schuller describes this solo more fully:

> For [Young], so sick that he could hardly stand, barely able to draw enough breath to sustain even a short phrase, nonetheless rose to the occasion and played a canticle of such overwhelming expressiveness as to put all the other playing into distant perspective . . . In his twelve halting, recitativelike bars he played a bare forty-five notes . . . , this half of Webster's majestic and ornate solo . . . Lester was undoubtedly also expressing his feelings for Billie – perhaps he sensed it would be his last chance to do so – and kept his solo, like her singing, pared-down to essentials.[62]

It is Holiday's singing, though, that draws out the purity and expressiveness of Young in that she brings together all the parts of this performance into a memorable whole. In her first chorus of the blues and in answering Webster's and Young's – especially Young's – solos, she sings like the horns she admires: she sings with the beat – sometimes on it, but clearly with it – in song that is almost as melodious as Young's powerful solo.

Roy Eldridge's solo is closer to Holiday's counterpoint in "They Can't Take That Away from Me" or "The Man I Love": within the fireworks of his virtuosity, he plays a pattern of musical clichés – not unlike the Gershwins' lyrical cliché that "someday he'll come along" – in a different time signature altogether. And after this solo, Holiday answers it in the next chorus by virtually talking the lyrics: "treat me right baby / I'll stay home every day," and the other lyrics are spoken/sung against silence, with the ensemble answering/filling-in between the words.[63] The last chorus – "Love is just like a faucet" – brings everything together, anchored, I think, in the harmony of Jerry Mulligan's melodic bass and Holiday's blues lyrics. What is anchored, after all, is the ensembled "answer" of music, its ability to create a rhythmic Gestalt, an overall pattern, a shape of action. Even the "often less-than-first-rate" lyrics that Schuller describes[64] – here, Holiday's own lyrics, that liken love to a faucet in a remarkably flat, "everyday" metaphor – are overwhelmed in this musical gift that does not, I think, turn on and off. Rather, it rhymes in its gestural sounds, "gone" and "on," and offers the rhyming, rhythmic, ensembled music that, at her best, is Billie Holiday's gift to us. The ensembled musicians – Billie Holiday, Ben Webster, Lester Young, Roy Eldridge, Jerry Mulligan – gather up the power of rhyming: words, sounds, rhythms. This, I suspect, is the "action" – the "living event" – of her ensembled music.

CULTURE, FORMS, AND THE ANSWERS OF POPULAR MUSIC

In their study of Bakhtin, Gary Morson and Caryl Emerson contrast Bakhtin's notion of "answerability" with that of "responsibility": "there is an ethical component in answerability as well, of course," they write,

> but it is more abstract and less tied to a specific act. One's obligation in answerability is to rescue the other from pure potential; reaching out to another consciousness makes the other coalesce, and turns the other's "mere potential" into space that is open to the living event.[65]

Such "answerability," I believe, is predicated on the possibility of grasping phenomena whole, momentarily, in terms of their value. Moreover, its abstraction acts formally: it detaches meaning from one context and situates it in another by making the act of performance – the interchange of dialogue – the motor of its achievement. In her musical performances Billie Holiday creates such detachment – of meaning and context, meaning and gesture, words and music, phonetic and prosodic energies – in performances of rhythmic decomposition so that the cliché and banality of "I'll Be Seeing You," as Brackett notes, can unite its audience to the human sufferer. She uses that detachment to create an "answering" whole that relocates meaning.

Such "whole relocations," I believe, situate Holiday – and also the Gershwins, Porter, and Waller – within cultural modernism. Modernism itself – both Enlightenment modernity and twentieth-century modernism – created this very kind of relocation of social life, of personal experience, of linguistic forms, and of what constitutes truth and value altogether. A useful figure for such global transformation, as I mentioned earlier, is "anagogic." The term "anagogic" is odd yet powerful. In the *Merriam Webster's Dictionary*, as I noted in Chapter 2, it is described as an "interpretation of a word, passage, or text (as of Scripture or poetry) that finds beyond the literal, allegorical, and moral sense a fourth and ultimate spiritual or mystical sense." *Anagogy* designates a global meaning that is not quite reducible to this or that particular part or "kernel" of truth – whether it be the social formations, psychological experience, or linguistic structures I have traced in Gershwin, Porter, and Waller. That is, such global meaning is not something which can stand in place of something else, but a whole way of apprehending phenomena, a "take" of experience charged with its "aura," its power, in which the subjects of experience are not so much in possession of their experience as they are swept up in an experience or understanding that stakes a powerful claim upon them. Holiday's singing is such a "take," not only on music but on the very experience of the early twentieth century, with the commercialization of its new musical forms, the intimacies of mass communication, its powerful urban concentrations. But twentieth-century popular music more generally can be understood this way. Such a "take" anagogically *reorients* experience and understanding by erasing the hierarchical opposition between fact and meaning, nature and culture, absolute music and its ephemeral performances by alloying formalism and semantics. This, I am arguing, is a signal aspect of modernism that is realized in the popular music of Gershwin, Porter, Waller, and Holiday.

In an authoritative analysis, "Towards a New Reading of Gershwin," Charles Hamm argues that the "progressivist" model of musical history that organizes understanding in relation to a succession of musical styles necessarily examines the phenomenon of music – and of any other artifacts of human individual and communities – outside of "cultural life."[66] For Gershwin this has meant that he has been studied and analyzed in relation to an "authentic" jazz "performed by black musicians for black audiences" (310) and in relation to the innovative stylistics of contemporary "classical" composers, especially Charles Ives (308–09). Hamm suggests that "alternative periodizations of the history of music, based upon economic and social relationships rather than musical style" would allow us to understand Gershwin's music in new ways (319–20). Specifically, he suggests a periodization that includes

(a) From prehistory to the birth of Europe (until *c.* 500)
(b) Church music (from *c.* 500 to *c.* 1520)
(c) Court and town (from *c.* 1520 to *c.* 1740)
(d) Concert life (from *c.* 1740 to World War I)
(e) Mass media (from World War I to the present). (320)[67]

"Gershwin's music," he says – but his sense could be extended to all the great musicians I am studying in *Modernism and Popular Music* –

> comes into different focus when measured against these new frameworks. His first compositions appear at the very beginning of an era of "Mass media" or "repetition," rather than several decades into a "modern" or "twentieth-century" style period. The critical issues of his time become the impact of the electronic mass media on the invention, production, and consumption of music – not experiments in abstract manipulation of tones. (320)

Hamm is describing the way that historical musicology had traditionally "embraced the notion of 'autonomous art'" – the very Enlightenment transcendentalism I discussed in Chapter 1 – and he notes that "some music historians are now beginning to question the long-held tenets of their discipline, proposing . . . that music is best understood as a product of social and economic forces, not as an autonomous object" (318–19). That is, he is arguing (quoting the literary scholar Jerome McGann) that "works of art are 'modelling rather than mirroring forms.' That is, works of literature (or music) do not 'point to a prior, authorizing reality, they themselves *constitute* – in both the active and passive sense – what must be taken as reality'" (319). This is the very argument Stravinsky makes when he describes the "reflective system between the language structure of the music and the structure of the phenomenal world."[68]

The key term Hamm uses, I think, is the "*consumption* of music." Hamm is describing an analysis of music that emphasizes the ways it is part of the lives of those who experience it rather than a monument to those who compose it. And it is this "performative" sense of music that is best captured in Holiday's ensemble performances. Moreover, "consumption" is instructive in other ways as well. The popular music of the 1920s and 1930s takes its place, as Hamm suggests, within a consumer society in which desire rather than need organizes experience, the very organization of social relations, personal feelings, and even communal linguistic structures that governs the arts, sciences, and quotidian experience of what I am calling cultural modernism. We can see social, personal, and linguistic elements of this new order here and there, but the whole impact of it, I believe – its *anagogic* impact – is notable in the ensemble music of Holiday. In her music the received hierarchies of "modern" understanding and experience in the world – the elevation of composer over performer, meaning over sound, the proper linguistic usages of Samuel Johnson over the argot of everyday language, and tempered music over local performances – are both called upon and overturned. Such overturning is the abiding quality of modernism, inhabiting popular music as well as the high arts and sciences of the early twentieth century.

Conclusion: popular music and the revolution of the word

Throughout *Modernism and Popular Music* I have noted the ways that popular music is, in many ways, essentially performative, and in the Introduction I argued that the interpretive disciplines of the human sciences are particularly well positioned to engage with such performativity. I also suggested that such "interpretive disciplines" in important ways emerged within cultural modernism. Colin MacCabe's study, *James Joyce and the Revolution of the Word*, taking its title from Eugene Jolas's manifesto published in *transition* in 1929, situates Joyce at the heart of the modernist "revolution" that, as I mentioned earlier, made engagement with performance rather than the comprehension of authorial meaning its signal manner of comprehension. "Instead of constructing a meaning," MacCabe argues, "Joyce's texts concern themselves with the position of the subject in language,"[1] and such positioning, he claims, follows from the "fact that meaning is distributed through material and is constantly, therefore, open to further interpretations" (15). This performative engagement – shared with other modernist disciplines such as psychology, sociology, dialogics – is a function of grasping the materiality of language, as opposed to its "transcendental" meanings which, like Bach's music, seem independent of time, place, and the "accidents" of performance. Moreover, the "further interpretations" of performance entail kinds of active rewriting we have encountered in the Gershwins and Porter taking up popular forms, and the "jazz" of Waller and Holiday re-singing them. That is, such performative engagement, as I hope I have demonstrated, is particularly pronounced in popular music, whose "materiality" rings in our ears and taps our feet. Just as Billie Holiday creates senses of sadness or solitude that are strangely *impersonal* in that they are only locatable, if at all, in the sonic materiality of music, so, MacCabe says, such unlocatable – and, perhaps, dislocated – meanings are provoked by Joyce's fiction, and, I might add, in the project of "high" modernism altogether. Quoting Joyce's observation about *Dubliners* that there is a "special odour of corruption which, I hope, *floats* over my stories," MacCabe notes that "there is no single message inscribed in the code, and the meaning of the text is produced by the reader's own activity although the text determines that a certain odour of corruption will float, always in suspension, over any such meaning" (29). This is a "revolution" indeed, in reading, in experience, in the very notions of "truth," "authority," and even "coherence" that we have inherited from the Enlightenment. Finally, it is an activity that is particularly provoked by the popular arts at their best.

In a fascinating article "Words in Motion: The Movies, the Readies, and 'the Revolution of the Word,'" Michael North argues that Jolas's "revolution of the word" was particularly interested in the popular art of the movies so that there might be "a revolution of the word accomplished quite literally by bringing to language the physical dynamism and energy associated with film."[2] In 1927, North notes, Jolas described the "need [for] new words, new abstractions, new hieroglyphics, new symbols, new myths." "The mutation now going on," Jolas wrote,

> which is helped dynamically by the new technological means such as the cinema, the radio, and other mechanical forces, is about to create a linguistic interpenetration that will doubtless have its effect on the final morphological process of modern languages.[3]

"What Jolas means here," North says, glossing this passage, "is that the new media, simply as vastly powerful methods of communication, facilitate the interpenetration of national languages, but also that as languages themselves the new media merge with the existing national languages to create entirely new forms" (210). North is arguing for the inclusion of the cinema into our own – and into the "high" modernists' own – working definition of modernism, and he describes, as his title says, projects (by Bob Brown, contributing to *transition*) for the creation of "words in motion" in the forms of cinematic representations of language. North notes that "other writers for *transition* also," besides Erwin Panofsky, writing about film, as well as Brown

> insisted that "mobility" is the essence of film art, and several demanded a literature that would mimic that movement . . . [A]s Jolas put it, "we need the twentieth century word. We need the word of movement, the word expressive of the great new forces around us." Words need to move, to become a literal cinematography, because only in this way can they cut against old, accepted literary usages and also reach a wide popular audience. (213)

Brown envisioned "readies" – moving, visual words, parallel to "movies." But all around Jolas, Brown, and Panofsky were the moving words of popular music.

I have tried to describe those "moving words" throughout *Modernism and Popular Music*, to describe the "revolutions" that can be found in the brilliant words and music of the Gershwins, Porter, Waller, Holiday. In a short essay in *transition* that appeared a few years before the "Revolution of the Word" manifesto, Jolas published an essay entitled "The Revolution of Language and James Joyce" which, espousing high modernist "principles," explicitly separates the avant-garde from the "monotonous repetitiousness" and "worn-out verbal patterns" of the "traditional meaning of words,"[4] an argument that certainly understands the modernist project as self-consciously opposed to the hackneyed language of Tin Pan Alley. In this essay, he nevertheless also articulates aspects of "the disintegration of words and their reconstruction" (1928: 109) which describes many of the musical performances of language I have been describing in this study in relation to the rhythmic decomposition, montage, and whole of an aesthetics of popular music. "Audibility as a factor of prose," Jolas writes, "has always been of secondary importance in the history of literature. In the new work of Mr. Joyce, this element should be considered as of primary importance" (112). "Before the prosaic language," he writes, "there was the rhythmic one, before the epistolary language there were gestures and metaphors" (113). In the "revolution" that Jolas describes – including the "polyglot" of Joyce's expression (113) – we can hear versions of Ira Gershwin's contention that "the literary cliché," as he wrote in 1959, "is an integral part of lyric writing. The phrase that is trite and worn-out when appearing in print usually becomes, when heard fitted to an appropriate musical turn, revitalized, and seems somehow to revert to its original provocativeness."[5]

The "modernist" revolution Jolas describes is psychological as well as social, conditioned by "the discoveries of the subconscious by medical pioneers as a new field";[6] it is linguistic and, I could say, a powerful example of signifyin'. Above all, as a "revolution" it lends itself to anagogic comprehension, articulating the pity rather than the terror that Stephen Dedalus described. "In reading Work in Progress," Jolas contends,

> let us not forget that it is a joyous creation. The universe, through these newly minted words, these grotesque and striking dissociations, these rhythms and timbres, appears flooded with laughter. The eternal flux of time through space is exteriorized with the humor of an insurgent mind. He moves by a sequence that inheres in the form itself. He has his focus on a scheme of sounds that deviates

from the norm merely because we have not yet had the courage to get out of the beaten track. (115–16)

Needless to say, the popular music I have discussed in *Modernism and Popular Music* – the music we have listened to throughout these pages – is not the "revolution" of *Finnegans Wake*, the revolution of high modernism. Yet it is essentially "gestural," as Jolas says here, polyglot, playing with desire, riffing on language, and offering, in its finest examples – in the Gershwins, Porter, Waller, and Holiday – a sense that all of our actions and feelings and relationships can be comprehended under the category of music. And in that comprehension arises pleasure and fellow feeling, pity for the human sufferer. The popular music of the 1930s, I am contending – standards, jazz, enduring recordings – responds to the same world that high modernism does, in which people struggle to find community and home in the new and fantastic environment of the early twentieth century.

Notes

NOTES TO THE PREFACE

1 Theodor Adorno, *Aesthetic Theory*, trans. C. Lenhardt (New York: Routledge & Kegan Paul, 1984), pp. 17–18.

2 Robert Witkin, *Adorno on Popular Culture* (London: Routledge, 2003), pp. 179–80; italics added.

3 Igor Stravinsky, *Themes and Conclusions* (Berkeley: University of California Press, 1982), p. 147.

4 Daniel Albright, *Stravinsky: The Music Box and the Nightingale* (New York: Gordon and Breach, 1989), p. 4.

NOTES TO THE INTRODUCTION

1 Alfred Appel, Jr., *Jazz Modernism: From Ellington and Armstrong to Matisse and Joyce* (New York: Knopf, 2002), p. 13.

2 On leisure, see Campbell, *The Romantic Ethic and the Spirit of Modern Consumerism* (London: Alcuin Academics, 2005), p. 26.

3 Michel Foucault, "What Is an Author?", trans. Josué Harari, in Robert Con Davis and Ronald Schleifer (eds.), *Contemporary Literary Criticism: Literary and Cultural Studies* (White Plains: Longman, 1994), pp. 342–53. Theodor Adorno, in Fredric Jameson's account, recapitulates Enlightenment modernity's particular relation to notation – a theme of great importance in the following chapters – under the category of nominalism. "What is in many ways the most central sense of the term nominalism as Adorno uses it through *Aesthetic Theory*," Jameson argues, is that of "an event, and in particular as something that happened to the history of art itself. The historical paradigm remains the familiar one of the emergence of modernity (as we have learned to understand it in Marx's account of the commodity form, and in Weber's account of rationalization) and of modernism (as it is registered in the forms of the arts, most emblematically, from the European perspective, in Baudelaire). This mythic 'fall' – into capitalism and into modernization – was, as we have seen, already paradoxically inscribed in the very title of *Dialectic of Enlightenment*, where a repressive mimetic and self-sublating process of abstraction

and control – projected back into the origins of human history . . . – now suddenly, in the eighteenth century, seems to know a dialectical leap in which, brutally canceling its older magical and superstitious, overtly mimetic forms, it pursues the mimetic process on a higher level of abstraction, keeping faith with the deeper impulse of mimesis by systematically expunging all traces of mimesis itself, in what Adorno and Horkheimer will call the *Bilderverbot*, the ban on graven images of a henceforth secular, skeptical, mathematizing thought" (Fredric Jameson, *Late Marxism: Adorno, or, The Persistence of the Dialectic* [London: Verso, 1990], p. 161). Adorno, as will become apparent, is an important figure for the project of this book, in large part because he so thoroughly studied the homologous relationship between aesthetics and cultural formations.

4 Charles Hamm, *Putting Popular Music in Its Place* (Cambridge University Press, 1995), p. 320.

5 Joseph Horowitz notes that "in Europe, especially, 'jazz' could mean American popular music of all kinds. Europeans enthusiastically embraced it, however understood, as unique, exotic, fascinating, and fresh – 'American'" (*Classical Music in America: A History of Its Rise and Fall* [New York: Norton, 2005], p. 461).

6 For summaries of Adorno's argument see Theodore Gracyk, "Adorno, Jazz, and the Aesthetics of Popular Music," *The Musical Quarterly*, 76 (1992), 526–42; and Keith Negus, *Popular Music in Theory: An Introduction* (Hanover, NH: Wesleyan University Press, 1996). For a thoroughgoing critique of Adorno's position, see Richard Middleton, *Studying Popular Music* (Philadelphia: Open University Press, 1990).

7 Karl Marx and Friedrich Engels, *The Communist Manifesto*, in *Marx and Engels: Basic Writings on Politics and Philosophy*, ed. Lewis Feuer (New York: Anchor Books, 1959), p. 12.

8 See Ronald Schleifer, *Modernism and Time: The Logic of Abundance in Literature, Science, and Culture 1880–1930* (Cambridge University Press, 2000).

9 Kenneth Hudson, *The Archaeology of the Consumer Society: The Second Industrial Revolution in Britain* (Cranbury, NJ: Fairleigh Dickinson University Press, 1983), p. 12; see also Schleifer, *Modernism and Time*, pp. 121–22.

10 See especially Bruno Latour, *We Have Never Been Modern*, trans. Catherine Porter (Cambridge, MA: Harvard University Press, 1993).

11 Such "formality," I believe, is the basis of what Adorno describes as "nominalist" descriptions of traditional belief in the era of Enlightenment modernity insofar as the nominalism Jameson describes asserts that magical and "superstitious" beliefs can be seen as arbitrary "nominal" designations for deeper and transcendentally "formal" truths (see notes 3 and 60).

12 Mary Poovey, *A History of the Modern Fact: Problems of Knowledge in the Sciences of Wealth and Society* (Chicago University Press, 1998), pp. 3–4.

13 Igor Stravinsky, *Themes and Conclusions* (Berkeley: University of California Press, 1982), p. 147; Daniel Albright, *Stravinsky: The Music Box and the Nightingale* (New York: Gordon and Breach, 1989), p. 4.

14 Jonathan Culler, "Convention and Meaning: Derrida and Austin," in Robert Con Davis and Ronald Schleifer (eds.), *Contemporary Literary Criticism: Literary and Cultural Studies* (White Plains: Longman, 1994), p. 319.

15 A. J. Greimas, *Structural Semantics*, trans. Danielle McDowell, Ronald Schleifer, and Alan Velie (Lincoln: University of Nebraska Press, 1983), p. 133.

16 See also Ronald Schleifer, *Intangible Materialism: The Body, Scientific Knowledge, and the Power of Language* (Minneapolis: University of Minnesota Press, 2009) for the working out of this definition of language in relation to mathematical physics and evolutionary biology. In Chapter 1 below, I present particular examples of such linguistic overdetermination in the etymologies of *fret*, *accidentals*, and *modernism*.

17 Elmar Holenstein, *Roman Jakobson's Approach to Language*, trans. Catherine Schelbert and Tarcisius Schelbert (Bloomington: Indiana University Press, 1976).

18 See Bruno Latour, *The Pasteurization of France*, trans. Alan Sheridan and John Law (Cambridge, MA: Harvard University Press, 1988), p. 220; and also Latour's *We Have Never Been Modern* and *Pandora's Hope: Essays on the Reality of Science Studies* (Cambridge, MA: Harvard University Press, 1999) and my discussion of his work in Chapter 1.

19 Andreas Huyssen, *After the Great Divide: Modernism, Mass Culture, Postmodernism* (Bloomington: Indiana University Press, 1986), p. vii.

20 See David Yaffe, *Fascinating Rhythm: Reading Jazz in American Writing* (Princeton University Press, 2006), esp. pp. 96–98; Michael North, *The Dialect of Modernism* (New York: Oxford University Press, 1994); Appel, *Jazz Modernism*.

21 Theodor Adorno, *The Philosophy of Modern Music*, trans. Anne Mitchell and Wesley Blomster (New York: Seabury Press, 1973), p. 6.

22 Middleton, *Studying Popular Music*, p. 58. Keith Negus presents a fine survey of studies examining the place of music in everyday life, and in so doing, he responds to Adorno's notion of the passive, manipulated audience of popular music with a sense of an "active audience." One survey he cites describes the fact that "depending on age, 75–90 per cent of all music listening occurs in connection with some other parallel activity." He warns, however, that "if we pursue this theme too far we will be led to a dichotomy: music as foreground or music as background. Such a distinction can be misleading, implying that music can be identified as central/foreground or peripheral background, when more often it is an integral *part* that should be understood in relation to other very particular cultural practices and activities" (*Popular Music in Theory* 28). His entire chapter "Audiences" offers a fine context for the discussion of the role of the audience I am pursuing here. This sense of "integral part," erasing the opposition of foreground and background, is precisely the performative work (and "realization") of "semantic formalism."

23 David Brackett, *Interpreting Popular Music* (Cambridge University Press, 1995), pp. 16, 24. See also Roland Barthes, "The Death of the Author," in *Image-Music-Text*, trans. Stephen Heath (New York: Noonday Press, 1977), p. 148.

24 In "What Is an Author?", Foucault answers Barthes with a historical analysis of authorship which situates its emergence as part of Enlightenment modernity. "The coming into being of the notion of 'author,'" he begins, "constitutes the privileged moment of *individualization* in the history of ideas, knowledge, literature, philosophy, and the sciences" (342), and he goes on to suggest that the advent of the "author," its privileged moment, "occurred in the seventeenth or eighteenth century" (347).
25 *The Philosophy of Modern Music*, xii.
26 Brackett, *Interpreting Popular Music*, p. 24; see also my Chapter 1.
27 See Middleton, *Studying Popular Music*, pp. 103–26 for a description of a "new musicology" to account for this situation.
28 Hamm, *Putting Popular Music in Its Place*, 320; I focus on this argument in Chapter 6.
29 Middleton, *Studying Popular Music*, 58.
30 J. Hillis Miller, "The Search for Grounds in Literary Study," in Robert Con Davis and Ronald Schleifer (eds.), *Rhetoric and Form* (Norman: University of Oklahoma Press, 1985), p. 20. See also Chapter 2.
31 For a detailed formal account of these categories – organized in relation to the "semantic formalism" of speculation – see Ronald Schleifer, "The Semiotics of Speculation: A. J. Greimas and the Example of Literary Criticism," *Genre*, 42 (2009), 165–86.
32 Gracyk, "Adorno, Jazz," p. 530; Gracyk is citing Adorno, *Aesthetic Theory* pp. 160–61.
33 See Charles Hamm, *Yesterdays: Popular Song in America* (New York: Norton, 1979), p. 376.
34 See Schleifer, "The Semiotics of Speculation" for an elaboration of the appropriation of Dante's term *anagogic* in relation to Miller.
35 Jean-François Lyotard, "Answering the Question: What Is Postmodernism?" in his *The Postmodern Condition: A Report on Knowledge*, trans. Geoff Bennington and Brian Massumi (Minneapolis: University of Minnesota Press, 1984), p. 77.
36 Gunther Schuller, *The Swing Era: The Development of Jazz 1930–1945* (New York: Oxford University Press, 1989), p. 536.
37 Middleton, *Studying Popular Music*, p. 58.
38 Campbell, *Romantic Ethic*, p. 59.
39 Campbell also describes the opposition of satisfaction and pleasure in terms of the contrast between pain and pleasure. Since pain and pleasure "are not really opposites," he writes, "they cannot be regarded, in Benthamite fashion, as if they were the motivational north and south poles of conduct. Pain is a sensation, and as such can be identified and described: we may note that it is an 'aching', 'throbbing' or 'burning' pain, and is located in our foot or our head. Pleasure, on the other hand, is less an individual sensation than a quality of an experience and if asked to locate and describe pleasure we are normally forced to respond by elaborating on the nature of that experience" (63). Pleasure, he concludes, arises from *changing* stimuli: "pleasure," he says,

"appears to arise from a pattern and more usually a sequence of stimuli" so that "pleasure thus appears to be a tune made from the notes of individual stimuli, whilst pain is one or more notes of excessive volume" (64). For this reason he suggests that "it should not be surprising that some people develop a taste for 'explosive bangs' in their favourite tune" (64). In relation to this last comment, Stravinsky comes immediately to mind, whom Adorno negatively compares to Schoenberg. For a discussion of the manner in which the semiotics of pain can situate this specific "sensation" as a more general, qualitative "experience," see Schleifer, *Intangible Materialism*, Chapter 5.

40 Simon Frith, "The Good, the Bad, and the Indifferent: Defending Popular Culture from the Populists," *Diacritics*, 21 (1991), 107.

41 As I note in Chapter 5, Peter Townsend describes four "aspects" of jazz in an attempt to define "jazz as music": "repertoire, improvisation, rhythm and individual technique"; he calls these aspects "the stable elements in any consensus as to [the] musical definition" of jazz (*Jazz in American Culture*, Edinburgh: Edinburgh University Press, 2000], p. 31). Townsend's categories nicely correspond to wholeness (repertoire), montage (improvisation), and rhythmic decomposition (rhythm), which I am discussing here.

42 Robert Witkin, *Adorno on Popular Culture* (London: Routledge, 2003), p. 185.

43 Adorno, "On Popular Music," in his *Essays on Music*, ed. Richard Peppert (Berkeley: University of California Press, 2002), p. 441.

44 For a more detailed discussion of Adorno's conception of wholeness – one that suggests the ways it is *performed* in relation to the "swarm of things" he mentions below – see the discussion of metonymy in Chapter 4, particularly note 16.

45 Adorno, *Aesthetic Theory*, pp. 148–49; trans. modified by Jameson in *Late Marxism*, p. 172.

46 Albright, *Stravinsky*, p. 4.

47 Adorno, *Aesthetic Theory*, p. 89; trans. modified by Jameson in *Late Marxism*, p. 180.

48 Adorno, *Aesthetic Theory*, p. 56.

49 Claude Lévi-Strauss, *The Raw and the Cooked*, trans. John Weightman and Doreen Weightman (New York: Harper Colophon Books, 1975), p. 16.

50 Adorno, *Aesthetic Theory*, p. 223.

51 Adorno, *Aesthetic Theory*, p. 173; Jameson is quoting Adorno in *Late Marxism*, p. 223.

52 Adorno, *Aesthetic Theory*, p. 321; Jameson, *Late Marxism*, p. 181.

53 Stravinsky, *Themes and Conclusions*, p. 147.

54 Theodor Adorno, *Negative Dialectics*, trans. E. B. Ashton (New York: Continuum, 1973), pp. 17–18.

55 In his valorization of suffering over celebration in art, Adorno is also valorizing need over desire, in the opposition I described earlier in this chapter and describe again in Chapter 2 in relation to the classical economics of Enlightenment modernity and neoclassical economics of twentieth-century cultural modernism. He shares this valorization with Freud.

56 Witkin, *Adorno on Popular Culture*, pp. 179–80.

57 Raymond Williams, *The Politics of Modernism* (London: Verso, 1989).

58 See Angela Davis, *Blues Legacies and Black Feminism: Gertrude "Ma" Rainey, Bessie Smith, and Billie Holiday* (New York: Pantheon, 1998).

59 Middleton, *Studying Popular Music*, p. 106.

60 Such notational centricity is closely related to Adorno's sense of "nominalism" discussed in notes 3 and 11. Adorno's sense of nominalism as *notation* might be seen in an off-hand remark he makes in *Aesthetic Theory*: "if you listen to or read Beethoven's most articulated music with attention," he writes, "you will notice that it resembles a continuum of nothingness" (265). For Adorno, reading the score and listening to the music are interchangeable acts; nominalism is complete. In fact, Adorno's rejection of jazz improvisation as, in the words of Robert Witkin, "an example of thoroughly standardized music . . . [living] off an amalgam of utterly rigid and standard schemas and a variety of 'deviations' or 'excesses' which never overcame the fundamental conformity of the basic structure" (105) was, I believe, a function of a nominal *reading* of musical forms rather than a performative experiencing of them. Witkin's discussion of Winthrop Sargeant is powerful in the ways it demonstrates the fact that "the creative exhilaration felt by musicians and audiences alike . . . comes from the battle between the unexpected, restless challenging rhythm played against the fundamental regularity of the stated and implied pulse" (113). The exhilaration of musicians and audiences I described earlier is precisely what is lost in the equation of reading and hearing. Witkin concludes by noting that "the ethnomusicological perspective that [Sargeant] adopts is almost entirely missing from Adorno's work" (115).

61 See also Charles Keil, "Motion and Feeling through Music," *Journal of Aesthetics and Art Criticism*, 24 (1966), 337–49.

62 Middleton, "Popular Music Analysis and Musicology: Bridging the Gap," in Richard Middleton (ed.), *Reading Pop: Approaches to Textual Analysis in Popular Music* (Oxford University Press, 2000), p. 104.

63 Lévi-Strauss, *The Raw and the Cooked*, p. 105.

64 Keil, "Motion and Feeling," p. 338.

65 See Schleifer, *Intangible Materialism*, pp. 13–14, 159–60; "The Semiotics of Speculation."

66 J. L. Austin, "Three Ways of Spilling Ink," in his *Philosophical Papers* (Oxford University Press, 1979), pp. 272–87.

67 J. L. Austin, *How to Do Things with Words* (Cambridge, MA: Harvard University Press, 1962).

68 For a concise exposition of Austin's "speech-act theory," see Culler, "Convention and Meaning."

69 Colin MacCabe, *James Joyce and the Revolution of the Word* (New York: Palgrave, 2003), p. 15.

70 Recently, I have called them "speculative sciences"; see *Intangible Materialism* and "Speculation."

71 Middleton, *Studying Popular Music*, p. 104.

72 In Chapter 1, I note that the traditional literary criticism of modernism, focusing on the "spatial form" of modernist texts, also emphasizes these features which Middleton is describing in musicology.
73 Steven Mithen, *The Singing Neanderthals: The Origins of Music, Language, Mind and Body* (Cambridge, MA: Harvard University Press, 2006), p. 74.
74 Keil, "Motion and Feeling," p. 349 n. 33.
75 Middleton, "Popular Music Analysis," p. 106.
76 Middleton, "Popular Music Analysis," p. 120.
77 John Casti, *Complexification: Explaining a Paradoxical World through the Science of Surprise* (New York: HarperPerennial, 1995), pp. 79–80. See also Schleifer, *Intangible Materialism*, pp. 58–63 and "The Semiotics of Speculation."
78 Middleton, "Popular Music Analysis," p. 105; he is citing Maróthy.
79 Frith, "The Good, the Bad," p. 107.

NOTES TO CHAPTER 1

1 Modris Eksteins, *Rites of Spring: The Great War and the Birth of the Modern Age* (New York: Vintage, 1990), p. xiv.
2 Carl Van Vechten, *Music and Bad Manners* (New York: Knopf, 1916), p. 34.
3 Eksteins, *Rites of Spring*, p. 12.
4 Steiner's essay "On Difficulty," in *On Difficulty and Other Essays* (New York: Oxford University Press, 1980), pp. 18–47, argues that a defining feature of modernist poetry – and philosophy, too, I suspect, given his reliance on Heidegger – is that it is difficult on four different levels: that it is obscure in the ways that words we don't know are obscure; that it is foreign in the manner that a foreign language *modally* organizes experience differently; that its intended goal – intended by its author or its form – is the *defamiliarization* of habitual experience; and that, unintentionally, it confronts its audience with the necessarily mysterious frameworks – what I am calling in this book *anagogic* frameworks, but which Steiner, following Heidegger, conceives as linguistic frameworks – that reveal the largest metaphysical questions concerning life and death, individual versus collective experience, and other such questions within the most ordinary of experiences.
5 Carol Oja, "Gershwin and American Modernists of the 1920s," *The Musical Quarterly*, 78 (1994) 652.
6 See also Horowitz's account of the way that "American classical music closed ranks against Gershwin" (*Classical Music* 460–72). Horowitz also describes the "lavish" admiration Europeans "bestowed on Gershwin" (463) – noting particularly the admiration of Ravel and Schoenberg (464) – and he argues that Gershwin's work in "art" music, particularly his Concerto in F and *Porgy and Bess*, "straddled two musical worlds" (465n). In the latter, Horowitz argues, "when he hits stride, as in Robbins's funeral with its ceremony of lament and keening widow's song, *Porgy* is – a rarity in American music, because the

American experience is so much shorter and more sanguine than centuries of European vicissitude – at once a human and an epic tragedy" (467).

7 Adorno, *Philosophy of Modern Music*, p. 6. In this stance – which he consistently assumes in his discussions of everything but absolutely "great art" (see notes 16 and 55) – Adorno is situating himself within the position of what Colin Campbell describes as the "manipulationist" notion of the origin of consumer wants. "What the producers of goods and services actually manipulate, through their agents, are not consumers or their wants but, in the first instance at least, the symbolic meanings which are attached to products. They, in effect, manipulate messages" (*Romantic Ethic* 47). Campbell goes on to ask "how does receipt of a message lead to the creation of a want in the consumer?" (47). Adorno answers this in his assumption, according to Fredric Jameson, that the goal of art, in Stendhal's description, is a promise of happiness ("*promesse de bonheur*"), which, Adorno believes, is "false happiness, just . . . deceptive pleasure" (*Late Marxism* 146). As I suggested in the Introduction, however, the pleasures of popular music are not necessarily "deceptive," but can be found, in part, in popular music's celebration of "suppressed life" by means of its wholeness, rhythmic decomposition, and montage effects.

Still, one should not dismiss Adorno's answer to Campbell's question too quickly. As Jameson has argued, "the Adorno-Horkheimer theory of the Culture Industry provides a theoretical description of mass cultural experience which can scarcely be reduced to sheer opinionated or elitist vituperation against 'bad art'" (*Late Marxism* 145). Earlier Jameson notes that "degraded individual works of 'art' are therefore not here evaluated [by Adorno and Horkheimer] for purely aesthetic reasons, from some rigid 'standard' of high art . . . ; rather, they have become so many symptoms of the degradation of subjectivity" (108). Adorno, according to Jameson, pursues "as scandalously and as baldly as possible" the proposition that "all art is 'great art'; there are no degrees in the aesthetic experience of even partial, promising, middling, incomplete aesthetic experience; there is only the thing itself, or else its absence" (132), and because of this there exist "people radically unable to have aesthetic experience in the first place" (137). Still, "what is inauthentic in the offerings of the Culture Industry, then," Jameson paraphrases the Adorno-Horkheimer argument, "is not the remnants of experience within them, but rather the ideology of happiness they simultaneously embody: the notion that pleasure or happiness ('entertainment' would be their spurious synthesis) already exists, and is available for consumption" (147).

8 W. B. Yeats, *Collected Poems* (New York: Macmillan, 1956), p. 323, in "The Statues." Adorno is cited in Gracyk, "Adorno, Jazz," p. 528.

9 Cornel West, "The New Cultural Politics of Difference," in *The Cornel West Reader* (New York: Basic Books, 1999), pp. 119–39.

10 See Lawrence Birken, *Consuming Desire: Sexual Science and the Emergence of a Culture of Abundance, 1881–1914* (Ithaca: Cornell University Press, 1988).

11 Cornel West argues that Europe itself, between 1492 and "the last European century," Matthew Arnold's time, came to define itself against external and

internal "others." West chooses the year 1492 because it designates both the encounter with external others in Columbus's discovery of the "new world" of the Americas and the expulsion of internal others with Spain's forcing out of the Jews. Jews, other seeming non-Caucasians, sexual deviants, women as well as other "foreigners," West argues, all helped to define the "Age of Europe" ("Cultural Politics" 121; see also Cornel West, "Historicizing the Postmodern Debate: Arnold, Eliot, Trilling, and Fannon on the Crisis in Modern Culture," unpublished lecture presented at the University of Oklahoma, November 2, 1988). For self-proclaimed "Europeans" defining themselves against these "others," the wealth, democratization, and mobility facilitated by the second Industrial Revolution were indeed as shocking as Stravinsky's strange rhythms, Joyce's dislocated discourse, Picasso's curious vision, and even the "trash" of popular music. Those oppressed by the "Age of Europe" were less upset. See also Stephen Kern's powerful detailed study of the transformations of this period (*The Culture of Time and Space: 1880–1918* [Cambridge, MA: Harvard University Press, 1983]); and my discussions of this theme (Schleifer, *Rhetoric and Death: The Language of Modernism and Postmodern Discourse Theory* [Urbana: University of Illinois Press, 1990] and *Modernism and Time: The Logic of Abundance in Literature, Science, and Culture 1880–1930* [Cambridge University Press, 2000]).

12 Middleton, *Studying Popular Music*, p. 4.

13 See Marshall Berman, *All That Is Solid Melts into Air: The Experience of Modernity* (New York: Simon and Schuster, 1982).

14 James Joyce, *A Portrait of the Artist as a Young Man* (New York: Viking, 1964), p. 204.

15 Wilfred Owen, "Strange Meeting" (1918), in M. H. Abrams (general ed.), *The Norton Anthology of English Literature*, 3rd edn. (New York: Norton, 1974), p. 2296. See also Paul Fussell, *The Great War and Modern Memory* (New York: Oxford University Press, 1975) for this reading of *The Waste Land.*

16 In this context it is striking that in *Negative Dialectics* Adorno asserts that "the need to lend a voice to suffering is a condition of all truth" (17–18) because what he leaves out is truth conditioned by voices of the celebration of ordinary life experiences and, also, voices of pity, which do not give voice to suffering but acknowledge it in ordinary fellow-feeling. As Jameson notes, for Adorno there is "one crucial thematic differentiation between 'genuine art' and that offered by the Culture Industry: both raise the issue and the possibility of happiness in their very being, as it were, and neither provides it; but where the one ['genuine art'] keeps faith with [happiness] by negation and suffering, through the enactment of its impossibility, the other assures us it is taking place" (*Late Marxism* 147).

17 Cited in Witkin, *Adorno on Popular Culture*, p. 112.

18 Aaron Copland, *Music and Imagination* (New York: Mentor, 1952), p. 92.

19 Middleton, *Studying Popular Music*, p. 58.

20 For an account of these collaborations, see Negus, *Popular Music in Theory.*

21 Copland, *Music and Imagination*, p. 96.

22 For a thoroughgoing history of the modernist arts, see Peter Gay, *Modernism: The Lure of Heresy from Baudelaire to Beckett and Beyond* (New York: Norton, 2008).

23 See Schleifer, *Modernism and Time*, chapters 1 and 3 for detailed discussions.

24 Susan Buck-Morss, *The Dialectics of Seeing: Walter Benjamin and the Arcades Project* (Cambridge, MA: MIT Press, 1989), p. 70. "This new nature," Buck-Morss goes on, "its powers still unknown, can appear ominous and terrifying to the first generations confronting it . . . who have yet to learn to master, not this nature itself, but humanity's relationship to it. Such mastery demands being receptive to the expressive power of matter, a mimetic, not an instrumental skill; and it is the central intellectual task of the modern era" (70). Middleton devotes a chapter of his study of popular music to Benjamin's relation to the new technology (*Studying Popular Music* 34–63).

25 David Landes, *The Wealth and Poverty of Nations* (New York: Norton, 1999), pp. 41, 40.

26 Wilfrid Mellers, "God, Modality, and the Meaning in Some Recent Songs of Bob Dylan," *Popular Music*, 1 (1981) 145.

27 Oja, "Gershwin and American Modernists," pp. 648–49. Horowitz offers a parallel argument when he notes that "to the degree that Gershwin and Ives, Melville and Whitman are all talents unfinished or unpolished, they arguably remain true to 'America' – its youth, its sprawling diversity, its cockiness of adventure. 'Many American composers, I believe, have been interested in working things out for themselves to a great extent,' wrote Ives in his *Memos*. He was of course thinking of himself – but Gershwin, though in constant search of teachers, also fits" (*Classical Music* 471).

28 E.g., Birken, *Consuming Desire*; Buck-Morss, *Dialectics*; Kern, *Time and Space* Landes, *Wealth and Poverty;* Poovey, *Modern Fact;* Schleifer, *Modernism and Time.*

29 Latour, *We Have Never Been Modern*, p. 10.

30 Latour, *We Have Never Been Modern*, p. 67.

31 Bruno Latour, *Pandora's Hope*, p. 151. In Chapter 2, I examine the way that William Carlos Williams pursues the poetry of discovering not "a substance *in addition to* attributes," but *qualities of experience* in addition to attributes. In this, I argue, Williams is pursuing the modernist program of discovering, as Paul Klee had said, "the essential nature of the accidental" (cited in Malcolm Bradbury and James McFarlane, "The Name and Nature of Modernism," in *Modernism: 1890–1930*, ed. Bradbury and McFarlane [Harmondsworth: Penguin Books, 1976], p. 48). The sense of focusing on and emphasizing qualities of experience might well be a good working definition of poetry altogether. Such a definition also emphasizes the performative aspect of experiencing art. It is also, as I mention in Chapter 6, part of the power of Billie Holiday's music.

32 Andy Hamilton, "The Aesthetics of Imperfection," *Philosophy*, 65 (1990) 325.

33 This might not be true of Pasteur (who died in 1895), but it is true, I think, of his younger contemporary Joyce (who was born in 1892) or Einstein (who was

born in 1879). As we have seen, Andreas Huyssen argues that twentieth-century cultural modernism followed the same impulse toward "purity" as that of the seventeenth century. "Modernism," he writes, "constituted itself through a conscious strategy of exclusion, an anxiety of contamination by its other: an increasingly consuming and engulfing mass culture" (*Great Divide* vii). While this is true, as Latour argues it is not altogether true. In relation to popular music this is particularly clear in the way that "continental modernists, as is well known, embraced American popular culture as a weapon of artistic rebellion" even as, Oja argues, American modernists distanced themselves from its "contamination" ("Gershwin and American Modernists" 650). As I have suggested elsewhere, it is the embracing of "impurity" that might well define postmodernism in relation to modernism (see Schleifer, *Rhetoric and Death: The Language of Modernism and Postmodern Discourse Theory* [Urbana: University of Illinois Press, 1990]). For more detailed discussions concerning the relation between modernism and postmodernism, see Jean-François Lyotard, "Note on the Meaning of 'Post-,'" in his *The Postmodern Explained: Correspondence 1982–1985* (Minneapolis: University of Minnesota Press, 1992), pp. 64–68, and his "Answering the Question"; David Jobling, Tina Pippin, and Ronald Schleifer (eds.), *A Postmodern Bible Reader* (Oxford: Blackwell Publishers, 2001), Introduction.

34 Cited in Isaac Goldberg, *George Gershwin: A Study in American Music* (New York: Frederick Ungar Publishing, 1958), p. 275; see also Jeffrey Melnick, "Tin Pan Alley and the Black-Jewish Nation," in Rachel Rubin and Jeffrey Melnick (eds.), *American Popular Music* (Amherst: University of Massachusetts Press, 2001), pp. 36–37.

35 Elizabeth Deeds Ermarth, *Realism and Consensus in the English Novel* (Princeton University Press, 1983), pp. 17–18.

36 Mellers, "God, Modality," p. 45.

37 Brackett, *Interpreting Popular Music*, p. 24. Traditional literary-critical treatments of modernism also participate in focusing on what Joseph Frank called the "spatial form" of modern literature which valorizes written texts over aural performances. Thus, in a very influential study, Frank argued that "the reader is forced to read *Ulysses* in the same manner as he reads modern poetry, that is, by continually fitting fragments together and keeping allusions in mind until, by reflexive reference, he can link them together to their complements . . . Joyce cannot be read – he can only be reread" (Joseph Frank, "Spatial Form in Modern Literature," in his *The Widening Gyre* [Bloomington: Indiana University Press, 1963], pp. 18, 19).

38 Middleton, *Studying Popular Music*, p. 104.

39 See Middleton, *Studying Popular Music*, p. 4.

40 Brackett, *Interpreting Popular Music*, p. 19. See also Simon Frith, "What Is Good Music?", *Canadian Music Review*, 10 (1990), 99–100.

41 Frith, "The Good, the Bad," p. 107.

42 Mellers, "God, Modality," p. 145.

43 In music, an "accidental" note is marked by a diacritical marking (e.g., sharp #, or flat ♭, or the natural sign ♮); and, as the OED notes, it is "strictly so

called only when they occur before particular notes, and not in the *signature* of the various keys." This "strict" definition asserts that such accidentals are "non-diatonic" or "chromatic" notes, not part of the diatonic scale implicit in the key signature. That it is called an "accidental" reinforces the sense of the dominance of the general category over the particular instances. In the special case of the key of C, accidentals are marked by flats and sharps; in other keys flats and sharps systematically appear as inherent elements of the diatonic scale and an accidental can be marked by a natural sign, ♮.

44 Brackett, *Interpreting Popular Music*, p. 28.

45 Hamm, *Putting Popular Music in Its Place*, p. 3. Andy Hamilton also notes that "before the fourteenth century notation had been only a sort of shorthand to guide an accomplished performer, who was otherwise a musician of oral and traditional training. The transformation of the score from mnemonic device to what is often (mistakenly) regarded as the rigid repository of the art-work was a process that lasted many centuries – and was not complete until the second half of the nineteenth century" ("Aesthetics of Imperfection" 325).

46 Hamm is citing Carl Dahlhaus, *Foundations of Music History* (Cambridge University Press, 1983), pp. 150, 155. For a telling modern-day example of the difference between the scholar's approach to music and the performer's, see Charles Rosen's "informal" lectures on music. There he describes the ways that scholarly "writing about music [might not be] meant for the performer." "I once played Beethoven's Sonata in A Major for Piano and Cello, opus 69, with Pierre Fournier, who always seemed to me the supreme model of elegance and sensitivity. Lewis Lockwood's study of the sketches and manuscript of this sonata had recently appeared, and I told Fournier that it was interesting to see that Beethoven had worked out on paper the derivation of the second theme from the first, literally by writing one directly underneath the other . . . Fournier was impressed, but remarked, 'I have been playing this piece for fifty years, and I never noticed that they were really the same theme.' Would his performance have improved if he had noticed it? I doubt it" (Charles Rosen, *The Frontiers of Meaning: Three Informal Lectures on Music* [New York: Hill and Wang, 1994], p. 73). Calling the two themes "the same" is precisely the modern gesture of discovering "essences" in the varieties of experience.

47 Brackett, *Interpreting Popular Music*, pp. 19–20. In *Highbrow/Lowbrow*, Lawrence Levine describes this as well: "in the early decades" of the twentieth century, he writes, "the masterworks of the classical composers were to be performed in their entirety by highly trained musicians on programmes free from the contamination of lesser works or lesser genres, free from the interference of audience or performer, free from the distractions of the mundane; audiences were to approach the masters and their works with proper respect and proper seriousness, for aesthetic and spiritual elevation rather than mere entertainment was the goal. This transition was not confined to the worlds of symphonic and operatic music or of Shakespearean drama; it was manifest in other important areas of expressive culture as well" (*Highbrow/Lowbrow*

[Cambridge, MA: Harvard University Press, 1988], p. 146). For a history of the "sacralization" of music in nineteenth-century America, see Horowitz, *Classical Music*.

48 Hermann Keller, *The Well-Tempered Clavier by Johann Sebastian Bach*, trans. Leight Gerdine (London: George Allen & Unwin, 1976), pp. 24–25.

49 Siglind Bruhn, *J. S. Bach's Well-Tempered Clavier: In-Depth Analysis and Interpretation*, Vol. 1. (Hong Kong: Mainer International, 1993), p. 11.

50 See Schleifer, *Rhetoric and Death*; *Modernism and Time;* "The Beatles, Postmodernism, and Ill-Tempered Musical Form: Cleaning My Gun; or, The Use of Accidentals in *Revolver*," in Russell Reising (ed.), *'Every Sound There Is': The Beatles'* Revolver *and The Transformation of Rock & Roll.* (Hants, GB: Ashgate Publishers, 2002), pp. 222–33; Jobling *et al.*, *A Postmodern Bible Reader.*

51 Ralph Kirkpatrick, *Interpreting Bach's* Well-Tempered Clavier*: A Performer's Discourse of Method* (New Haven: Yale University Press, 1984), p. 7.

52 Cited in Kirkpatrick, *Interpreting Bach*, p. 6.

53 Toby Miller, *The Well-Tempered Self: Citizenship, Culture, and the Postmodern Subject* (Baltimore: Johns Hopkins University Press, 1993), p. x.

54 On Descartes's inventions, see Stephen Gaukroger, *Descartes: An Intellectual Biography* (New York: Oxford University Press, 1995), p. 94.

55 Adorno, "On Popular Music," pp. 437–38. This is part and parcel of his notion, as he suggests in a footnote to this assertion, that the essence of popular music is determined by "the externally super-imposed, commercial character of those patterns which aims at canalized reactions or, in the language of the regular announcement of one particular radio program, at 'easy listening'" (428; see also Negus, *Popular Music in Theory*, pp. 8–12). In his study of Adorno and popular culture, Robert Witkin reiterates this point: Adorno "insists that popular music is formulaic and standardized and that the form of the music is completely unresponsive to its contents, from which it does not differ in any essential way" (*Adorno on Popular Culture*, 123; see also 98).

Adorno takes jazz as a representational "'exemplar' of all popular music" (see Gracyk, "Adorno, Jazz," 526; see also 527). As I have already mentioned, this is a confusion of terminology that was common throughout the early development of the popular music of Tin Pan Alley, where the term "jazz" was constantly used in relation to what we now call the "standard" songs of the 1920s and 1930s. Such a confusion is no accident, I believe, because it is precisely the performative and improvisatory within "jazz" that, perhaps less explicitly, characterizes "popular music" more generally. I examine this "confusion" of terminology in greater detail in Chapter 2.

56 Lyotard, "Answering the Question," p. 79. In fact, Lyotard makes the presence of a "postmodern" moment a defining feature of twentieth-century modernism in his essay "Answering the Question: What is Postmodernism?" There he argues that the so-called *post*-modern is a constituent element or "moment" of modernism altogether insofar as any sense of "modernism" needs to disrupt any grounded sense of reality: "Modernity," he argues, "in whatever age it appears, cannot appear without the shattering of belief and without discovery

of the 'lack of reality' of reality, together with the invention of other realities" (77). Modernism for Lyotard – both "classical" Enlightenment modernity and twentieth-century modernism – warrants its designation insofar as it makes things new. But, as I argue here, "making things new" takes on particular force in the twentieth century in relation to the makings of mass commodification. For a detailed examination of Lyotard's position – and of the relationship between modernism and postmodernism – see Jobling *et al.*, *Postmodern Bible*, Introduction, esp. pp. 5–8.

57 Michael Kennedy and Joyce Bourne, *The Concise Oxford Dictionary of Music* (New York: Oxford University Press, 1996), pp. 400–01.

58 The double meaning of *fret* I describe is distinct from the double meaning of *modernism. Modernism*'s two meanings exist on levels of the literal meaning ("new") and of the performative assertion against another meaning ("not traditional"), while *fret*'s two meanings stem from different linguistic histories: "fret" as "concern" derives from the Old English *fretan*, "to devour," while the "fret" of the banjo derives from Old French *frette*, "a band or ferrule." (There is a third "fret" as in the fretwork of architecture that derives, probably, from the combination of the Old French *frette* with the Old English *frætwa*, "ornament.") The combination here of the two distinct linguistic traditions of English, the Germanic and Romance languages, underlines the traditional differences between *fret* and *fret*. Most important, it underlines the accidental nature of this double meaning: the accident of the coincidence of these words' *sounds* arbitrarily designating different meanings. The uses of the term *accidental* are, interestingly, more historical: the adjective ("accidental or chance occurrence") becomes a substantive technical term in musicology that, as it approaches a common noun, loses all sense of its history and becomes a "transcendental" designation.

59 *Sense* is another term that means alternatively "faculty of sensation" and simply "meaning." All of these examples demonstrate the overdetermination of language I mentioned in the Introduction.

60 Keil, "Motion and Feeling," p. 345.

61 Daniel Rosen has pointed out in a remarkably generous reading of an earlier draft of this chapter that the modality of minor keys is also more complicated than my discussion sometimes suggests: "strictly speaking," he noted in a personal correspondence, "any alterations noted in a key signature are considered accidentals. But I ordinarily refer only to pitches that are outside the tonic key as accidentals. And the accidentals within the minor key are not ordinarily included in the key signature, since it usually involves the use of flats and sharps simultaneously (i.e. G-minor, with two flats, requires an F♯ as its leading tone). A tone outside the key is the meaning that I think you give to the term 'accidental' in your definition. Now, C# is essentially within the key of E-minor. Remember, our system actually incorporates into its 'mechanism' three forms of the minor mode – the natural, the harmonic, and the melodic. The C# is, of course, one of the scale tones in the melodic form of E-minor." In the *Oxford English Dictionary*, the earliest usage of "accidental" to mean

"present by chance; non-essential" is 1386; the earliest musical usage to mean "signs of chromatic alteration . . . not in the *signature* of various keys" is 1806.

62 Cited in Bradbury and McFarlane, "Nature of Modernism," p. 48.

63 James Joyce, *Ulysses* (New York: Random House, 1961), p. 190.

64 Campbell, *Romantic Ethic*, pp. 136–37.

65 Campbell notes that "our interest . . . in the modern economy as a system of consumption rather than one of production means that we have good grounds for making a different evaluation from Weber concerning which Protestant teachings are of most relevance" (193–94); then he goes on to describe the reaction to Calvinism, best represented by Leibniz and the Cambridge Platonists (107ff). The anti-Calvinist reaction, he argues, participated in Enlightenment reason, individualism, and, to a lesser extent, imperialism even as it validated consumption (that is, pleasure seeking) in addition to ascetic productionism.

66 Poovey, *Modern Fact*, p. 55.

67 Jameson, *Late Marxism*, p. 161.

68 For a thoroughgoing treatment of the response of American modernists to the late Romantic genteel poets and critics of the late nineteenth century, see Frank Lentricchia, *Modernist Quartet* (Cambridge University Press, 1994). Adorno was particularly critical of the late Romantic music of composers such as Rachmaninov, Tchaikovsky and Sibelius who, Witkin notes, "perpetuated the decayed contents of bourgeois ideology, conjuring the appearance of spiritual values, inwardness and heroic individualism that had been all but extinguished by modern social conditions" (*Adorno on Popular Culture* 88–89). Adorno's critique of late Romantic music in the classical tradition is based on the same grounds as his rejection of popular music.

69 See Campbell, *Romantic Ethic*, pp. 26–27 for a discussion of the relation of the emergence of consumerism to romantic love.

70 Witkin, *Adorno on Popular Culture*, p. 88.

71 Campbell, *Romantic Ethic*, p. 216. Campbell argues earlier that for Romanticism, "the perception of beauty became linked to the gaining of privileged insights" (182), a position that comports nicely with Adorno's sense of the homologous relationship between art and social life I describe in the Introduction. In the passage I am citing here, Campbell goes on to assert, as Adorno does, that where such idealism "is absent, and largely materialistic and utilitarian beliefs prevail, then it seems only too likely that romantic poems, novels and music, will be employed as little more than the raw material for a leisure and recreation industry; with dreams used less to raise the vision of an imaginatively apprehended ideal world with which to counter this one, than to overcome boredom and alienation" (216). I should say that Campbell consistently uses the term "idealism" not in terms of transcendental "ideas," but rather as the possibility of imagining worlds different from our own, contrary-to-fact understanding that is not the opposite of "materialism"; see, for instance, his insistence that idealism should be understood as "activity aimed at fulfilling an ideal" (213). It is, of course, such contrary-to-fact understanding that governs Adorno's work.

NOTES TO CHAPTER 2

1 John Coates, untitled review of Regenia Gagnier, *The Insatiability of Human Wants: Economics and Aesthetics in Market Society* and of Michael Tratner, *Deficits and Desires: Economics and Sexuality in Twentieth-Century Literature* in the *Journal of Aesthetics and Art Criticism*, 60 (2002), pp. 369–70.

2 Kant, the great philosopher of Enlightenment modernity, had explicitly separated art and economics – judgment and practical reason – but the new twentieth century had destroyed their "purity" and made allies of them. Stephen Dedalus makes such "Kantian" separation his creed in *A Portrait of the Artist*, where he describes "interested" art that provokes desire and loathing as "pornographical or didactic" and therefore impure, "improper art," while "the esthetic emotion" is "static" and by means of which "the mind is arrested and raised above desire and loathing" (*Portrait* 205). But both Joyce and Leopold Bloom in *Ulysses* are less scrupulous.

3 See Karl Marx, *Capital*, Vol. 1, *The Process of Capitalist Production*, trans. Samuel Moore and Edward Aveling (New York: International Publishers, 1967), chapters 6, 7.

4 Campbell, *Romantic Ethic*, p. 64.

5 Birken, *Consuming Desire*, p. 25. It is also important to note that the productionist measures of the value of commodified labor, namely, food, clothing, shelter, were the great commodities of the first Industrial Revolution of the late eighteenth and early nineteenth centuries in the form of railroads transporting foodstuff, the great textile mill, and the boom in furniture manufacture, while the explosion in consumer goods – the bicycles, automobiles, telephones, phonographs, higher education, light bulbs, etc. I already mentioned in Chapter 1 – were part and parcel of the new "neolithic" revolution of the turn of the twentieth century, what has been called the second Industrial Revolution between 1875 and 1945 (see Schleifer, *Modernism and Time* pp. 46–47; and my "Narrative Discourse and a New Sense of Value: Meaning and Purpose in the Neoclassical Economics of Alfred Marshall," in Carol Jacobs and Henry Sussman (eds.), *Rereading Narrative* [Stanford University Press, 2003], pp. 157–73, 257–79).

6 Birken, *Consuming Desire*, p. 34. He notes that "the productivist ideology . . . emphasized, on the one hand, the *productivity*, and, on the other hand, the *neediness*, of human beings" (27). Several important studies of the ways this transformation affected the literary arts include those of Regenia Gagnier and Michael Tratner. Gagnier notes, for instance, that in the marginal economists "the idea of needs – which were finite and the focus of political economy – was displaced by the idea of tastes, which were theoretically infinite" (*The Insatiability of Human Wants: Economics and Aesthetics in Market Society* [University of Chicago Press, 2000], p. 94). Tratner focuses on the ways that the Keynesian "'revolution' . . . carried much further the valuing and channeling of desire, developing macroeconomic strategies for stimulating and even creating consumer demand on a mass scale" (*Deficits and Desires:*

Economics and Sexuality in Twentieth-Century Literature [Stanford University Press, 2001], p. 3). I should add here that "idiosyncratic desire" and "taste" are more like the performances of popular music than the settled texts of art music.

7 Although I mention physics, art, and psychology, these three kinds of reassessments of knowledge can also be found in Darwin's work. This is most clear, I think, in the category of retrospective understanding. Stephen Jay Gould has done important work in examining the systematic method of retrospective analysis in the theory of evolution – see especially his *Wonderful Life: The Burgess Shale and the Nature of History* (New York: Norton, 1989) – and his magisterial *The Structure of Evolutionary Theory* (Cambridge, MA: Harvard University Press, 2002) demonstrates the ways that evolutionary theory also participates in alternating levels of analysis and a sense of the overdeterminations that govern its objects of study. See also Schleifer, *Intangible Materialism*, pp. xi–xiii, 120–24 for a discussion of Gould. In *Consuming Desire*, Birken argues that "if Machiavelli discovered power as the underlying basis of the political realm, and if Locke discovered labor as the unifying substance of the political-economic realm of the male sex, Darwin discovered desire as the fundamental ground of both sexes . . . In the Darwinian state of nature, there were only genderless, desiring creatures" (7).

8 See Timothy Scheurer, "Introduction: The Tin Pan Alley Years (1890–1950)," in Timothy Scheurer (ed.), *American Popular Music: Readings from the Popular Press Volume I: The Nineteenth Century and Tin Pan Alley* (Bowling Green: Bowling Green State University Popular Press, 1989), p. 87.

9 David Sanjek, "They Work Hard for Their Money: The Business of Popular Music," in Rachel Rubin and Jeffrey Melnick (eds.), *American Popular Music* (Amherst: University of Massachusetts Press, 2001), p. 10.

10 Sanjek, "They Work Hard," pp. 11, 12.

11 Hamm, *Yesterdays*, p. 309.

12 Jason Toynbee, *Making Popular Music: Musicians, Creativity and Institutions* (London: Arnold, 2000), p. xix. The Gennett Record Company of Richmond, Indiana was founded in 1919, as a subsidiary of the Starr Piano Co., and went on to become one of the earliest labels to release many important early masterpieces from a multitude of artists, many of whom today are literally jazz legends, including Jelly Roll Morton, King Oliver, Louis Armstrong, Bix Beiderbecke, Don Murray, Tommy Dorsey, etc., etc. (www.shellac.org/wams/wgen.html).

13 Hamm, *Yesterdays*, pp. 376–77. One great exception to this was Billie Holiday's recording of "Strange Fruit" in 1939. For a history of this song, see David Margolick, *Strange Fruit: Billie Holiday, Café Society, and an Early Cry for Civil Rights* (Philadelphia: Running Press, 2000). Another exception was Waller's "Black and Blue," which I discuss in Chapter 5.

14 Michael Alexander, *Jazz Age Jews* (Princeton University Press, 2001), p. 158.

15 Melnick, "Tin Pan Alley and the Black-Jewish Nation," p. 31. Melnick describes the striking interplay between Jewish Americans and African Americans in

New York. "What comes through most clearly in Armstrong's 'Ain't Misbehavin', '" a song, Melnick argues, based on Gershwin's music which helped Armstrong achieve stardom, "is his musical assertion that he and Gershwin, white and black, jazz, popular song, and symphonic music all shared space in the modern city" (31). I return to the relationship between Jewish and African American music later in this chapter. In *Fascinating Rhythm*, his study of the representation of jazz in American literature, David Yaffe offers a fine chapter examining "Blacks and Jews in words and music."

16 Hamm, *Yesterdays*, p. 377. Melnick, "Tin Pan Alley," p. 31.

17 Campbell, *Romantic Ethic*, p. 31.

18 Eric Hobsbawm, *The Age of Empire 1875–1914* (New York: Pantheon Books, 1987), p. 180.

19 See Schleifer, *Modernism and Time*, pp. 127–36.

20 Sanjek, "They Work Hard," p. 19; Tratner, *Deficits and Desires*.

21 As we have already seen, in *The Romantic Ethic and the Spirit of Modern Consumerism*, Colin Campbell rethinks Weber's thesis from the point of view of consumption and pleasure (as opposed to production and need).

22 Timothy Scheurer, "'Thou Witty': The Evolution and Triumph of Style in Lyric Writing, 1890–1950," in Scheurer (ed.), *American Popular Music*, p. 105.

23 Hamm, *Yesterdays*, p. 297.

24 Harris cited in Scheurer, "Thou Witty," p. 106.

25 Nancy West and Penelope Pelizzon, in *Tabloid, Inc.: Crimes, Newspapers, Narratives* (Columbus: Ohio State University Press, 2010), write eloquently about the powerful ways the tabloid press informed another form of popular modernist art in the 1930s, the film noir.

26 Melnick, "Tin Pan Alley," p. 29; for another account of Armstrong in this revue see Yaffe, *Fascinating Rhythm*, pp. 72, 99.

27 William Carlos Williams, *The Autobiography of William Carlos Williams* (New York: New Direction, 1951), p. 359.

28 In Margaret Ferguson, Mary Jo Salter, and Jon Stallworthy, *The Norton Anthology of Poetry*, shorter fifth edn. (New York: Norton, 2005), p. 830.

29 In Ferguson *et al.*, *Norton Poetry*, p. 1053.

30 In Ferguson *et al.*, *Norton Poetry*, pp. 829–30.

31 Aaron Fox, *Real Country: Music and Language in Working-Class Culture* (Durham, NC: Duke University Press, 2004), p. 233.

32 Appel, *Jazz Modernism*, p. 13.

33 Cited in Morroe Berger, "Fats Waller: The Outsider Insider," *Journal of Jazz Studies*, 1 (1973), p. 8.

34 George Gershwin and Ira Gershwin, *The Music and Lyrics of George and Ira Gershwin: Special Centenary Edition* (Miami: Warner Bros. Publications, 1998), p. 409; video available on YouTube.

35 Adorno, *Aesthetic Theory*, pp. 148–49; trans. modified by Jameson, *Late Marxism*, p. 172.

36 The words here are taken from Armstrong's recording, which differs somewhat – in its "accidental" jazz performance – from published versions of this

song, e.g., *'Fats' Waller: Piano-Styles and Original Songs* (New York: Jazz Giants, n.d.).

37 Cited in Albright, *Stravinsky*, p. 17.

38 Cole Porter, *Cole* (New York: Delta, 1971), p. 110.

39 Billie Holiday, "Fine and Mellow," in Henry Louis Gates, Jr., and Nellie Y. McKay (eds.), *The Norton Anthology of African American Literature* (New York: Norton, 1997), p. 35.

40 Fox, *Real Country*, p. 220.

41 Viktor Shklovsky coined the term "defamiliarization" in 1917 in what was surely a powerfully *modernist* moment in the understanding of literature (see "Art as Technique," in *Russian Formalist Criticism: Four Essays*, trans. Lee Lemon and Marion Reis [Lincoln: University of Nebraska Press, 1965]). In this gesture of what came to be called Russian Formalism the "autonomy" of art, which Hamm discusses, is particularly pronounced. In his analysis, Shklovsky was primarily interested in the ways that Tolstoy's everyday realism of ordinary cliché created social, emotional, linguistic, and transformational power.

42 Adorno, "On Popular Music," p. 442.

43 Gracyk, "Adorno, Jazz," p. 537.

44 Hamm, *Putting Popular Music in Its Place*, p. 310.

45 Yaffe notes that "the word 'jazz' has been associated with everything from an African word for 'jism' to a synonym for 'fuck' – a meaning upheld even by Jazz at Lincoln Center Artistic Director Wynton Marsalis" (*Fascinating Rhythm* 4). Later he notes that "the word 'jazz,' of course, comes up in writing more often than the music is actually confronted. F. Scott Fitzgerald coined the term the 'jazz age' without offering his views on Ellington and Armstrong, but as Fitzgerald himself noted, the word's meaning in the 1920s was multivalenced: 'The word jazz in its progress toward respectability,' he wrote, 'has meant first sex, then dancing, then music.' Add 'drinking' to the list," Yaffe concludes, "and Fitzgerald would have been concerned with music the very least" (12).

46 Ferruccio Busoni, *Sketch of a New Aesthetic of Music*, in *Three Classics in the Aesthetic of Music* (New York: Dover, 1962), p. 84; cited in Hamilton, "The Aesthetics of Imperfection," p. 323.

47 Cited in Hamilton, "The Aesthetics of Imperfection," p. 323.

48 "One of the peculiar features of Western music during the last 200 years," Peter Townsend writes, "has been its exclusion of improvisation. In earlier times, composers and performers, among them Mozart, Beethoven, and J. S. Bach, were accomplished improvisers. Improvisation of one kind or another has been endemic in the folk musics of the world. In some 'classical' forms, such as Indian music, improvisation is central to the musical culture. European 'serious' music of the nineteenth and twentieth centuries is an ethnomusicological exception in its complete severance from improvisatory methods" (*Jazz in American Culture* 8). Townsend also goes on to discuss the element of rhythm in jazz: "rhythmic energy is like improvisation in being a discounted,

even a dubious, value within the system of Western music. It has a lower position in the hierarchy of musical elements than harmony, melody and form. Rhythm is the least cerebral, the most bodily of the components of music" (20). In his extended discussion of rhythm (20–27) he touches on the ways that improvisation encompasses rhythm (as does Aaron Copland, *Music and Imagination*).

49 Adorno participates in this "museum art" ethos when he likens the concert hall to a cathedral: "to 'enter' a symphony," he writes, "means to listen to it not only as something before one, but as something around one as well, as a medium in which one 'lives'. It is this surrounding quality that comes closest to the idea of 'symphonic absorption'" (cited in Witkin, *Adorno on Popular Culture* 125).

50 Melnick, "Tin Pan Alley," p. 43.

51 Alexander, *Jazz Age Jews*, p. 137.

52 Alexander is citing Eric Lott, *Love & Theft: Blackface Minstrelsy and the American Working Class* (New York: Oxford University Press, 1995), p. 234.

53 Appel, *Jazz Modernism*, p. 37.

54 Melnick, "Tin Pan Alley," p. 44.

55 Townsend, *Jazz in American Culture*, p. 9. Alec Wilder notes that jazz musicians are attracted to song in which "the melody should be spare, containing a minimal number of notes, and the harmony should be similarly uncluttered . . . However, the principal jazz interest in any song lies in its 'changes': its harmony" (*American Popular Song* [New York: Oxford University Press, 1972], p. 128). Wilder, a successful songwriter himself, wrote what Charles Hamm calls the only "detailed study of the musical style of [Tin Pan Alley's] songs" (*Yesterdays* 357). His thesis, as Hamm notes in citing Wilder, is that "during the thirty-year period between 1885 and World War I [what I am calling the first wave of Tin Pan Alley], American music underwent many fundamental changes. Finally, when these changes – rhythmic, harmonic, melodic – were consolidated, a unique kind of song emerged: American song' (*American Popular Song* 3). Wilder's analyses are highly detailed, technical and often idiosyncratic and cranky. Middleton spends some time examining the assumptions of traditional musicology in Wilder's work (*Studying Popular Music* 108–10).

56 Yaffe, *Fascinating Rhythm*, pp. 16–17; see also Hamm, *Putting Popular Music in Its Place*, p. 307.

57 See also Appel, *Jazz Modernism*.

58 Kern, *Time and Space*, p. 177.

59 Hamilton, "Aesthetics of Imperfection," p. 339.

60 Middleton, *Studying Popular Music*, p. 7.

61 Virginia Woolf, "Mr. Bennett and Mrs. Brown," in *Collected Essays, Volume 1* (New York: Harcourt, Brace, and World, 1967), pp. 320, 321. For a thoroughgoing examination of Woolf's observation, see Peter Stansky, *On or About December 1910: Early Bloomsbury and Its Intimate World* (Cambridge, MA: Harvard University Press, 1996).

62 W. H. Auden, "In Memory of Sigmund Freud," in *Selected Poetry of W. H. Auden* (New York: Modern Library, 1959), p. 57.
63 Walter Benn Michaels, "American Modernism and the Poetics of Identity," *Modernism/Modernity*, 1 (1994), pp. 39, 40.
64 George Edwards, *The Evolution of Finance Capitalism* (New York: Longmans, 1938), p. 29; see also Schleifer, *Modernism and Time*, pp. 119–32.
65 Alex Ross gives a nice account of twelve-tone music: "in the mad year of hyperinflation, Schoenberg offered a kind of stabilization – the conversion of a chaotic musical marketplace to a planned economy. There was a nationalistic thrust, too, to Schoenberg's return to order; at a time when Russian, French, and American composers were seizing headlines with their Jazz Age antics, Schoenberg was reasserting the primacy of Austro-German composition, its ancient arts of counterpoint and thematic development" (*The Rest Is Noise: Listening to the Twentieth Century* [New York: Farrar, Straus and Giroux, 2007], p. 197). See also Mary Poovey's description of the general occurrence, "at different moments in different disciplines" at the turn of the twentieth century, of methods of understanding, like the periodic table, which "gradually elevated rule-governed, autonomous models over observed particulars. After the late nineteenth century, at least in the natural and social sciences, expert knowledge producers sought not to generate knowledge that was simultaneously true to nature and systematic but to *model* the *range of the normal* or sometimes simply to create the most sophisticated models from available data, often using mathematical formulas. As the units of such models, postmodern facts [as she distinguishes these phenomena from the "modern" Enlightenment facts] are not necessarily observed particulars; instead, as digital 'bits' of information, the 'phenomenological laws' of physics, or poststructuralist signifiers with no referent, they are themselves already modeled and thus exist at one remove from what the eye can see, although they are no less the units by which we make what counts as knowledge about our world" (*Modern Fact* 3–4).
66 For a thoroughgoing structuralist account of the concept of the anagogic, see my essay "The Semiotics of Speculation." In that essay, following Hillis Miller, I situate anagogical interpretation in relation to social, psychological, and linguistic interpretations.
67 Nat Hentoff, "The Real Lady Day," in Leslie Gourse (ed.), *The Billie Holiday Companion* (New York: Shirmer Books, 1997), p. 154.
68 See Mithen, *Singing Neanderthals*.
69 Holiday's performance of "Night and Day" is widely available. See, for instance, *Love Songs Billie Holiday*, Sony Music Entertainment 1996, CK 64853.
70 Ralph Ellison, *Shadow and Act* (New York: Signet Books, 1966), p. 243.
71 See Jameson, *Late Marxism*, pp. 49–58; Schleifer, *Modernism and Time*, pp. 84–94.
72 North, *Dialect of Modernism*.
73 Stravinsky, *Themes and Conclusions*, p. 147.

NOTES TO CHAPTER 3

1 Cited in Alexander, *Jazz Age Jews*, p. 158.
2 Hamm, *Putting Popular Music in Its Place*, p. 322.
3 Cited in Isaac Goldberg, *George Gershwin*, pp. 275–76.
4 Mikhail Bakhtin, *Speech Genres and Other Late Essays*, trans. Vern McGee (Austin: University of Texas Press, 1986), p. 72.
5 Middleton, *Studying Popular Music*, p. 7.
6 Deena Rosenberg, *Fascinating Rhythm: The Collaboration of George and Ira Gershwin* (London: Lime Tree Press, 1992), p. 135.
7 Rosenberg, *Collaboration*, p. 146.
8 Goldberg, *George Gershwin*, p. 41.
9 Hamm, *Putting Popular Music in Its Place*, p. 311.
10 Melnick, "Tin Pan Alley," 43.
11 See Rosenberg, *Collaboration*, p. 135 and *passim*; Rosenberg discusses many of the examples in Figure 2.
12 Rosenberg, *Collaboration*, p. xviii.
13 In his usual cranky style, Alec Wilder describes the chorus as "monotonous" (despite the fact that he concedes it "is part of our musical language"), and describes the verse as "a monotony of imitative phrases which no amount of adroit harmony can leaven" (*American Popular Song* 139).
14 Cited in Rosenberg, *Collaboration*, p. 160.
15 Ira Gershwin, *Lyrics on Several Occasions* (New York: Knopf, 1959), p. 163.
16 See Ronald Schleifer, "Rural Gothic: The Sublime Rhetoric of Flannery O'Connor," in David Mogen, Scott Sanders, and Joanne Karpinski (eds.), *Frontier Gothic: Terror and Wonder at the Frontier in American Literature* (Madison, NJ: Fairleigh Dickinson University Press, 1993), pp. 175–86.
17 Fox, *Real Country*, p. 229.
18 Ira Gershwin, *Lyrics*, p. 342.
19 A feminine rhyme is one which rhymes two-syllable words – or the final two syllables of longer words – on the accented penultimate syllable rather than the final syllable: *dinner/sinner*.
20 Ira Gershwin, *Lyrics*, p. 343.
21 Rosenberg, *Collaboration*, p. 159.
22 Again Wilder crankily notes that, although "Nice Work" is "especially fine," "a very clever song," he is "slightly embarrassed, however, by its cadence, since it is a somewhat lordly allusion to a phrase from *I Got Rhythm*. No doubt the Gershwins were right: everyone *did* know the earlier song. But it does seem a bit like boasting" (*American Popular Song* 158–59).
23 Joan Peyser, *The New Music: the Sense Behind the Sound* (New York: Delacourt Press, 1971), p. 57.
24 Cited in Rosenberg, *Collaboration*, p. 108.
25 Jonathan Culler, "Apostrophe," in his *The Pursuit of Signs* (Ithaca: Cornell University Press, 1981), p. 142.

26 A. J. Greimas, "La linguistique structurale et la poétique," in *Du Sens* (Paris: Seuil, 1970), p. 279; my translation. I make this argument in my discussion of Tourette's Syndrome in Chapter 3 of *Intangible Materialism* and in the far different context of a comparison of Descartes and Foucault in *Analogical Thinking: Language, Collaboration, and Criticism* (Ann Arbor: University of Michigan Press, 2000), pp. 190–91. In important ways, the "quotation" of rhymes is a strong example of analogical thinking on the level of material sound.

27 Ira Gershwin, *Lyrics*, p. 31.

28 William Carlos Williams, *Autobiography*, p. 146.

29 George and Ira Gershwin, *The Music and Lyrics of George & Ira Gershwin: Special Centenary Edition* (Miami: Warner Bros. Publications, 1998), p. 77.

30 See Rosenberg, *Collaboration*, p. 161.

31 Rosenberg, *Collaboration*, p. 337.

32 Ira Gershwin, *Lyrics*, p. 258.

33 Culler, "Apostrophe," p. 142.

34 George and Ira Gershwin, *Music and Lyrics*, p. 337.

35 Ira Gershwin, *Lyrics on Several Occasions*. New York: Knopf, 1997, p. 234.

36 George and Ira Gershwin, *Music and Lyrics*, p. 53.

37 Walter Benjamin, "N [Re the Theory of Knowledge, Theory of Progress]," trans. Leigh Hafrey and Richard Sieburth, in *Benjamin: Philosophy, Aesthetics, History*, ed. Gary Smith (University of Chicago Press, 1989), p. 45.

38 Rosenberg, *Collaboration*, pp. 179–80.

39 Bahktin, *Speech Genres*, p. 60.

40 Of course the first mode of performance also includes, at the extreme, the precise renderings of a score. Aaron Copland notes that "the improvising performer [that includes Holiday following the lyrics in her way as well as Waller improvising "I Got Rhythm" that I examine in Chapter 5] is the very antithesis of that tendency in contemporary composition that demands absolute exactitude in the execution of the printed page. Perhaps M. Stravinsky and those who support his view of rigorous control for the performer have been trying to sit on the lid too hard. Perhaps the performer should be given more elbow room and a greater freedom of improvisatory choice . . . Most jazz improvisers are not entirely free either, partly because of the conventionality of jazz harmonic formulas, and partly because of the over-used melodic formulas. Recent examples of group improvisations by Lennie Tristano and some few other jazz men are remarkable precisely because they avoid both these pitfalls. When American musicians improvise thus freely, and we are able to rehear their work through recordings, the European musician is the first to agree that something has been developed here that has no duplication abroad" (*Music and Imagination*, 96–97).

41 Mikhail Bakhtin, *The Dialogic Imagination*, trans. Caryl Emerson and Michael Holquist (Austin: University of Texas Press, 1981), p. 341.

42 See Schleifer, *Rhetoric and Death*, pp. 102–09.

43 Mikhail Bakhtin [V. N. Voloshinov], *Marxism and the Philosophy of Language*, trans. Ladislav Matejka and I. R. Titunik (Cambridge, MA: Harvard University Press, 1986), pp. 141–60.
44 See Hugh Kenner, *Joyce's Voices* (Berkeley: University of California Press, 1979), pp. 15–17.
45 William Carlos Williams, *Autobiography*, p. 146; this is the import of Colin MacCabe's argument, discussed in my Introduction and Conclusion.
46 Kenner, *Joyce's Voices*.
47 Cited in Rosenberg, *Collaboration*, p. 135.
48 Bakhtin, *Marxism*, p. 102.
49 For an insightful discussion of the lack of quotation marks in Joyce and its relation to the "revolution" of cultural modernism, see MacCabe, *James Joyce*. MacCabe argues there that the work of quotation marks is to absolutely distinguish between the "performed" language of characters and the "transcendental" language of an omniscient narrator, a voice from nowhere that articulates "truth" in the same way that Newton's equations or Bach's fugues articulate the "truth" of physics or harmony.
50 Wilder, *American Popular Song*, p. 157.
51 Rosenberg, *Collaboration*, p. 346.
52 Gilles Deleuze, *The Logic of Sense*, trans. Mark Lester (New York: Columbia University Press, 1990), p. 287.
53 Rosenberg, *Collaboration*, p. xx.

NOTES TO CHAPTER 4

1 Raymond Williams, *The Long Revolution* (Harmondsworth: Penguin Books, 1961), p. 63.
2 The performative nature of subjectivity and desire has been examined at great length by scholars following the work of Jacques Lacan, which I pursue in this chapter. For representative examples see Judith Butler, *Gender Trouble: Feminism and the Subversion of Identity* (New York: Routledge, 1990); Shoshana Felman, *The Scandal of the Speaking Body: Don Juan with J. L. Austin, or Seduction in Two Languages*, trans. Catherine Porter (Stanford University Press, 2002); Jane Gallop, *Reading Lacan* (Ithaca: Cornell University Press, 1985).
3 Lévi-Strauss, *The Raw and the Cooked*, p. 16. See also Middleton, "Popular Music Analysis," p. 106.
4 See note 52 for a particular example in Porter's "What Is This Thing Called Love?" of the phenomenon of a not quite fully achieved anticipation.
5 Robert Jourdain, *Music, the Brain, and Ecstasy: How Music Captures Our Imagination* (New York: Quill, 2002), p. 340.
6 Stephen Greenblatt, "Culture," in Frank Lentricchia and Thomas McLaughlin (eds.), *Critical Terms for Literary Study* (University of Chicago Press, 199[illegible]), p. 227.
7 Lévi-Strauss, *The Raw and the Cooked*, p. 22.
8 Campbell, *Romantic Ethic*, p. 61.

9 Frith, "The Good, the Bad," p. 107.
10 Cole Porter, *Cole* (New York: Delta, 1971), p. 235.
11 Cited in Charles Schwartz, *Cole Porter: A Biography* (New York: Da Capo Press, 1977), pp. 117–18.
12 Porter, *Cole*, p. 206.
13 Within his high praise for the harmonics of this song, Alec Wilder notes, however, that a "pleasant conceit occurs in measure twenty-eight where the lyric says 'major to minor,' for an A-flat minor chord is present. Unfortunately, under the word 'major,' it is the same minor chord. But one should not ask for a miracle" (*American Popular Song* 248). Here, the major chord is under the word "change." In a late recording of this song (1957), Ella Fitzgerald consistently sings before the beat up until this final verse, when she sings behind the beat, slowing down to a different time scheme altogether as she sings "how strange the change from major to minor" (1993). Thus the figure of musical performance – "major to minor" – elicits the syncopation of "a second rhythmic line countering the first," as Robert Jourdain notes (*Music and Ecstasy* 129), that syncopates not only music and lyrics, but performance and text.
14 Felman, *Scandal of the Speaking Body*.
15 Porter, *Cole*, p. 239.
16 Adorno, *Aesthetic Theory*, p. 259. Adorno's description of wholeness, which I described in the Introduction, seems to be fully synecdochical in that, as he says, "the detail virtually contains the whole and leads to the exposition of the whole, at the same time, it is produced out of the conception of the whole" ("On Popular Music" 441). But the dialectic he describes that encompasses decomposition (into a metonymic "swarm of things") and metonymic montage transforms the synecdochical part–whole relationship into a dialectic of metonymy and synecdoche.
17 In relation to Peirce's "index," see Frank Wilson's remarkable study of the evolution and function of the human hand, particularly his discussion of the relation of hands to musical performance. "Musical skill," he writes, "provides the clearest example and the cleanest proof of the existence of a whole class of self-defined, personally distinctive motor skills with an extended training and experience base, strong ties to the individual's emotional and cognitive development, strong communicative intent, and very high performance standards . . . [Instrumental] musical skill [provides] evidence of the existence of a whole *family* of physically and cognitively demanding, hierarchically structured, creatively rich human skills that (like sign) have communicative content and are 'put out through the hand'" (*The Hand: How Its Use Shapes the Brain, Language, and Human Culture* [New York: Vintage Press, 1999], p. 207). In *Intangible Materialism*, I examine the evolution of the hand in relation to Peirce's notion of the index and its referential function; see especially Chapter 4. Peirce mentions different functions, but he is clear that these functions work together and never individually (although one or another function may receive greater emphasis).

18 Roman Jakobson, "Two Aspects of Language and Two Types of Aphasic Disturbances," in *Language in Literature*, ed. Krystyna Pomorska and Stephen Rudy (Cambridge, MA: Harvard University Press, 1987), pp. 95–114.

19 Lévi-Strauss, *The Raw and the Cooked*, p. 22. In his discussion, Jakobson calls *both* of the rhetorical figures of metonymy and synecdoche "metonymy" and opposes them to the rhetorical figure "metaphor" even though, as I have mentioned, synecdoche is significantly different from metonymy. He does not distinguish the part for the whole (the sailors' "hands") and the contiguity for the whole (the King's "crown") when describing the spatial and temporal extensiveness of metonymy as opposed to metaphor.

20 That Jakobson doesn't pursue this way of understanding metonymy as marked by the accidental contingencies of non-signifying *things* follows, I believe, from his global project of developing a *science* of meaning. Such a scientific project – part and parcel of the Enlightenment modernity I discussed in Chapter 1 – pursues the articulation of unmarked universals. It is for this reason that he erases the distinction between metonymy and synecdoche just as tempering erases the distinction between G♯ and A♭. If metonymy chooses a contingent or accidental factor as the figure, synecdoche – expressing the whole through a part – chooses an *essential* factor as a figure, the king's head in "head of state," for example, as opposed to metonymy's "crown." For discussions of linguistic marking, see Holenstein, *Roman Jakobson's Approach to Language*, pp. 130–33; Ronald Schleifer, *A. J. Greimas and the Nature of Meaning* (Lincoln: University of Nebraska Press, 1987), pp. 50–55.

21 Porter, *Cole*, p. 94.

22 Jakobson, "Two Aspects," p. 113.

23 Lacan, *Écrits: A Selection*, trans. Alan Sheridan (New York: Norton, 1977), p. 259.

24 Jacques Lacan, *The Four Fundamental Concepts of Psycho-Analysis*, trans. Alan Sheridan (Harmondsworth: Penguin Books, 1977), p. 25.

25 Keil, "Motion and Feeling," p. 345.

26 In "The Freudian Thing," Lacan attempts to describe this ambiguous operation in terms of "*Adaequatio rei et intellectus [the correspondence of thing and thought]*." "Intellects like ours," he writes, "will certainly be adequate to this thing that speaks to us, which speaks within us, and in escaping behind the discourse that says nothing but to make us speak, it would be strange indeed if it did not find to whom it might speak" (*Écrits* 131). Like much of Lacan's writing, this is a dense description that might well be understood in terms of Lévi-Strauss's definition of music as a seemingly natural "thing" in which culture is already present in the form of sense experience. As such, music speaks to us, within us even as it "says nothing" but to provoke us to respond, in language and/or in feeling.

27 Porter, *Cole*, p. 143.

28 The slashes are linguistic marks indicating phonemic sound, rather than meaning. The /de/ looks like a morpheme (the smallest unit of sense in a language,

usually a syllable) but functions here like a phoneme (the smallest unit of distinguishable sound in a language).

29 Lacan, *Écrits*, p. 287.
30 Gallop, *Reading Lacan*, pp. 151–52.
31 Jacques Derrida, *Positions*, trans. Alan Bass (University of Chicago Press, 1979), p. 58.
32 Friedrich Nietzsche, *The Birth of Tragedy*, in *The Birth of Tragedy and The Case of Wagner*, trans. Walter Kaufmann (New York: Vintage, 1967), p. 141; Campbell also examines the "enjoyable discomfort" of longing in relation to his description of pleasure, *Romantic Ethic*, pp. 85–88.
33 Porter, *Cole*, p. 110.
34 Nietzsche, *Birth*, p. 74.
35 Wallace Stevens, *The Palm at the End of the Mind: Selected Poems and a Play*, ed. Holly Stevens (New York: Vintage, 1972), p. 217.
36 Richard Rorty, "Philosophy as a Kind of Writing: An Essay on Derrida," in his *Consequences of Pragmatism* (Minneapolis: University of Minnesota Press, 1982), p. 94.
37 Wilder, *American Popular Song*, p. 239.
38 Porter, *Cole*, pp. 123–24.
39 T. S. Eliot, *Selected Poems* (New York: Harcourt Brace, 1964), p. 65.
40 Lacan, *Écrits*, p. 130.
41 Porter, *Cole*, p. 141.
42 Wilder, *American Popular Song*, p. 238.
43 While Gershwin's songs are usually 16 bars, he rarely uses this standard chord progression. None of the songs mentioned in Chapter 3 do.
44 Porter, *Cole*, p. 236.
45 Yeats, *Collected Poems*, p. 70.
46 Sharon Cameron, *Lyric Time: Dickinson and the Limits of Genre* (Baltimore: Johns Hopkins University Press, 1979), p. 218.
47 Lacan, *Écrits*, p. 287.
48 Lévi-Strauss, *The Raw and the Cooked*, p. 22.
49 Emmanuel Levinas, "Ethics as First Philosophy," trans. Seán Hand and Michael Temple, in *The Levinas Reader*, ed. Seán Hand (Cambridge: Blackwell, 1989), pp. 82–83.
50 John Aggleton and Andrew Young. "The Enigma of the Amygdala: On Its Contribution to Human Emotion," in Richard Lane and Lynn Nadel (eds.), *Cognitive Neuroscience of Emotion* (Oxford University Press, 2000), p. 113. See also Daniel McNeill, *The Face* (Boston: Little Brown, 1998); and Schleifer, *Intangible Materialism*, Chapter 2.
51 Porter, *Cole*, p. 93.
52 Wilder offers a fine technical description of Porter's effect (and, insofar as it is not quite graspable, his *affect*). "The chorus [in "What Is This Thing Called Love?"] is highly unusual," he writes. "In the first place, it begins on the minor seventh, a *b* flat in the key of C, and its supporting harmony is a C chord. The melody then resolves, unexpectedly, to F minor, instead of F major. In the bass

there is a pedal point of *c* for four measures. From the nature of the melody up to the close of the first section, the listener must anticipate a cadence in C minor. Yet the cadence is, remarkably, in C major and the melody note, *e* natural to make the effect more dramatic, is the determining factor" (*American Popular Song* 228). In this description, Wilder is offering a specific technical example of the listener's not fully achieved "anticipation" that Lévi-Strauss describes.

53 Martin Heidegger, *What Is a Thing?*, trans. W. B. Barton and Vera Deutsch (Chicago: Henry Regnery Company, 1967), p. 5.

54 Porter, *Cole*, p. 94.

55 Jourdain, *Music and Ecstasy*, p. 340.

56 Lacan, *Écrits*, p. 302.

57 Porter, *Cole*, p. 152.

NOTES TO CHAPTER 5

1 Henry Louis Gates, Jr., *The Signifying Monkey: A Theory of African-American Literary Criticism* (New York: Oxford University Press, 1988), p. 52.

2 Cited in Gates, *Signifying Monkey*, pp. 81–82.

3 Gates spends time discussing "(re)naming" in relation to the word "signifyin(g)" itself, distinguishing between the standard "dictionary entry" "signifying" and the black, oral "signifyin'." Although I do not follow this distinction here, it is an important one to note. "Some black genius or a community of witty and sensitive speakers emptied the signifier 'significatin' of its received concepts and filled this empty signifier with their own concepts. By doing so, by supplanting the received, standard English concept associated by (white) convention with the particular signifier, they (un)wittingly disrupted the nature of the sign = *signified/signifier* equation itself" (46). In this analysis, I should note, Gates is effecting the combination of public and private scenes I am claiming for Waller's music. As we saw in Chapter 4, Lacan would argue that the "empty signifier" is filled not so much with concepts as with "things" – objects or seeming referents – that function to seemingly anchor the unarticulated feeling (desire?) that empty signifiers provoke. That the subject of signifyin' can be a community as well as an individual also links this process to the "communal" music of the Gershwin brothers. For a fine analysis of the "signifying" (and "double-voiced") performances of James Brown, see Brackett *Interpreting Popular Music*, Chapter 4. The insult, homage, and confrontation of Gates's catalogue are gestures of decomposition, wholeness, and montage.

4 Cited in Gates, *Signifying Monkey*, p. 54.

5 Jacques Derrida, "Me-Psychoanalysis: An Introduction to the Translation of 'The Shell and the Kernel' by Nicholas Abraham," trans. Richard Klein, *Diacritics*, 9 (1979), pp. 4–5.

6 Gates, *Signifying Monkey*, pp. 58–59.

7 Here I would like to add a more or less technical linguistic comment on the process/concept of *signifying*. Gates describes this process in a

vocabulary that is a little different from the one I am using here. "Black people vacated this signifier, then – incredibly – substituted as its concept a signified that stands for the system of rhetorical strategies peculiar to their own vernacular tradition. Rhetoric, then, has supplanted semantics in this most literal meta-confrontation within the structure of the sign. Some historical black community of speakers most certainly struck directly at the heart of the matter, on the ground of the referent itself, thereby demonstrating that even (or especially) the concepts signified by the signifier are themselves arbitrary" (47). Here Gates uses "rhetoric" where I am using "reference," even though in a crucial moment in this discussion – one that addresses the historical timeliness of a black community and of discourse itself – he "grounds" rhetoric in referentiality. The issue of the referentiality of the sign is a vexed one in discussions of linguistics – it is a significant distinction between "structural" linguistics and "empirical" linguistics – and I am suggesting that the political/ethical dimension of language is closely tied to "signifyin(g)" this concept. In other words, where Gates describes signifyin(g) as equating the linguistic "signified" with "rhetorical figures" rather than with the traditional notion of "concept" (48–51), it might also be understood as equating "reference" or "referential gesture" with the signified. What this referential gesture necessarily does, I argue here, is powerfully to *assert* – but also to *perform* – visibility against the cypherlike invisibility of slavery and racism. Peirce's referential "index," grounded in gestures of the hand, enacts this performance/assertion (see Schleifer, *Intangible Materialism*, Chapter 4). These performances are, of course, necessarily improvisatory, and in the *politics* of signifyin' one might also see the implicit political gesture of jazz more generally. Yet insofar as they are "rhetorical" in Gates's terms, they are also systematic, an instance of semantic formalism insofar as the formal gesture of rhetoric is also – also *performs* – its meaning.

8 Ralph Ellison, *Invisible Man* (New York: Vintage Books, 1972), pp. 7–8.

9 Thomas "Fats" Waller, *Satch Plays Fats: A Tribute to the Immortal Fats Waller by Louis Armstrong* (Columbia Legacy, CK 64927, 2000).

10 Hamm, *Putting Popular Music in Its Place*, p. 316.

11 Ellison, *Shadow and Act*, p. 64.

12 For a fine discussion of both this fact and the issue of race in Waller's music, see David Cayer's "Black and Blue and Black Again: Three Stages of Social Imagery in Jazz Lyrics," *Journal of Jazz Studies*, 1, no. 2 (1974) 38–71. This essay examines racial stereotypes in Waller's earlier song "Porter's Love Song to a Chambermaid" and, notably for any discussion of the improvisatory nature of *signifyin'*, it also examines alternative lyrics in some of its recordings. Brackett also discusses in detail African American music as a "musicological subject" (*Interpreting Popular Music* 115 ff.).

13 Derrida, "Me-Psychoanalysis," pp. 4–5.

14 Yaffe, *Fascinating Rhythm*, pp. 72–73.

15 Yaffe details Armstrong's relation to Jewishness as well as suggesting his relation to Waller's stride music: "Louis Armstrong got his first trumpet from

the Karnosky family, Jews who hired him to deliver coal to the whores of Storyville, his first joint from Mezz Mezzrow, a mediocre Jewish clarinet player, pledged allegiance to Joe Glaser, a Jewish gangster manager, and wore a star of David around his neck for most of his life" (*Fascinating Rhythm* 18).

16 In the 1955 recording (also reproduced on *Satch Plays Fats*) he does pronounce *face*, but even in that recording he scat sings after saying the word and adds a full extra bar to the song.

17 Yaffe glosses Ellison's phrase: "when, according to Ellison's description, [Armstrong] 'bends that military instrument into a beam of lyrical sound,' Ellison is probably alluding to Armstrong's first cornet lessons as a boy imprisoned at the Colored Waifs' Home . . . According to Ellison, even though Armstrong learned the instrument in a military capacity, the blues, with their 'bent' thirds and sevenths, gave Armstrong the freedom to find lyricism. While he is singing a song called '(What Did I Do To Be So) Black and Blue,' his performance has no trace of self-pity" (*Fascinating Rhythm* 74–75).

18 Louis Armstrong & His Hot Five, also available on Waller, *Satch Plays Fats*.

19 Paul Machlin, *Stride: The Music of Fats Waller* (Boston: Twayne Publishers, 1985), p. 8.

20 Joel Vance, *Fats Waller: His Life and Times* (London: Robson Books, 1979), p. 6. A fine visual representation of stride playing – with the video focusing on the left-hand bass in the foreground – is a video of Jim Hession performing Waller's "Minor Drag." See Jim Hession/Minor Drag/Harlem Full/Fats Waller/Stride on YouTube. I discuss "The Minor Drag" later in this chapter.

21 Marchlin, *Stride*, p. 9.

22 Toni Morrison's novel *Jazz* (New York: Vintage, 2004) begins with an extended description of a rent party in 1920s Harlem.

23 Vance, *Fats Waller*, pp. 40–41.

24 As I noted in Chapter 3, Jeffrey Melnick pointed out that "Gershwin was so well known for his 'black' compositions that Langston Hughes was inspired to joke that during the 1920s 'any Harlem Negro of any social importance at all would be likely to say casually: . . . "As I said to George –," referring to George Gershwin'" ("Tin Pan Alley" 43).

25 A reissue of "The Minor Drag" can be found on *The Very Best of Fats Waller* See also Jim Hession's performance mentioned in note 20.

26 Vance, *Fats Waller*, p. 49.

27 Cited in Edward Myer, *Giant Strides: The Legacy of Dick Wellstood* (Lanham, MD: Scarecrow Press, 1999), p. 17.

28 Cited in Myer, *Giant Strides*, p. 18.

29 Peter Townsend modifies this assertion somewhat in *Jazz in American Culture* when he argues that "improvisation is often taken to be a defining and unique feature of jazz, but neither of these adjectives is strictly justifiable" (*Jazz in American Culture* 7). Nevertheless, he does argue, as I

mentioned in Chapter 2, that "improvisation of one kind or another has been endemic in the folk musics of the world. In some 'classical' forms, such as Indian music, improvisation is central to the musical culture. European 'serious' music of the nineteenth and twentieth centuries is an ethnomusicological exception in its complete severance from improvisatory methods" (8).

30 Ellison, *Shadow and Act*, p. 151.
31 Townsend, *Jazz in American Culture*, p. 31.
32 Ellison, *Shadow and Act*, p. 209.
33 Appel, *Jazz Modernism*, p. 13.
34 Townsend, *Jazz in American Culture*, p. 47.
35 Jacqui Malone, *Steppin' on the Blues: The Visible Rhythms of African American Dance* (Urbana: University of Illinois Press, 1996), pp. 5, 3; see also Townsend, *Jazz in American Culture*, pp. 55–61.
36 Ellison, *Shadow and Act*, p. 189.
37 The "Filthy" nickname is noted by Vance, *Fats Waller*, p. 33.
38 A reissue of this recording of "I Got Rhythm" can be found on *The Very Best of Fats Waller*; for Gershwin's music, see Figure 5.
39 Townsend citation from *Jazz in American Culture*, p. 10.
40 Ellison, *Shadow and Act*, p. 226.
41 Berger, "Outsider Insider," p. 6.
42 Machlin, *Stride*, p. 83.
43 Cited in Machin, *Stride*, p. 84, and clearly heard on the recording.
44 Berger, "Outsider Insider," p. 14.
45 Ellison, *Shadow and Act*, pp. 161–62.
46 Frith, "The Good, the Bad," p. 107.
47 Machlin, *Stride*, p. 38.
48 Ellison, *Shadow and Act*, p. 243.
49 In "Parker's Back," for instance, O'Connor's character has a tattoo of Jesus's face on his back, and someone tells him "the eyes of God are on you." O'Connor, though, isn't signifyin': rather, she's trying to capture religious mystery by literalizing figures of speech (see Schleifer, "Rural Gothic: The Sublime Rhetoric of Flannery O'Connor," in David Mogen, Scott Sanders, and Joanne Karpinsky (eds.), *Frontier Gothic: Terror and Wonder at the Frontier in American Literature* [Madison, NJ: Fairleigh Dickinson University Press, 1993], pp. 175–86).
50 Waller, *Piano-Styles*, p. 20.
51 Machlin, *Stride*, p. 36.
52 Roland Barthes, *Camera Lucida*, trans. Richard Howard (New York: Hill and Wang, 1981), p. 26.
53 Cited in Berger, "Outsider Insider," p. 8.
54 The performance Berger quotes is available on *The Definitive Fats Waller* (where it is designated "'E' Flat Blues" even though Waller describes it, as Berger notes, as the B Flat Blues; it sounds B-flat on the recording).
55 Ellison, *Shadow and Act*, p. 67.
56 Berger, "Outsider Insider," pp. 3–4.

NOTES TO CHAPTER 6

1 Quoted in Robert O'Meally, *Lady Day: The Many Faces of Billie Holiday* (New York: Arcade Publishing, 1991), p. 41.
2 Citation from O'Meally, *Lady Day*, p. 55.
3 Cited in O'Meally, *Lady Day*, p. 56.
4 John Hammond, cited in Humphrey Lyttelton, *The Best of Jazz II: Enter the Giants 1931–1944* (New York: Taplinger, 1982), p. 204.
5 Schuller, *The Swing Era*, p. 540.
6 In this, Farah Jasmine Griffin (*If You Can't Be Free, Be a Mystery: In Search of Billie Holiday* [New York: Free Press, 2001]) is following Robert O'Meally's important biography *Lady Day*.
7 Cited in Griffin, *If You Can't Be Free*, p. 85.
8 O'Meally, *Lady Day*, pp. 115, 110.
9 One significant theme of David Brackett's important study *Interpreting Popular Music* is that the category of "author" is problematic in popular music. As I noted in earlier chapters, he contends (as do Middleton, Tagg, and many others) that the focus on the written score in traditional musicology is not the best way to study popular music. Citing Roland Barthes's observation in "The Death of the Author" that a "text's unity lies not in its origin but in its destination," he suggests that the very "popularity" of music – what I have described in Part I as its embeddedness in a culture of *consumption* – emphasizes its *temporal* and local nature (*Interpreting Popular Music* 16, 24). In his superb chapter comparing the recorded performances (in 1944) of Bing Crosby and Billie Holiday singing "I'll Be Seeing You," he notes that his discussion of the *impersonal* category of "*topoi* in the biographical literature of Billie Holiday is really a way of discussing the concept of authorship in popular music" (49). Brackett also describes the ways that Holiday "created" her persona, almost impersonally, in relation to the fact that a career as an "entertainer [was] one of the few non-menial fields open to African-Americans at the time" (45) Brackett also vividly describes the racism and sexism in American culture and particularly in commercial popular music at the time (41–43).
10 Washington, cited in Griffin, *If You Can't Be Free*, p. 88.
11 It also led that other master of form, Glenn Gould, to disparage the musicality of Bach's *Well-Tempered Clavier*, both in word and, at times, in deed. Thus, he performs the Book II F-minor prelude and fugue, among the most musically beautiful pieces in *The Well-Tempered Clavier*, at speeds that transform them into the exercises he claims they are. Such mechanical exercising creates what Viktor Zuckerkandl calls a "sound system," the "equal distribution of tones throughout tonal space, [that] represents, musically considered, the dissolution of all order: between the tones of the chromatic scale there are . . . no dynamic relations; every tone is as good as every other" (*Sound and Symbol: Music and the External Word*, trans. Willard Trask [Princeton University Press, 1956], pp. 58–59).
12 John Holland, *Emergence: From Chaos to Order* (Reading, MA: Persius Books, 1998), p. 6.

13 Stravinsky, *Themes and Conclusions*, p. 147.
14 In *Modernism and Time* I suggest that Stravinsky's observations about art also shed light on the "modernist" mathematics of Bertrand Russell and the physics of Albert Einstein, and they all take their place within the context of cultural modernism as responses to the abundance of the second Industrial Revolution (181). Mary Poovey makes a similar point about the changing concept of the "modern fact" at the turn of the twentieth century in *A History of the Modern Fact* (3–4), which I noted in the Introduction.
15 Schuller, *The Swing Era*, p. 540.
16 Albright, *Stravinsky*, p. 4.
17 Poovey, *Modern Fact*, esp. 3–4.
18 Comment by Henderson in O'Meally, *Lady Day*, p. 24.
19 Schuller, *The Swing Era*, p. 536.
20 Brackett, *Interpreting Popular Music*, p. 61.
21 Schuller is describing Holiday's performance of Duke Ellington's "Solitude." "In my view," he writes, "this is perhaps the most powerful – and oddly neglected – recorded performance of her career. It is more than a song; it is more than a musical performance. To hear her sing the words 'haunt' and 'taunt,' stretched to the maximum intensity, taut and vibrato-less, is to experience the ultimate anguished meaning of those words. The listener is irresistibly drawn into *her* solitude . . . The mood of utter loneliness is heightened by Roy Eldridge's faraway, faintly audible muted obbligato behind [Holiday] and by Eddie Heywood's wistful solo (with some lovely high-register passages in third) almost managing to sustain [Holiday's] unearthly mood" (*The Swing Era* 545). This recording is available on *Billie Holiday: 1940–1942 (*Chronological Classics, 2006), ASIN: BOO265XSAQ. This performance is also available on YouTube (youtube.com).
22 Michaels, "American Modernism," p. 39.
23 Mithen, *Singing Neanderthals*.
24 Peter Townsend notes that "improvisation can be 'on' the sense of the song or can allude to well-known previous versions of it, or to an artist's own earlier interpretations. Jazz players often work with a particular song over a period of years, and find nuances within it that spring from a continual re-evaluation of the piece. After the 1941 recording of 'All of Me' that features Billie Holiday and Lester Young improvising vocally and instrumentally on the theme, Holiday reduced the tempo of the piece for a more serene version eight years later" (*Jazz in American Culture* 18). In Chapter 5, I mentioned how Louis Armstrong retained some of the qualities of the 1929 recording of "Black and Blue" in the big-band recording of 1955.
25 Middleton, "Popular Music Analysis."
26 O'Meally, *Lady Day*, p. 37.
27 Holiday's probable father, Clarence Holiday, was a rhythm guitar player. "In terms of musical influence," O'Meally notes, "Billie was probably most turned on by her father's easy-seeming and yet complexly accurate sense of time. If Bobby Tucker and others said Holiday's time was as perfect as a metronome's (more so, since no metronome could accent or style the beat as Holiday could),

perhaps it is because from the beginning of her conscious life, she was aware that her father's job was that of the perfect jazz band's perfect timekeeper. He . . . nonchalantly swung the band by keeping time much better than a clock" (75).

28 See also Brackett's observation on how Holiday exemplifies the category of "vocal with small group" (*Interpreting Popular Music* 58–61).

29 O'Meally, *Lady Day*, p. 121. O'Meally goes on to say that "Basie specialized not just in the keeping of flawless tempos but in the magic of musical understatedness. Both as a soloist and an arranger, Basie kept things to a minimum, never using two notes where one would do" (121).

30 Stuart Nicholson, *Billie Holiday* (Boston: Northeastern University Press, 1995), p. 93.

31 Lyttelton, *The Best of Jazz*, pp. 207–08.

32 Deleuze, *Logic of Sense*, p. 288.

33 Most people writing about Holiday note a change in her work with the recording of "Strange Fruit" in 1939. As I already noted, O'Meally dates "the first great Billie Holiday period" as "the early years of her recording at Columbia, from 1935 to 1939" (*Lady Day* 115). At the time of the recording of "Strange Fruit," Brackett writes, "she began to develop a more theatrical way of presenting herself onstage; her recordings from this time until the end of the forties undoubtedly enhanced the sense of the 'dramatic songstress' developed in her stage act" (*Interpreting Popular Music* 49). Schuller also notes that the recording of "Strange Fruit" "was to alter her career. Its controversial success was also to affect her singing, not so much in style, but in choice of material and type of accompaniment" (*The Swing Era* 543), which was a turn away from the kind of ensemble music I am focused on here. Of course, she never did fully abandon ensemble music, as is suggested by her late performance of "Fine and Mellow" I discuss later in this chapter.

34 Nicholson, *Billie Holiday*, pp. 82–83.

35 Bruce Crowther and Mike Pinfold, *Singing Jazz: The Singers and Their Styles* (San Francisco: Miller Freeman, 1997), p. 74.

36 Nicholson, *Billie Holiday*, p. 86.

37 Merlin Donald, *Origins of the Modern Mind: Three Stages in the Evolution of Culture and Cognition* (Cambridge, MA: Harvard University Press, 1991), p. 186.

38 Merlin Donald, *A Mind So Rare: The Evolution of Human Consciousness* (New York: Norton, 2001), p. 272.

39 Griffin, *If You Can't Be Free*, p. 196.

40 Brackett notes that many critics noticed the exaggeration of this quality of a "'semi-recitative style' (the idea that she is 'reciting' rather than 'singing' . . .)" in her recordings of the 1950s (*Interpreting Popular Music* 43). The recording of "Fine and Mellow" cited below is a good example of this.

41 Angela Davis, *Blues Legacies*, p. xv.

42 O'Meally, *Lady Day*, pp. 36–37.

43 Schuller, *The Swing Era*, p. 536.

44 Davis, *Blues Legacies*, p. xv; italics added.

45 Stravinsky, *Themes and Conclusions*, p. 147.
46 Lyttelton, *The Best of Jazz*, p. 201.
47 Schuller, *The Swing Era*, p. 536.
48 Oswald Ducrot and Tzvetan Todorov, *Encyclopedic Dictionary of the Sciences of Language*, trans. Catherine Porter (Baltimore: Johns Hopkins University Press, 1979), p. 104.
49 In a sense, the very mathematics and mathematical science of Bertrand Russell and Albert Einstein can be understood as "semanticized." Einstein is a good case in point: he devised his own notational conventions in articulating the Special Theory of Relativity that allowed him kinds of simplicity – and semanticization – of his mathematical formulas. In fact, his 1905 paper on special relativity is notable for its paucity of mathematical demonstrations. Einstein reconceived physics, so to speak, so that the issue of "frames of reference" became the object of study as well as the assumed basis of study (see Schleifer, *Modernism and Time* 167). As I noted earlier, Mary Poovey makes a similar, more general argument about the place of frames of reference in relation to the changing idea of "facts" in the early twentieth century (*Modern Fact* 3–4).
50 Donald, *Origins*, p. 167.
51 Donald notes that "one corroboration of Darwin's intuition comes from behavior genetics. The genetics of rudimentary musical skills appear to be different from verbal skill; in virtually all studies of the structure of intelligence, musical talent is isolated as a separate factor from verbal skill. Moreover, language follows a completely different developmental course from musical ability . . . Finally, aphasias (loss of language function) usually result from left-hemisphere injury, while aprosodias (impaired voice modulation) and amusias (selective loss of musical ability) more often follow injury to the right" (*Origins* 40; see also 182). Donald's descriptions of the neural and cognitive functioning of rhythm, in fascinating detail, contribute to this argument about the "sense" of music (see *Origins* 186–87; and *A Mind So Rare* 271–74). In *The Singing Neanderthals*, Steven Mithen offers a sweeping study of the evolution of music and its meanings that focuses on its adaptive features rather than its formal features. Nevertheless, his study also suggests the powerful functional *meanings* of music. Mithen describes the ways that prosody, across different cultures, governs child–adult verbal – or I might say "phonic" – interactions (69–84).
52 See the whole of Donald, *Origins*, for this argument. Donald enlarges on this discussion in *A Mind So Rare*.
53 Donald, *Origins*, p. 170.
54 Schuller, *The Swing Era*, p. 537.
55 Donald, *A Mind So Rare*, p. 253; Stanley Cavell, *Must We Mean What We Say?* (Cambridge University Press, 1976), p. 204.
56 Davis, *Blues Legacies*, p. 167.
57 Zuckerkandl, *Sound and Symbol*, p. 1.
58 Video reproductions of this performance are widely available. See Joel J. Feigenbaum, director, *Lady Day: The Many Faces of Billie Holiday* for a VHS reproduction (Kultur Video: Asin 6302037034), 1995. White Star has produced

a DVD version of this title (Asin 000056B03), 1995. This performance is also available on YouTube (youtube.com).

59 Nicholson notes that "in the late 1930s, this young autodidact was negotiating with ease complex songs from the canons of a Cole Porter or a George Gershwin. Her grasp and understanding of form and structure were such that they also brought great symmetry to her vocal variations, and the best are minor miracles of organizing harmonic and rhythmic ideas to maximum effect" (*Billie Holiday*, 127).

60 Mikhail Bakhtin, *Art and Answerability*, trans. Vadim Liapunov and Kenneth Brostrom (Austin: University of Texas Press, 1990).

61 Nat Hentoff, "The Real Lady Day," p. 154.

62 Schuller, *The Swing Era*, pp. 561–62. Burnett James's general description of Young's music is also apt here: "There was plenty of feeling in Lester's playing; but it was not, like much jazz of varying sorts, feeling only. When Lester began to play you were aware immediately of a subtle and conscious intellect forming and fashioning the texture and substance of his solos" (*Essays on Jazz* [New York: Da Capo Press, 1990], p. 69).

63 Holiday, "Fine and Mellow," 34.

64 Schuller, *The Swing Era*, p. 536.

65 Gary Morson and Caryl Emerson, *Mikhail Bakhtin: Creation of a Prosaics* (Stanford University Press, 1990), p. 76.

66 In Hamm, *Putting Popular Music in Its Place*, p. 309.

67 In this "overview of Western music history" Hamm is following "a team of European musicologists, in preparation for the writing of Volume VII of *Music in the Life of Man: A World History*, a multi-volume global history sponsored by UNESCO" (*Putting Popular Music in Its Place* 320). These scholars, he notes, include Janos Karpati, Budapest; Jens Brincker, Finn Gravesen, Carsten E. Hatting, and Niels Krabbe, Copenhagen.

68 Stravinsky, *Themes and Conclusions*, p. 147. It is also Poovey's argument about the reconception of the notion of "fact" at the turn of the twentieth century (*Modern Fact*; see also Schleifer, *Intangible Materialism*).

NOTES TO CONCLUSION

1 MacCabe, *James Joyce*, p. 4.

2 Michael North, "Words in Motion: The Movies, the Readies, and 'the Revolution of the Word,'" *Modernism/Modernity*, 9 (2009), p. 206.

3 Cited in North, "Words in Motion," p. 210.

4 Eugene Jolas, "The Revolution of Language and James Joyce," *transition*, 11 (1928) 109.

5 Ira Gershwin, *Lyrics*, p. 163.

6 Jolas, "Revolution of Language," p. 109.

Bibliography

Adorno, Theodor. *Aesthetic Theory*, trans. C. Lenhardt. New York: Routledge & Kegan Paul, 1984.

Negative Dialectics, trans. E. B. Ashton. New York: Continuum, 1973.

"On Popular Music," in *Essays on Music*, ed. Richard Peppert. Berkeley: University of California Press, 2002, pp. 437–69.

The Philosophy of Modern Music, trans. Anne Mitchell and Wesley Blomster. New York: Seabury Press, 1973.

Aggleton, John and Andrew Young. "The Enigma of the Amygdala: On Its Contribution to Human Emotion," in Richard Lane and Lynn Nadel (eds.), *Cognitive Neuroscience of Emotion*. Oxford University Press, 2000, pp. 106–28.

Albright, Daniel. *Stravinsky: The Music Box and the Nightingale*. New York: Gordon and Breach, 1989.

Alexander, Michael. *Jazz Age Jews*. Princeton University Press, 2001.

Appel, Jr., Alfred. *Jazz Modernism: From Ellington and Armstrong to Matisse and Joyce*. New York: Knopf, 2002.

Auden, W. H. "In Memory of Sigmund Freud," in *Selected Poetry of W. H. Auden*. New York: Modern Library, 1959, pp. 54–58.

Austin, J. L. *How to Do Things with Words*. Cambridge, MA: Harvard University Press, 1962.

"Three Ways of Spilling Ink," in his *Philosophical Papers*. Oxford University Press, 1979, pp. 272–87.

Avakian, George. Original liner notes to *Satch Plays Fats: A Tribute to the Immortal Fats Waller by Louis Armstrong*. Columbia Legacy, CK 64927, 2000.

Bakhtin, Mikhail. *Art and Answerability*, trans. Vadim Liapunov and Kenneth Brostrom. Austin: University of Texas Press, 1990.

The Dialogic Imagination, trans. Caryl Emerson and Michael Holquist. Austin: University of Texas Press, 1981.

[V. N. Voloshinov], *Marxism and the Philosophy of Language*, trans. Ladislav Matejka and I. R. Titunik. Cambridge, MA: Harvard University Press, 1986.

Speech Genres and Other Late Essays, trans. Vern McGee. Austin: University of Texas Press, 1986.

Barthes, Roland. *Camera Lucida*, trans. Richard Howard. New York: Hill and Wang, 1981.

"The Death of the Author," in *Image-Music-Text*, trans. Stephen Heath. New York: Noonday Press, 1977, pp. 142–48.

Benjamin, Walter. "N [Re the Theory of Knowledge, Theory of Progress]," trans. Leigh Hafrey and Richard Sieburth, in *Benjamin: Philosophy, Aesthetics, History*, ed. Gary Smith. University of Chicago Press, 1989, pp. 43–83.

Berger, Morroe. "Fats Waller: The Outsider Insider," *Journal of Jazz Studies*, 1, no. 1 (1973) 3–20.

Berman, Marshall. *All That is Solid Melts into Air: The Experience of Modernity*. New York: Simon and Schuster, 1982.

Birken, Lawrence. *Consuming Desire: Sexual Science and the Emergence of a Culture of Abundance, 1881–1914*. Ithaca: Cornell University Press, 1988.

Brackett, David. *Interpreting Popular Music*. Cambridge University Press, 1995.

Bradbury, Malcolm and James McFarlane. "The Name and Nature of Modernism," in Bradbury and McFarlane (eds.), *Modernism: 1890–1930*. Harmondsworth: Penguin Books, 1976, pp. 19–55.

Bruhn, Siglind. *J. S. Bach's Well-Tempered Clavier: In-Depth Analysis and Interpretation*, vol. 1. Mainer International: Hong Kong, 1993.

Buck-Morss, Susan. *The Dialectics of Seeing: Walter Benjamin and the Arcades Project*. Cambridge, MA: MIT Press, 1989.

Busoni, Ferruccio. *Sketch of a New Aesthetic of Music*, in *Three Classics in the Aesthetic of Music*. New York: Dover, 1962.

Butler, Judith. *Gender Troubles: Feminism and the Subversion of Identity*. New York: Routledge, 1990.

Cameron, Sharon. *Lyric Time: Dickinson and the Limits of Genre*. Baltimore: Johns Hopkins University Press, 1979.

Campbell, Colin. *The Romantic Ethic and the Spirit of Modern Consumerism*. London: Alcuin Academics, 2005. Reprint of the 1987 edn.

Casti, John. *Complexification: Explaining a Paradoxical World through the Science of Surprise*. New York: HarperPerennial, 1995.

Cavell, Stanley. *Must We Mean What We Say?* Cambridge University Press, 1976.

Cayer, David. "Black and Blue and Black Again: Three Stages of Social Imagery in Jazz Lyrics," *Journal of Jazz Studies*, 1, no. 2 (1974) 38–71.

Chalmers, David. *The Conscious Mind: In Search of a Fundamental Theory*. Oxford University Press, 1996.

Coates, John. Untitled review of Regenia Gagnier, *The Insatiability of Human Wants: Economics and Aesthetics in Market Society* and Michael Tratner, *Deficits and Desires: Economics and Sexuality in Twentieth-Century Literature*, in *Journal of Aesthetics and Art Criticism*, 60 (2002) 369–72.

Copland, Aaron. *Music and Imagination*. New York: Mentor, 1952.

Crowther, Bruce and Mike Pinfold. *Singing Jazz: The Singers and Their Styles*. San Francisco: Miller Freeman, 1997.

Culler, Jonathan. "Apostrophe," in his *The Pursuit of Signs*. Ithaca: Cornell University Press, 1981, pp. 135–54.

"Convention and Meaning: Derrida and Austin," in Robert Con Davis and Ronald Schleifer (eds.), *Contemporary Literary Criticism: Literary and Cultural Studies*. White Plains: Longman, 1994, pp. 308–19.

Dahlhaus, Carl. *Foundations of Music History*. Cambridge University Press, 1983.

Davis, Angela Y. *Blues Legacies and Black Feminism: Gertrude "Ma" Rainey, Bessie Smith, and Billie Holiday*. New York: Pantheon, 1998.

Deleuze, Gilles. *The Logic of Sense*, trans. Mark Lester. New York: Columbia University Press, 1990.

Derrida, Jacques. "Me-Psychoanalysis: An Introduction to the Translation of 'The Shell and the Kernel' by Nicholas Abraham," trans. Richard Klein. *Diacritics*, 9 (1979) 4–12.

Positions, trans. Alan Bass. University of Chicago Press, 1979.

Donald, Merlin. *A Mind So Rare: The Evolution of Human Consciousness*. New York: Norton, 2001.

Origins of the Modern Mind: Three Stages in the Evolution of Culture and Cognition. Cambridge, MA: Harvard University Press, 1991.

Ducrot, Oswald and Tzvetan Todorov. *Encyclopedic Dictionary of the Sciences of Language*, trans. Catherine Porter. Baltimore: Johns Hopkins University Press, 1979.

Edwards, George. *The Evolution of Finance Capitalism*. New York: Longmans, 1938.

Eksteins, Modris. *Rites of Spring: The Great War and the Birth of the Modern Age*. New York: Vintage, 1990.

Eliot, T. S. *Selected Poems*. New York: Harcourt Brace, 1964.

Ellison, Ralph. *Invisible Man*. New York: Vintage Books, 1972. (Originally published in 1952.)

Shadow and Act. New York: Signet Books, 1966.

Ermarth, Elizabeth Deeds. *Realism and Consensus in the English Novel*. Princeton University Press, 1983.

Feigenbaum, Joel J. (director). *Lady Day: The Many Faces of Billie Holiday*. Kultur Video: ASIN 6302037034, 1995 (VHS). White Star: ASIN 000056B03, 1995.

Felman, Shoshana. *The Scandal of the Speaking Body: Don Juan with J. L. Austin, or Seduction in Two Languages*, trans. Catherine Porter. Stanford University Press, 2002.

Ferguson, Margaret, Mary Jo Salter, and Jon Stallworthy. *The Norton Anthology of Poetry*, shorter fifth edn. New York: Norton, 2005.

Fitzgerald, Ella. "'S Wonderful," "They Can't Take That Away from Me," and "Ev'ry Time We Say Goodbye," in *The Best of the Song Books*. Verve: 314 519 804–2, 1993.

Foucault, Michel. "What Is an Author?", trans. Josué Harari, in Robert Con Davis and Ronald Schleifer (eds.), *Contemporary Literary Criticism: Literary and Cultural Studies*. White Plains: Longman, 1994, pp. 342–53.

Fox, Aaron. *Real Country: Music and Language in Working-Class Culture*. Durham, NC: Duke University Press, 2004.

Frank, Joseph. "Spatial Form in Modern Literature," in his *The Widening Gyre*. Bloomington: Indiana University Press, 1963, pp. 3–62.
Freud, Sigmund. *Beyond the Pleasure Principle*, trans. James Strachey. New York: Bantam Books, 1959.
Frith, Simon. "The Good, the Bad, and the Indifferent: Defending Popular Culture from the Populists," *Diacritics*, 21 (1991) 102–15.
"What Is Good Music?" *Canadian Music Review*, 10 (1990) 92–102.
Fussell, Paul. *The Great War and Modern Memory*. New York: Oxford University Press, 1975.
Gagnier, Regenia. *The Insatiability of Human Wants: Economics and Aesthetics in Market Society*. University of Chicago Press, 2000.
Gallop, Jane. *Reading Lacan*. Ithaca: Cornell University Press, 1985.
Gates, Jr., Henry Louis. *The Signifying Monkey: A Theory of African-American Literary Criticism*. New York: Oxford University Press, 1988.
Gaukroger, Stephen. *Descartes: An Intellectual Biography*. New York: Oxford University Press, 1995.
Gay, Peter. *Modernism: The Lure of Heresy from Baudelaire to Beckett and Beyond*. New York: Norton, 2008.
Gershwin, George and Ira Gershwin. *The Music and Lyrics of George & Ira Gershwin: Special Centenary Edition*. Miami: Warner Bros. Publications, 1998.
Gershwin, Ira. *Lyrics on Several Occasions*. New York: Knopf, 1959.
Goldberg, Isaac. *George Gershwin: A Study in American Music*. New York: Frederick Ungar Publishing, 1958.
Gould, Stephen Jay. *The Structure of Evolutionary Theory*. Cambridge, MA: Harvard University Press, 2002.
Wonderful Life: The Burgess Shale and the Nature of History. New York: Norton, 1989.
Gracyk, Theodore. "Adorno, Jazz, and the Aesthetics of Popular Music," *The Musical Quarterly*, 76 (1992) 526–42.
Greenblatt, Stephen. "Culture," in Frank Lentricchia and Thomas McLaughlin (eds.), *Critical Terms for Literary Study*. University of Chicago Press, 1995, pp. 225–32.
Greimas, A. J. "La linguistique structurale et la poétique," in *Du Sens*. Paris: Seuil, 1970, pp. 271–83.
Structural Semantics, trans. Danielle McDowell, Ronald Schleifer, and Alan Velie. University of Nebraska Press: Lincoln, 1983.
Griffin, Farah Jasmine. *If You Can't Be Free, Be a Mystery: In Search of Billie Holiday*. New York: Free Press, 2001.
Hamilton, Andy. "The Aesthetics of Imperfection," *Philosophy*, 65 (1990) 323–40.
Hamm, Charles. *Putting Popular Music in Its Place*. Cambridge University Press, 1995.
Yesterdays: Popular Song in America. New York: Norton, 1979.
Heidegger, Martin, *What Is a Thing?* trans. W. B. Barton and Vera Deutsch. Chicago: Henry Regnery Company, 1967.

Hentoff, Nat. "The Real Lady Day," in Leslie Gourse (ed.), *The Billie Holiday Companion*. New York: Shirmer Books, 1997, pp. 153–60.

Hobsbawm, Eric. *The Age of Empire 1875–1914*. New York: Pantheon Books, 1987.

Holenstein, Elmar. *Roman Jakobson's Approach to Language*, trans. Catherine Schelbert and Tarcisius Schelbert. Bloomington: Indiana University Press, 1976.

Holiday, Billie. *Billie Holiday: Original Keys for Singers, Transcribed from Historic Recordings*. Milwaukee: Hal Leonard Corporation, 2002.

"I'll Be Seeing You," Commodore CCD 7001.

"The Man I Love," in *Love Songs Billie Holiday*, Sony Music Entertainment 1996, CK 64853.

"Night and Day," in *Love Songs Billie Holiday*, Sony Music Entertainment 1996, CK 64853.

"Solitude," in *Billie Holiday: 1940–1942*. Chronological Classics, 2006. ASIN BOO265XSAQ.

"They Can't Take That Away from Me," in *Love Songs Billie Holiday*, Sony Music Entertainment 1996, CK 64853.

"Fine and Mellow," in *Norton Anthology of African American Literature*, eds. Henry Louis Gates, Jr., and Nellie Y. McKay. New York: Norton, 1997, pp. 34–35.

Holland, John H. *Emergence: From Chaos to Order*. Reading, MA: Persius Books, 1998.

Horowitz, Joseph. *Classical Music in America: A History of Its Rise and Fall*. New York: Norton, 2005.

Hudson, Kenneth. *The Archaeology of the Consumer Society: The Second Industrial Revolution in Britain*. Cranbury, NJ: Fairleigh Dickinson University Press, 1983.

Huyssen, Andreas. *After the Great Divide: Modernism, Mass Culture, Postmodernism*. Bloomington: Indiana University Press, 1986.

Jakobson, Roman. "Two Aspects of Language and Two Types of Aphasic Disturbances," in his *Language in Literature*, ed. Krystyna Pomorska and Stephen Rudy. Cambridge, MA: Harvard University Press, 1987, pp. 95–114.

James, Burnett. *Essays on Jazz*. New York: Da Capo Press, 1990.

Jameson, Fredric. *Late Marxism: Adorno, or, The Persistence of the Dialectic*. London: Verso, 1990.

Postmodernism; or The Cultural Logic of Late Capitalism. Durham, NC: Duke University Press, 1991.

Jobling, David, Tina Pippin, and Ronald Schleifer, eds. *A Postmodern Bible Reader*. Oxford: Blackwell Publishers, 2001.

Jolas, Eugene. "The Revolution of Language and James Joyce," *transition*, 11 (1928) 109–16.

Jourdain, Robert. *Music, the Brain, and Ecstasy: How Music Captures Our Imagination*. New York: Quill, 2002.

Joyce, James. *A Portrait of the Artist as a Young Man*. New York: Viking, 1964.

Ulysses. New York: Random House, 1961.

Keil, Charles. "Motion and Feeling through Music," *Journal of Aesthetics and Art Criticism*, 24 (1966) 337–49.

Keller, Hermann. *The Well-Tempered Clavier by Johann Sebastian Bach*, trans. Leight Gerdine. London: George Allen & Unwin, 1976.

Kennedy, Michael and Joyce Bourne. *The Concise Oxford Dictionary of Music*. New York: Oxford University Press, 1996.

Kenner, Hugh. *Joyce's Voices*. Berkeley: University of California Press, 1979.

Kern, Stephen. *The Culture of Time and Space: 1880–1918*. Cambridge, MA: Harvard University Press, 1983.

Kirkpatrick, Ralph. *Interpreting Bach's Well-Tempered Clavier: A Performer's Discourse of Method*. New Haven: Yale University Press, 1984.

Lacan, Jacques. *Écrits: A Selection*, trans. Alan Sheridan. New York: Norton, 1977.

The Four Fundamental Concepts of Psycho-Analysis, trans. Alan Sheridan. Harmondsworth: Penguin Books, 1977.

Landes, David. *The Wealth and Poverty of Nations*. New York: Norton, 1999.

Latour, Bruno. *Pandora's Hope: Essays on the Reality of Science Studies*. Cambridge, MA: Harvard University Press, 1999.

The Pasteurization of France, trans. Alan Sheridan and John Law. Cambridge, MA: Harvard University Press, 1988.

We Have Never Been Modern, trans. Catherine Porter. Cambridge, MA: Harvard University Press, 1993.

Lentricchia, Frank. *Modernist Quartet*. Cambridge University Press, 1994.

Levinas, Emmanuel. "Ethics as First Philosophy," trans. Seán Hand and Michael Temple, in *The Levinas Reader*, ed. Seán Hand. Cambridge: Blackwell, 1989, pp. 75–87.

Levine, Lawrence. *Highbrow/Lowbrow*. Cambridge, MA: Harvard University Press, 1988.

Lévi-Strauss, Claude. *The Raw and the Cooked*, trans. John Weightman and Doreen Weightman. New York: Harper Colophon Books, 1975.

Lott, Eric. *Love & Theft: Blackface Minstrelsy and the American Working Class*. New York: Oxford University Press, 1995.

Lyotard, Jean-François. "Answering the Question: What Is Postmodernism?", in his *The Postmodern Condition: A Report on Knowledge*, trans. Geoff Bennington and Brian Massumi. Minneapolis: University of Minnesota Press, 1984, pp. 71–84.

"Note on the Meaning of 'Post-,'" in *The Postmodern Explained: Correspondence 1982–1985*. Minneapolis: University of Minnesota Press, 1992, pp. 64–68.

Lyttelton, Humphrey. *The Best of Jazz* (2 vols.), Vol. II: *Enter the Giants 1931–1944*. New York: Taplinger, 1982.

MacCabe, Colin. *James Joyce and the Revolution of the Word*. New York: Palgrave, 2003.

Machlin, Paul. *Stride: The Music of Fats Waller*. Boston: Twayne Publishers, 1985.

Malone, Jacqui. *Steppin' on the Blues: The Visible Rhythms of African American Dance*. Urbana: University of Illinois Press, 1996.

Margolick, David. *Strange Fruit: Billie Holiday, Café Society, and an Early Cry for Civil Rights*. Philadelphia: Running Press, 2000.

Marx, Karl. *Capital*, vol. 1, *The Process of Capitalist Production*, trans. Samuel Moore and Edward Aveling. New York: International Publishers, 1967.

Marx, Karl and Friedrich Engels. *The Communist Manifesto*, in *Marx and Engels: Basic Writings on Politics and Philosophy*, ed. Lewis Feuer. New York: Anchor Books, 1959, pp. 1–41.

McNeill, Daniel. *The Face*. Boston: Little Brown, 1998.

Mellers, Wilfrid. "God, Modality, and the Meaning in Some Recent Songs of Bob Dylan," *Popular Music*, 1 (1981) 143–57.

Melnick, Jeffrey. "Tin Pan Alley and the Black-Jewish Nation," in Rachel Rubin and Jeffrey Melnick (eds.), *American Popular Music*. Amherst: University of Massachusetts Press, 2001, pp. 29–45.

Meyer, Edward N. *Giant Strides: The Legacy of Dick Wellstood*. Lanham, MD: Scarecrow Press, 1999.

Michaels, Walter Benn. "American Modernism and the Poetics of Identity," *Modernism/Modernity*, 1 (1994) 38–56.

Middleton, Richard. "Popular Music Analysis and Musicology: Bridging the Gap," in Richard Middleton (ed.), *Reading Pop: Approaches to Textual Analysis in Popular Music*. Oxford University Press, 2000, pp. 104–21.

Studying Popular Music. Philadelphia: Open University Press, 1990.

Miller, J. Hillis. "The Search for Grounds in Literary Study," in Robert Con Davis and Ronald Schleifer (eds.), *Rhetoric and Form*. Norman: University of Oklahoma Press, 1985, pp. 19–36.

Miller, Toby. *The Well-Tempered Self: Citizenship, Culture, and the Postmodern Subject*. Baltimore: Johns Hopkins University Press, 1993.

Mithen, Steven. *The Singing Neanderthals: The Origins of Music, Language, Mind and Body*. Cambridge, MA: Harvard University Press, 2006.

Morrison, Toni. *Jazz*. New York: Vintage, 2004.

Morson, Gary Saul and Caryl Emerson. *Mikhail Bakhtin: Creation of a Prosaics*. Stanford University Press, 1990.

Negus, Keith. *Popular Music in Theory: An Introduction*. Hanover, NH: Wesleyan University Press, 1996.

Nicholson, Stuart. *Billie Holiday*. Boston: Northeastern University Press, 1995.

Nietzsche, Friedrich. *The Birth of Tragedy*, in *The Birth of Tragedy and The Case of Wagner*, trans. Walter Kaufmann. New York: Vintage, 1967.

North, Michael. *The Dialect of Modernism*. New York: Oxford University Press, 1994.

"Words in Motion: The Movies, the Readies, and 'the Revolution of the Word,'" *Modernism/Modernity*, 9 (2009) 205–23.

Oja, Carol. "Gershwin and American Modernists of the 1920s," *The Musical Quarterly*, 78 (1994) 646–68.

O'Meally, Robert. *Lady Day: The Many Faces of Billie Holiday*. New York: Arcade Publishing, 1991.

Owen, Wilfred. "Strange Meeting" (1918) in M. H. Abrams (general ed.), *The Norton Anthology of English Literature*, third edn. New York: Norton, 1974, pp. 2,295–96.

Peyser, Joan. *The New Music: The Sense Behind the Sound.* New York: Delacourt Press, 1971.

Poovey, Mary. *A History of the Modern Fact: Problems of Knowledge in the Sciences of Wealth and Society.* Chicago University Press, 1998.

Porter, Cole. *Cole.* New York: Delta, 1971.

100th Anniversary: Piano/Vocal. Miami: Warner Bros. Publications Inc., 1991.

Frank Sinatra Sings the Select Cole Porter. Capitol Records: CD 7 96611 2, 1991.

Music & Lyrics: A Treasury of Cole Porter. New York: Random House, 1972.

Reising, Russell. "Introduction: 'Of the Beginning,'" in *'Every Sound There Is': The Beatles'* Revolver *and the Transformation of Rock and Roll.* Hants.: Ashgate Publishers, 2002, pp. 1–14.

Rorty, Richard. "Philosophy as a Kind of Writing: An Essay on Derrida," in his *Consequences of Pragmatism.* Minneapolis: University of Minnesota Press, 1982, pp. 90–109.

Rosen, Charles. *The Frontiers of Meaning: Three Informal Lectures on Music.* New York: Hill and Wang, 1994.

Rosenberg, Deena. *Fascinating Rhythm: The Collaboration of George and Ira Gershwin.* London: Lime Tree Press, 1992.

Ross, Alex. *The Rest Is Noise: Listening to the Twentieth Century.* New York: Farrar, Straus and Giroux, 2007.

Sanjek, David. "They Work Hard for Their Money: The Business of Popular Music," in Rachel Rubin and Jeffrey Melnick (eds.), *American Popular Music.* Amherst: University of Massachusetts Press, 2001, pp. 9–27.

Scheurer, Timothy. "Introduction: The Tin Pan Alley Years (1890–1950)," in Timothy Scheurer (ed.), *American Popular Music: Readings from the Popular Press* (2 vols.), Vol. I: *The Nineteeenth Century and Tin Pan Alley.* Bowling Green: Bowling Green State University Popular Press, 1989, pp. 87–91.

"'Thou Witty': The Evolution and Triumph of Style in Lyric Writing, 1890–1950," in Timothy Scheurer (ed.), *American Popular Music: Readings from the Popular Press* (2 vols.), Vol. I: *The Nineteeenth Century and Tin Pan Alley.* Bowling Green: Bowling Green State University Popular Press, 1989, pp. 104–19.

Schleifer, Ronald. *A. J. Greimas and the Nature of Meaning.* Lincoln: University of Nebraska Press, 1987.

Analogical Thinking: Language, Collaboration, and Criticism. Ann Arbor: University of Michigan Press, 2000.

"The Beatles, Postmodernism, and Ill-Tempered Musical Form: Cleaning My Gun; or, The Use of Accidentals in *Revolver,*" in Russell Reising (ed.), *'Every Sound There Is': The Beatles'* Revolver *and The Transformation of Rock & Roll.* Hants.: Ashgate Publishers, 2002, pp. 222–33.

Intangible Materialism: The Body, Scientific Knowledge, and the Power of Language. Minneapolis: University of Minnesota Press, 2009.

Modernism and Time: The Logic of Abundance in Literature, Science, and Culture 1880–1930. Cambridge University Press, 2000.

"Narrative Discourse and a New Sense of Value: Meaning and Purpose in the Neoclassical Economics of Alfred Marshall," in Carol Jacobs and Henry Sussman (eds.), *Rereading Narrative*. Stanford University Press, 2003, pp. 157–73, 257–79.

Rhetoric and Death: The Language of Modernism and Postmodern Discourse Theory. Urbana: University of Illinois Press, 1990.

"Rural Gothic: The Sublime Rhetoric of Flannery O'Connor," in David Mogen, Scott Sanders, and Joanne Karpinski (eds.), *Frontier Gothic: Terror and Wonder at the Frontier in American Literature*. Madison, NJ: Fairleigh Dickinson University Press, 1993, pp. 175–86.

"The Semiotics of Speculation: A. J. Greimas and the Example of Literary Criticism," *Genre*, 42 (2009) 165–86.

Schleifer, Ronald and Nancy West. "The Poetry of What Lies Close at Hand: Photography, Commodities, and Post-Romantic Discourses in Hardy and Stevens," *Modern Language Quarterly*, 60 (1999) 33–57.

Schuller, Gunther. *The Swing Era: The Development of Jazz 1930–1945*. New York: Oxford University Press, 1989.

Schwartz, Charles. *Cole Porter: A Biography*. New York: Da Capo Press, 1977.

Shklovsky, Victor. "Art as Technique," in *Russian Formalist Criticism: Four Essays*, trans. Lee Lemon and Marion Reis. Lincoln: University of Nebraska Press, 1965.

Stansky, Peter. *On or About December 1910: Early Bloomsbury and Its Intimate World*. Cambridge, MA: Harvard University Press, 1996.

Steiner, George. "On Difficulty," in his *On Difficulty and Other Essays*. New York: Oxford University Press, 1980, pp. 18–47.

Stevens, Wallace. *The Palm at the End of the Mind: Selected Poems and a Play*, ed. Holly Stevens. New York: Vintage, 1972.

Stravinsky, Igor. *Themes and Conclusions*. Berkeley: University of California Press, 1982.

Townsend, Peter. *Jazz in American Culture*. Edinburgh University Press, 2000.

Toynbee, Jason. *Making Popular Music: Musicians, Creativity and Institutions*. London: Arnold, 2000.

Tratner, Michael. *Deficits and Desires: Economics and Sexuality in Twentieth-Century Literature*. Stanford University Press, 2001.

Vance, Joel. *Fats Waller: His Life and Times*. London: Robson Books, 1979.

Vannatta, Jerry, Ronald Schleifer, and Sheila Crow. *Medicine and Humanistic Understanding: The Significance of Narrative in Medical Practices*. Philadelphia: University of Pennsylvania Press, 2005, a DVD-ROM publication.

Van Vechten, Carl. *Music and Bad Manners*. New York: Knopf, 1916.

Waller, Thomas "Fats." *'Fats' Waller: Piano-Styles and Original Songs*. New York: Jazz Giants, n.d.

"I Got Rhythm" in *The Very Best of Fats Waller*, Collector's Choice Music: 2000.

"I'm Crazy 'Bout My Baby," in *The Definitive Fats Waller*, CD digital audio, 1996.

"The Minor Drag," in *The Very Best of Fats Waller*, Collector's Choice Music: 2000.

Satch Plays Fats: A Tribute to the Immortal Fats Waller by Louis Armstrong. Columbia Legacy, CK 64927, 2000.

West, Cornel. "Historicizing the Postmodern Debate: Arnold, Eliot, Trilling, and Fannon on the Crisis in Modern Culture," unpublished lecture presented at the University of Oklahoma, November 2, 1988.

"The New Cultural Politics of Difference," in *The Cornel West Reader*. New York: Basic Books, 1999, pp. 119–39.

West, Nancy and Penelope Pelizzon, *Tabloid, Inc.: Crimes, Newspapers, Narratives*. Columbus: Ohio State University Press, 2010.

Wilder, Alec. *American Popular Song*. New York: Oxford University Press, 1972.

Williams, Raymond. *The Long Revolution*. Harmondsworth: Penguin Books, 1961.

The Politics of Modernism. London: Verso, 1989.

Williams, William Carlos. *The Autobiography of William Carlos Williams*. New York: New Direction, 1951.

Wilson, Frank. *The Hand: How Its Use Shapes the Brain, Language, and Human Culture*. New York: Vintage Press, 1999.

Witkin, Robert W. *Adorno on Popular Culture*. London: Routledge, 2003.

Woolf, Virginia. "Mr. Bennett and Mrs. Brown," in her *Collected Essays* (5 vols.), Vol. 1. New York: Harcourt, Brace, and World, 1967, pp. 319–73.

Yaffe, David. *Fascinating Rhythm: Reading Jazz in American Writing*. Princeton University Press, 2006.

Yeats, W. B. *Collected Poems*. New York: Macmillan, 1956.

Zuckerkandl, Viktor. *Sound and Symbol: Music and the External Word*, trans. Willard Trask. Princeton University Press, 1956.

Index